Accelerating
the Tendering Cycle

A Legal Due Diligence Guide

Accelerating the Tendering Cycle

A Legal Due Diligence Guide

Paul Emanuelli

Northern Standard
Publishing
Toronto, Canada

Accelerating the Tendering Cycle: A Legal Due Diligence Guide

© Paul Emanuelli, 2012

March 2012

Emanuelli, Paul, 1970 –

    Accelerating the Tendering Cycle: A Legal Due Diligence Guide/Paul Emanuelli

ISBN: 978-0-9811458-1-5

Union printed and bound in Canada.

Northern Standard Publishing
Suite 329 – 639 Dupont Street
Toronto, Ontario M6G 1Z4

For my son
Robert Angelo Emanuelli
and for my daughter
Isabella Sophia Emanuelli

ACCELERATING THE TENDERING CYCLE: A LEGAL DUE DILIGENCE GUIDE

TABLE OF CONTENTS

About the Author

Paul Emanuelli has been recognized by *Who's Who Legal* as one of Canada's leading procurement lawyers. He is the General Counsel and Managing Director of the Procurement Law Office, which is ranked by *Global Law Experts* as Canada's top public procurement law firm. Paul's portfolio focuses on major procurement projects, developing innovative procurement formats, negotiating commercial transactions and advising institutions on the strategic legal aspects of their purchasing operations. Paul also has an extensive track record of public speaking, publishing and training. Paul is the author of *The Laws of Precision Drafting: A Handbook for Tenders and RFPs*, the textbook *Government Procurement* and the newsletter *National Tendering Law Update*. He also hosts the *Procurement Law Update* webinar series. Paul is a regular law columnist with the *Daily Commercial News* and *Purchasing b2b* magazine and has published dozens of articles, columns and essays for other leading publications including *The Lawyers Weekly, Municipal Lawyer, The Legal Edge, Summit Magazine, Progressive Purchasing Online, Caveat Emptor* and *The Law Times.* Paul has also trained and presented to thousands of procurement professionals from hundreds of institutions across Canada and internationally. He has a proven track record of successful collaboration with industry-leading organizations, having developed and delivered training programs through institutions such as Osgoode Hall Law School, the Ontario Bar Association, the Canadian Institute, the Purchasing Management Association of Canada, the Canadian Public Procurement Council, the Institute of Internal Auditors, the Atlantic Public Purchasing Association, the Ontario Public Buyers Association and the Caribbean Procurement Institute. Paul has also presented to a broad range of other industry organizations including the Strategy Institute, Federated Press, Insight, the Canadian IT Law Association, the Information Technology Association of Canada, the Law Society of Upper Canada, the Canadian Corporate Counsel Association, the Municipal Law Departments of Ontario and the Canadian Bar Association. Before launching the Procurement Law Office, Paul served 10 years as Crown Counsel with the province of Ontario, at Management Board Secretariat and then at Crown Law Office Civil, where he focused on procurement and information technology transactions and chaired the government's Procurement Lawyers Group. During that time he also served two terms as the Chair of the Ontario Bar Association's Public Sector Lawyers Section and four terms on the executive of the Toronto Computer Lawyers Group. He has also served on the Board of Directors of the Association of Law Officers of the Crown and on the Board of Directors of the Canadian IT Law Association. Paul graduated with a B.A. from the University of Toronto in 1993 and a J.D. from Osgoode Hall Law School in 1996. He was called to the Bar of Ontario in 1998. Paul can be reached at paul.emanuelli@procurementoffice.ca.

Acknowledgments

I would like to thank my Procurement Law Office colleagues Marilyn Brown, Maud Murray and Rosslyn Young for contributing articles to this handbook, as well as Greg Slater, Tanya Adams and the team at Thistle Printing for their support with typesetting and printing. Finally, I would like to extend a special note of thanks to my colleague Jennifer Marston for her invaluable assistance as editor.

I hope that our efforts serve you, the reader, well in your pursuit of due diligence in the procurement cycle.

Regards,

Paul Emanuelli

Lethbridge, Alberta
March 20, 2012

INTRODUCTION:
ASSESSING COMPLIANCE AND ACCELERATING PROCUREMENT

The cut and thrust of supplier competition, the ever-present threat of litigation, the increasing pressure to get value-for-money, the growing complexities of a round-the-clock interconnected global marketplace and the demand for faster and faster turnaround times make the hours, days and months fly by in an ever-accelerating blur of relentless procurement cycles. Then a crisis hits. Whether it's a story in the paper, auditors knocking at your door or a supplier serving you with a lawsuit, in that split second, everything stops. Past events replay before you in slow motion under the white hot glare of public scrutiny as the spectacle of second-guessing and finger pointing begins. At that moment, memories will fade, accountabilities will blur and everyone will claim someone else was taking care of due process on the file that's now on fire.

In recent years, public procurement has become unnecessarily complicated and high risk. It doesn't need to be. Whether you're living through a procurement crisis or proactively trying to avoid one, this handbook was prepared to help you navigate through and simplify the complexities of government procurement so you can meet your due diligence duties while also accelerating your tendering cycle.

Leveraging thousands of hours of legal research and years of practical experience, this handbook will help you gain a better picture of how your organization measures up to prevailing due diligence standards. Ongoing developments in the procurement field have put us under an unprecedented level of scrutiny and an unprecedented volume of compliance requirements. The ever-expanding and overlapping body of red tape flowing out of public inquiries, public commissions, task forces, auditor general reports, domestic and international trade treaties, statutes, regulations, government directives and best-practices guidelines must be untangled and reconciled against a relentless tide of case law that is washing over every aspect of the tendering cycle and reshaping the purchasing landscape.

Without an effective strategy for addressing all of these regulatory requirements, a procurement operation can quickly find itself stretched to the breaking point by the competing tensions of meeting standards while meeting deadlines. Yet, as experience has shown, institutions can fulfill these twin objectives through the deployment of a three-stage strategy that assesses current conditions, integrates a proper governance framework and implements an effective institutional training program.

While some of the factors informing the three-stage strategy are particular to public sector purchasing, the overall strategy also has practical application to purchasing operations in the private sector.

The first step of this three-stage strategy is to take an accurate snapshot of the current situation within your institution by applying clear criteria for measuring its strengths and weaknesses. This handbook provides an overview of the factors relied on by an expanding number of institutions to get a clearer picture of their current conditions. Those factors are divided into the eight critical target areas of institutional governance, project governance, forms and formats, document drafting, bidding risks, contract administration, training and innovation:

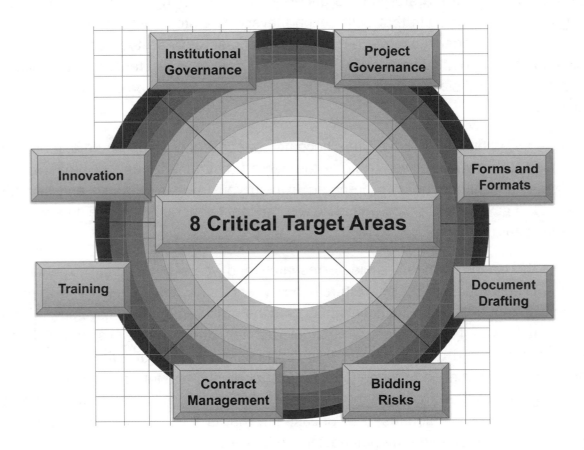

These eight critical target areas serve as the primary filters through which thousands of specific rules and requirements have been categorized. Using twenty four sub-categories referred to as due diligence indicators, the regulatory requirements have been sorted into a numerical indexing system so they can more effectively be used as benchmarks for measuring due diligence in the tendering cycle:

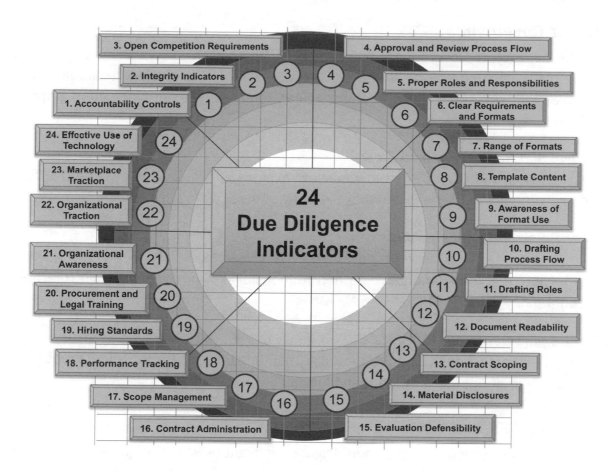

This handbook contains a number of leading case studies falling within these eight target areas that provide illustrative examples of the considerations that inform each of the due diligence indictors:

I. Institutional Governance

In Chapter 1 – Institutional Governance, due diligence indicators one, two and three focus on the institutional-level considerations of accountability controls, integrity indicators and open competition protocols:

1. Accountability Controls

Does your organization have the proper internal governance policies and procedures in place to keep pace with emerging due diligence standards?

2. Integrity Indicators

Does your organization have the necessary safeguards in place to address procedural improprieties, including unfair advantage, conflict of interest and evaluation bias?

3. Open Competition Requirements

Does your organization have the appropriate policies and procedures in place to comply with its open competition obligations and avoid trade treaty complaints based on inappropriate sole-sourcing, unauthorized branding and biased specifications?

II. Project Governance

In Chapter 2 – Project Governance, due diligence indicators four, five and six focus on the fundamentals of ensuring proper project approval and review processes, establishing clear project roles and responsibilities, defining clear requirements and selecting appropriate tendering formats:

4. Approval and Review Process Flow

Does your organization's project process flow avoid approval bottlenecks and effectively integrate key subject matter experts into the early stages of project planning?

5. Proper Roles and Responsibilities

Does your organization's project governance process establish a project governance framework that clearly documents roles and responsibilities in order to avoid role overlaps and accountability gaps?

6. Clear Requirements and Formats

Do your organization's project planning protocols mandate the preparation of clear requirements and the selection of appropriate tendering formats?

III. Forms and Formats

In Chapter 3 – Forms and Formats, due diligence indicators seven, eight and nine focus on the range of formats utilized by the institution, on whether its base templates are up-to-date and whether there is an adequate awareness across the institution of the legal implications of using the different types of tendering formats:

7. Range of Formats

Does your organization use a broad range of tendering formats based on domestic and international best practices?

8. Template Content

Do your organization's standard template terms comply with the expanding body of red-tape regulations flowing out of treaties, statutes, directives, good governance guidelines and case law developments?

9. Awareness of Format Use

Does your organization have a clear understanding of the legal liabilities created by certain tendering formats and is it properly avoiding the risks of bid repair, unfair process and bid shopping claims?

IV. Document Drafting

In Chapter 4 – Document Drafting, due diligence indicators ten, eleven and twelve focus on proper document drafting processes, clearly defined roles and responsibilities and document readability:

10. Drafting Process Flow

Does your organization have a clearly defined document drafting process that avoids duplication and delay and enables accelerated drafting?

11. Drafting Roles and Responsibilities

Does your organization have clearly identified roles and responsibilities for procurement advisors, legal counsel, technical experts and decision-makers in the drafting and assembly of its tendering documents?

12. Document Readability

Does your organization ensure better readability by using plain language in the main body of its tendering documents and properly incorporating technical content within appendices and schedules?

V. Bidding Risk

In Chapter 5 – Bidding Risk, due diligence indicators thirteen, fourteen and fifteen focus on the need for proper contract scoping, thorough material disclosures and defensible evaluation requirements:

13. Contract Scoping

Does your organization ensure that its solicitations are designed with clearly drafted requirements, properly aligned pricing and scoring structures and well-tailored legal agreements?

14. Material Disclosures

Does your organization have the proper material disclosure protocols built into its document drafting and tendering processes to mitigate against project delays and supplier extra-cost claims?

15. Evaluation Defensibility

Are your organization's evaluations based on clear compliance standards, transparent scoring mechanisms and defensible award processes?

VI. Contract Management

In Chapter 6 – Contract Management, due diligence indicators sixteen, seventeen and eighteen focus on clear contract administration accountability structures, proper scope management and solid supplier performance tracking systems:

16. Contract Administration Accountability
Does your organization have a proactive and clearly defined accountability structure for the contract administration stage of the procurement process?

17. Scope Management
Does your organization have proper scope-management practices to protect against improper scope increases?

18. Performance Tracking
Does your organization have the performance tracking measures in place to deal with problematic contractors and properly bar them from future work?

VII. Training
In Chapter 7 – Training, due diligence indicators nineteen, twenty and twenty-one focus on hiring and retention practices, the training of core procurement staff and the promotion of broader organizational awareness of proper procurement practices:

19. Hiring Standards
Are your organization's procurement hiring and retention practices properly targeted to the knowledge, skill set and experience required to meet prevailing due diligence standards?

20. Procurement and Legal Training
Are the core procurement staff within your purchasing and legal departments receiving the up-to-date training necessary to ensure that your organization is keeping pace with industry developments and meeting its due diligence duties?

21. Broader Organizational Awareness
Is your organization proactively avoiding procurement crises by promoting a broader organizational awareness of proper procurement practices?

VIII. Innovation
In Chapter 8 – Innovation, due diligence indicators twenty-two, twenty-three and twenty-four focus on whether procurement issues are being given sufficient attention by the senior levels of the institution, on the institution's interface with suppliers and on the use of technology throughout the tendering process:

22. Organizational Traction
Does your organization's procurement function have traction on senior management's agenda?

23. Marketplace Traction
Does your organization have effective market interface and monitoring policies and processes in place to deal with public access requests, debriefings and bid disputes, and is it protecting itself against bid rigging and improper lobbying?

24. Effective Use of Technology

Is your organization keeping up with industry practices and leveraging technological innovations to enhance and accelerate its tendering cycle?

By applying a sliding scale of compliance, you can ask yourself whether your organization is right on target in meeting these standards, or whether there are omissions in your procurement operations that place you at significant risk:

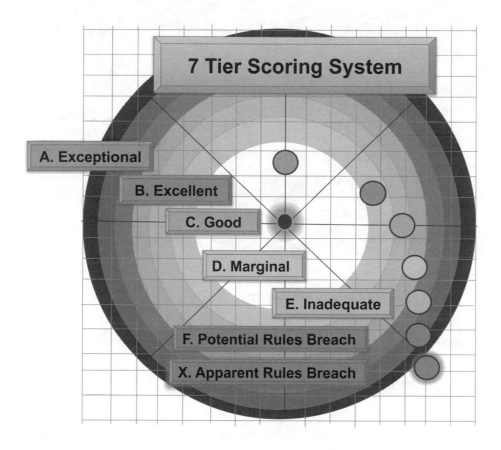

Since every institution is unique, each institution's due diligence footprint provides a different picture that informs how to implement remediation measures that can be tailored to address its specific circumstances:

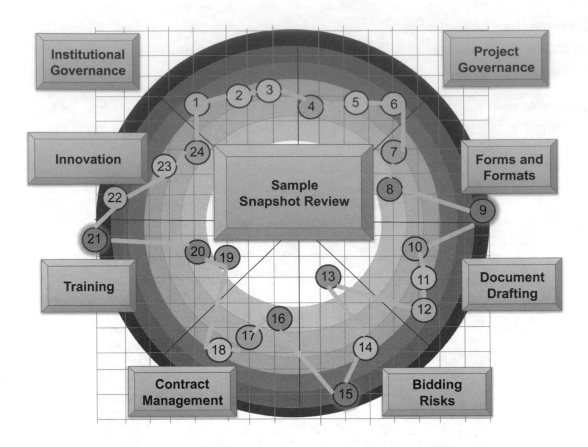

As discussed in the concluding chapter, entitled "Building Your Rapid Action Plan," once you have a sense of how your organization measures up to these due diligence standards you can then effectively turn your attention to implementing a strategy that includes a properly tailored good governance framework and an effective institutional training program. Until then, the case studies will speak for themselves.

Chapter 1:
INSTITUTIONAL GOVERNANCE

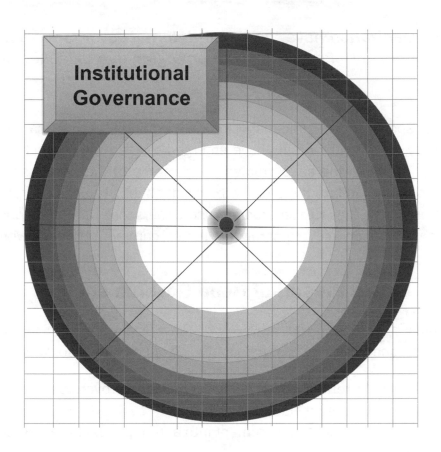

Introduction

Many of the issues that arise downstream in the procurement cycle can be attributed to a lack of proper practices and procedures at the institutional level of an organization. Institutions that are serious about meeting their due diligence duties should focus on establishing accountability controls that define roles and responsibilities, ethical rules that protect the integrity of their procurement process and open competition protocols that comply with trade treaty duties. Chapter 1 provides a series of case studies that focus on these critical areas of institutional governance.

Does your organization have the proper internal governance policies and procedures in place to keep pace with emerging due diligence standards?

Just as the federal sponsorship scandal and Toronto computer leasing scandal began to fade from public memory, new controversies have emerged to keep the spotlight firmly placed on public purchasing. The following case studies revisit some of the key lessons learned from those public inquiries and update the story with new questions relating to transparency in the budget approval process. These case studies also underscore the importance of balancing accountability with efficiency to avoid paralyzing the procurement process with red tape.

In Pursuit of Good Government

This article originally appeared in the March/April, 2006 issue of Municipal Lawyer, *the legal affairs magazine published by the International Municipal Lawyers Association.*

In recent years, a steady torrent of government spending controversies has put senior public officials in Canada in the hot seat, launching an ethics revolution that has transformed the once sleepy subject of government procurement into a front-page, prime-time and mainstream matter of national importance.

While there have been a number of recent Canadian contracting controversies, the two that serve as the most useful case studies on ethics in public sector spending are the federal government's Sponsorship Program and the City of Toronto's computer leasing contracts.

By way of background, in the wake of a near-win by separatist forces in the 1995 Quebec referendum, Canada's federal government established the Sponsorship Program. While the official objective was to promote federal government activities in Quebec as a means of fending off the separatist threat, millions of tax dollars were spent on improperly awarded and often haphazardly performed contracts. In some instances, public funds were improperly diverted for partisan political ends. After Canada's Auditor General released a highly critical report, the Prime Minister launched a public inquiry. On November 1, 2005, the Honourable Justice John. H. Gomery, the Quebec Superior Court judge who presided as Commissioner over the Inquiry, released the damaging report entitled *Commission of Inquiry into the Sponsorship Program and Advertising Activities* (the *"Gomery Federal Sponsorship Report"*) that led to the collapse of the federal government and to the electoral defeat of the ruling Liberal Party.

Like its federal counterpart, the City of Toronto faced its own spending scandal. In the wake of a runaway computer leasing contract that featured multi-million dollar cost-overruns, City Council struck two public inquiries to investigate both the specific leasing deal and the city's general technology procurement practices. On September 12, 2005, the Honourable Madam Justice Denise E. Bellamy, the Ontario Superior Court of Justice judge who presided as Commissioner over the two inquiries, submitted her report entitled *Toronto Computer Leasing Inquiry/Toronto External Contracts Inquiry Report* to the Mayor and Council of the City of Toronto. Volume 2 of the four-volume report, entitled "Good Government," included an extensive series of research papers (the *"Bellamy Toronto Good Government Report"*) focusing on procurement practices, conflict of interest, lobbying and municipal governance.

These two inquiries put a spotlight on public sector spending practices, calling for high-level remedial action to restore the credibility that was compromised by the public spending scandals. Public institutions need to counter this credibility gap by building winning conditions for their procurement professionals. Those winning conditions include clear centralized rules and practices and a broad range of flexible procurement tools that empower innovation. However, before any procurement team can function to full capacity, public institutions need to implement the following macro-level measures:

- enhancing independent external oversight of procurement activities;

- promoting values-based procurement and internal checks and balances; and

- defining clear roles and responsibilities within the organization.

With the *Gomery Federal Sponsorship Report* and the *Bellamy Toronto Good Government Report* serving as specific reference points, this article expands upon these due diligence measures and calls upon public institutions to restore public confidence in public sector spending.

Independent oversight is a key component of any system of checks and balances and is a cornerstone of the rule of law. For years the courts and the Canadian International Trade Tribunal have been effectively serving an oversight role over government procurement in Canada. An extensive body of case law has evolved to help govern the public tendering process. However, this type of oversight tends to focus on specific contract award competitions, rather than on activities such as lobbying that can occur behind closed doors and beyond the scope of a specific procurement process.

While lobbying activities are recognized as a legitimate and crucial component of the democratic process, when they are aimed at influencing the award of government contracts, such activities can compromise the integrity of government procurement and undermine public confidence in government spending. This has resulted in calls for the implementation of independent oversight functions beyond those traditionally fulfilled by courts and tribunals. As the U.S. Center for Democracy and Governance states in its February 1999 *Handbook for*

Fighting Corruption, independent government offices such as inspector generals, ombudsmen and anti-corruption agencies "improve accountability by overseeing government operations. In general, they look into allegations of mismanagement and review administrative systems to ensure they adhere to anti-corruption procedures." In addition to such arm's-length oversight bodies, the Center also recognizes the need for legislative oversight of government activities, noting that such oversight "provides a powerful check on executive authority, enhancing accountability where a dominant executive branch might otherwise operate with impunity."

The Canadian federal government's Sponsorship Program offers a case in point. In its November 2003 report entitled *Government-Wide Audit of Sponsorship, Advertising, and Public Opinion Research*, the Auditor General of Canada provided the initial catalyst for further scrutiny by revealing that:

> [T]he federal government ran the Sponsorship Program in a way that showed little regard for Parliament, the *Financial Administration Act*, contracting rules and regulations, transparency, and value for money:
>
> - Parliament was not informed of the program's objectives or the results it achieved and was misinformed as to how the program was being managed.
>
> - Those responsible for managing the program broke the government's own rules in the way they selected communications agencies and awarded contracts to them.
>
> - Partnership arrangements between government entities are not unusual in programs of mutual benefit. However, some sponsorship funds were transferred to Crown corporations using unusual methods that appear designed to provide significant commissions to communications agencies, while hiding the source of funds and the true nature of the transactions.
>
> - Documentation was very poor and there was little evidence of analysis to support the expenditure of more than $250 million. Over $100 million of that was paid to communications agencies as production fees and commissions.
>
> - Oversight mechanisms and essential controls at Public Works and Government Services Canada failed to detect, prevent, or report violations.

The Auditor General's findings triggered a Parliamentary committee investigation, which led to the Prime Minister striking the Gomery Inquiry. The findings from the November 2005 *Gomery Federal Sponsorship Report* served as a political *coup de grâce,* prompting a Parliamentary non-confidence motion, hastening the government's November 28, 2005, collapse, triggering the January 23, 2006, Canadian federal election and resulting in the defeat of the once-dominant Liberal Party after twelve years in power.

As this case study illustrates, independent oversight can be an effective mechanism for detecting and dealing with systemic procurement improprieties when it penetrates beyond the transaction-specific level. Institutional-level oversight functions, such as those performed by the Auditor General of Canada, need to be expanded to shine a brighter light on public sector spending practices. This can help serve as a deterrent against future improper practices and can help bolster accountability and public confidence in government spending.

Ethics and Accountability: Values-Based Procurement

A procurement organization should encourage values-based procurement by promoting a culture of ethics within the institution that includes: (i) mechanisms for internal regulation, reporting and self-governance; and (ii) measures to protect the security of tenure of employees responsible for enforcing internal governance rules. The *Gomery Federal Sponsorship Report* found that the Sponsorship Program was lacking in this regard. Amongst its "Major Findings," in Volume 1, the Report noted:

- a veil of secrecy surrounding the administration of the Sponsorship Program and an absence of transparency in the contracting process;

- the existence of a "culture of entitlement" among political officials and bureaucrats involved with the Sponsorship Program, including the receipt of monetary and non-monetary benefits;

- reluctance, for fear of reprisal, by virtually all public servants to go against the will of a manager who was circumventing established policies and who had access to senior political officials.

Such conditions, if allowed to persist, leave the situation ripe for future spending abuses. This clearly calls for remedial action. As the *Bellamy Toronto Good Government Report* states, "[i]t is widely recognized that public officials have a greater responsibility to uphold ethical standards to protect the 'public interest.'" With respect to government procurement practices in particular, the Report notes that:

> In surveying the literature and research on procurement, it quickly becomes evident that a primary focus of professional attention is on policies, procedures, directives, guidelines, techniques, best practices, etc. However, as also documented in the literature and validated in expert interviews, procurement is about more than the technical components. Almost universally, experts offered the view that ethics-related values

and principles are the essential foundation of public sector procurement in leading jurisdictions.

Promoting values-based procurement is a key component to a public institution's system of internal checks and balances. This calls for the implementation of mechanisms to enable both self-governance and reporting by individuals and monitoring by internal compliance offices within the institution.

Developing a code of conduct is a crucial element of such a system. In its 1997 *Practical Guide to Corruption Prevention*, Australia's New South Wales Independent Commission Against Corruption recognizes that "[a] code of conduct is an important management tool which can positively shape the culture of an organisation. Many organisations have found that adopting a clearly defined approach to ethical issues improves the organisation's reputation, helps to develop pride among staff and is good for business." The Commission calls for the broad implementation of such a code, stating that "significant cost savings can be made and loss of public confidence in organisations avoided if managers plan, develop and implement an integrated corruption prevention policy across their organization." In other words, promoting values-based procurement and internal checks and balances is simply good public policy and sound business strategy.

However, adequate protections need to be put in place to empower these policies. To give effect to such a system, a public institution should establish measures to protect those responsible for following and enforcing the rules. While the Guide notes that internal reporting systems account for a significant proportion of detected improprieties, it cautions that "corruption in the public sector is significantly under-reported. There are a number of reasons for this, one of which is a widespread fear of reprisals among public sector employees." Public institutions that are serious about promoting ethical procurement need to foster a culture that encourages all procurement staff to uphold values-based procurement without such fear of reprisal.

Just as independent decision-making has long been recognized as a crucial element of judicial independence and the rule of law, values-based procurement is a cornerstone of the public procurement process. Those responsible for administering and protecting the integrity of that process also require the degree of independent decision-making that is free from improper external influences. These safeguards are critical to building the winning conditions that protect a culture of ethics and promote values-based procurement.

Clear Roles and Responsibilities

A procurement organization should establish a clear and comprehensive set of roles and responsibilities within the institution including a clear division of roles between: (i) elected officials; (ii) senior management officials responsible for establishing and enforcing compliance with procurement rules; and (iii) front-line procurement professionals responsible for running specific projects. The *Gomery Federal Sponsorship Report* found that the Sponsorship Program lacked these necessary safeguards. Amongst its "Major Findings," the report noted:

- clear evidence of political involvement in the administration of the Sponsorship Program;

- insufficient oversight at the very senior levels of the public service which allowed program managers to circumvent proper contracting procedures and reporting lines;

- the refusal of Ministers, senior officials in the Prime Minister's Office and public servants to acknowledge their responsibility for the problems of mismanagement that occurred.

To guard against future abuses, it is crucial for public institutions to establish clearly defined roles and a system of checks and balances that protects the public interest against improper spending practices.

The *Bellamy Toronto Good Government Report* also uncovered a number of critical deficiencies in this regard at the municipal level of government and noted the importance of proper roles definition in the public procurement process:

> Experts and practitioners alike agree that a lack of internal clarity with respect to the relative roles and responsibilities of different players in the procurement process poses a high risk for both the integrity of the process and the likelihood of a value-for-money outcome. This includes roles and responsibilities for the central purchasing authority, the buying department, legal counsel, finance/budget staff, etc.

> The best practice in this area is relatively straightforward — to identify and describe these roles and responsibilities in clear and unambiguous terms as part of the overall purchasing policy and to embed these descriptions in training, guidelines, handbooks, checklists, case studies, etc. as part of ensuring a clear and consistent understanding across the organization.

Setting out the scope of roles and responsibilities is critical to avoiding overlapping accountability wherein no one is clearly accountable for decision-making or project outcomes, and to avoiding responsibility gaps which can leave critical issues unaddressed and unresolved.

Given the often complex and multi-disciplinary nature of a procurement project, it is crucial to establish a common universally understood allocation of roles, responsibilities and process roadmaps for the administration of both overall procurement practices and specific procurement projects. Front-line procurement staff should have a clear understanding of the scope of their discretion to make tactical planning decisions and should also be sequestered from inappropriate direct or indirect political interference.

While the *Bellamy Toronto Good Government Report* acknowledges that elected officials can play a legitimate role in the procurement process by providing overall spending approval and general oversight of the procurement system, it stresses that politicians should take a hands-off approach to specific contract award decisions:

> Experts suggest that in best practices jurisdictions — U.S. and Canada, federal, provincial/state, and municipal — elected officials understand the importance of remaining outside of the competitive tendering process. In this regard, it is generally viewed that one of the benefits of a having a highly professionalized procurement function is the ability to insulate and protect politicians from allegations of attempting to influence procurement decisions.

Unfortunately, the report notes that this ideal of enlightened hands-off political leadership is not always observed in practice, particularly at the municipal level of government, where elected officials often exercise an inordinate amount of direct influence over the procurement process:

> According to the experts, politicians do not always support fair and open competition, particularly when constituents are involved, i.e. not understanding that their direct intervention on behalf of a constituent would affect the fairness and equity of the process for other bidders.

The report goes on to cite a number of specific examples of political interference with public procurement at the municipal level of government, including instances where elected officials become involved in the development of specifications, review procurement documents outside of the formal internal approval process, meet with bidders and lobbyist once a tendering competition has been initiated, attempt to have staff waive mandatory requirements instead of disqualifying a particular bidder and directly entertain in-process and post-process bidder complaints instead of directing such complaints to the appropriate office.

Rather than micro-managing specific projects, the report suggests that a proper approach to ensuring accountability is to establish proper governing frameworks and support mechanisms for procurement staff. To maintain the integrity of the bidding process, contract award decisions need to be based on the objective application of transparent evaluation criteria. The integrity of the process and quality of the outcome can become compromised when the decision-making becomes politicized, is open to the influence of lobbying activities or is otherwise impacted by factors other than the objective application of predetermined transparent criteria.

A Call For Proactive Leadership

Recent high-profile spending controversies have triggered an instinctive call for greater controls over public purchasing practices. Public institutions should guard against misdirecting such remedial measures to the lower levels of an organization. While deflecting the issue may be the natural "scandal reflex" for some elected officials, the *Gomery Federal Sponsorship Report* clearly directs accountability for proper procurement practices to the highest levels of government. As the report states, "willful ignorance of administrative inadequacies will not absolve a Minister from responsibility for failures within the department." Imposing further constraints on front-line procurement professionals simply misses the point if such measures are not accompanied by systemic support mechanisms that enable individuals to properly perform their roles.

Rather than fettering discretion at the lower levels of an organization, a more progressive approach is to empower innovation by establishing and maintaining a consistent accountability framework. Public institutions need to develop a culture of innovation and improvement by ensuring adequate staffing and resources to properly manage all phases of the procurement cycle, adequate training at all levels of the procurement organization, a diverse framework of procurement tools and sufficient flexibility to enable procurement staff to exercise independent judgment. These remedial measures can only be implemented if the senior officials responsible for running the multi-billion dollar public procurement industry are prepared to step up to the challenge and deliver good government to the taxpayer.

Auditor General Finds Lack of Transparency in G8 Legacy Projects
Report of the Auditor General of Canada, Spring 2011

According to the spring 2011 report of the Auditor General of Canada, the government's funding and approval process for the G8 Legacy Infrastructure projects lacked the appropriate levels of transparency and documentation. As the report noted, rather than being clearly identified as funding for infrastructure projects in the Parry Sound-Muskoka region, the $50 million funding request was buried within Border Infrastructure Fund approvals for infrastructure projects earmarked to help ease border congestion. As the report stated, the real purpose for the funding was obscured in the legislative approval process:

The funding request was not made in a transparent manner

In November 2009, Supplementary Estimates (B) 2009–10 were tabled in the House of Commons. They included an item of $83 million for the "Border Infrastructure Fund relating to investments in infrastructure to reduce border congestion" (Exhibit 2.1). The Treasury Board of Canada Secretariat provided us with documentation showing that the intention was to use $50 million of this $83 million for G8 Summit projects. We noted, however, that this was not presented in the funding request made to Parliament through the Supplementary Estimates. Therefore, when Parliament considered the Supplementary Estimates as tabled, the request only indicated that money was to be used to reduce border congestion.

Treasury Board of Canada Secretariat officials explained to us that estimates contain, and combine, a large amount of expenditure information. Officials stated that it is government practice to present this information to Parliament at a very high level in order to ensure a manageable process.

In our view, by presenting the request for funding in the Supplementary Estimates in this way, the government was not being transparent about its purpose. Parliament was not provided with a clear explanation of how these funds were to be spent or informed that a special one-time exemption to the pre-existing terms and conditions of the Border Infrastructure Fund had been made to accommodate the G8 Fund.

The following year, because all $50 million was not expended during the 2009–10 fiscal year, the deadline for projects to be completed was extended to June 2010. Parliamentary approval to spend the remaining $10 million in unused funds in the next fiscal year was sought through the Supplementary Estimates (A) 2010–11. This time, the Supplementary Estimate item was labelled "Funding for Border Infrastructure Fund related to projects in support of the 2010 G8 Summit," which pointed out that funding was being sought for projects related to the G8 Summit. In our view, this is still not clear because it suggests that these projects were somehow related to border infrastructure, which was not the case.

The Auditor General recommended that in the future the Treasury Board of Canada Secretariat should "review the practices for determining the information that is presented to Parliament in the Estimates" with a view to ensuring that Parliament is presented with clear and accurate information about how the funds in question are to be used.

The Auditor General also noted that the government failed to properly document the decision-making process behind the selection of specific projects under the $50 million legacy fund. As the report indicates:

Of the 242 project proposals submitted, 33 projects were put forward by the Minister of Industry to the Minister of Infrastructure for consideration. Thirty-two projects were subsequently approved and funded, and one project was withdrawn by a municipality (Exhibit 2.2). However, due to the lack of supporting documentation, we could not conclude on the process to choose the projects put forward for funding consideration or determine why they were selected.

We are concerned about the lack of documentation in the process for selecting projects for funding. Supporting documentation is important, in our view, to show that the selection process was transparent, and provides a mechanism for accountability. When the Treasury Board approved Infrastructure Canada's submission for the G8 infrastructure program, it stated that the Treasury Board Policy on Transfer Payments be respected. Under this policy, any expenditure of public funds should demonstrate transparency, accountability, and value for money.

Transparency is fundamental to the proper accountability of decision-making in government procurement. When spending approvals are buried under budgets for unrelated initiatives, and when project-specific funding decisions are made behind closed doors in an undocumented fashion, this serves to undermine proper accountability for the expenditure of public resources and public confidence in the management of those resources.

Is Red Tape Paralyzing Public Purchasing? Considering the Bigger Picture

Recent high-profile public purchasing scandals have left little doubt that our government institutions need effective oversight to help promote transparency and accountability and to help ensure the proper spending of public dollars. However, these critical policy objectives must be balanced against the need to produce timely and cost-effective results.

With an ever-expanding line-up of reviewers, regulators and rejecters shining a spotlight on public purchasers, and with the ever-present risk of legal challenge, a critical question must be asked: Is red tape paralyzing public purchasing?

Recent scandals have spawned an increase in statutory and administrative rules aimed at imposing greater internal and external controls. In an era of increasingly stretched public resources, we should ask ourselves whether government institutions have achieved the proper balance between oversight measures on the one hand and efficient business practices on the other.

By imposing a high degree of oversight on their procurement processes, public institutions run the risk of obstructing and under-resourcing the "doers" within their organizations who are responsible for delivering results.

A Gomery Report background paper by Liane E. Benoit and Ned Franks entitled "For the Want of a Nail: The Role of Internal Audit in the Sponsorship Scandal" in *Restoring Accountability, Research Studies Volume 2: The Public Service and Transparency* (Ottawa: Public Works and Government Services Canada, 2006) offers the following caution:

> [W]hen the balance of "doers" to "checkers" gets too strongly tilted in favour of the latter, the oversight becomes oppressive and the corresponding impact on the morale and self-esteem of public servants can be significant. It is in no government's best interest to create so

> much tension among its employees — between the pressure on them
> to perform and the pressure on them to account for that performance
> — that they lose all latitude for creativity, innovation or common sense.

While no single oversight measure may, in itself, paralyze the system, the total accumulation of red tape can expose the purchasing process to death by a thousand paper cuts. Ironically, public institutions should consider imposing control measures over their control measures to avoid driving their purchasing cycle into bureaucratic gridlock.

The legal system is one of the leading contributors of red tape. In its 1981 decision in *Ontario v. Ron Engineering*, the Supreme Court of Canada applied a preliminary contract, known as "Contract A," to the tendering process. That decision will likely go down in history as the case that launched a thousand lawsuits.

In a pyrrhic victory, the purchaser won the right to keep a reneging bidder's bid security. However, since then, the courts have relied on Contract A to impose a broad range of legal duties on purchasers and grant a broad range of legal rights to suppliers.

The often-stated judicial policy aims of "protecting the integrity of the bidding process" and "ensuring fairness to bidders" have resulted in a quarter-century of piecemeal justice delivered on an often unpredictable and inconsistent case-by-case basis. The net result has been increased legal risk and uncertainty for public purchasers, with little business advantage gained in return.

The cumulative adverse impact of this legal red tape on the efficiency of the procurement cycle has been immeasurable. Public purchasers must now deliver results under extreme time pressures while navigating a legal maze of implied duties and guarding against the ever-present risk of legal challenge.

Yet, suppliers and their lawyers continue to advance – and the courts continue to entertain – new legal theories that would help suppliers launch even more lawsuits. It begs the ultimate question: can a legal regime geared to giving so many rights to unsuccessful suppliers translate into a purchasing system that serves the best interest of the taxpayer and the public?

Striking the right balance between accountability and action should be the ultimate policy objective of the public purchasing system. The system needs to run cleanly and transparently but it also needs to run efficiently and expeditiously.

Public institutions should consider taking a solid step towards reversing the tide of red tape by realigning their procurement operations so that more resources are directed towards equipping and training their purchasing professionals.

A well-trained and focused procurement operation, guided by an effective and minimally intrusive oversight system, coupled with a less litigation-friendly legal environment, would go a long way to reducing inefficiency and delivering positive results to the public.

World Bank Advises Mexico
to Cut Red Tape and Increase Efficiency
Procurement Assessment Report for Mexico, 2007

The World Bank's November 2007 review of Mexico's government procurement system offers a clear warning to all jurisdictions that want to avoid red tape entanglements. In the report, the World Bank notes that Mexico's government procurement system places too much emphasis on outdated oversight and control processes that cause confusion and bureaucratic gridlock while failing to add value, integrity or transparency to government spending practices. To help modernize the procurement process, the World Bank recommends a cultural shift away from control-focused processes and towards a strategic procurement philosophy aimed at promoting fiscal management and supporting the government's broader initiatives.

To properly leverage the strategic value of procurement, the World Bank recommends that procurement not be viewed as a process to be administered and controlled. Rather, it should be viewed more broadly as an integral part of an institution's overall objectives:

> A major transformation of the prevailing mindset on the nature of the procurement function is necessary. Decision makers have traditionally considered public procurement as an administrative and control function, but the modern concept is that procurement is a strategic function of the government used to promote better fiscal management and to support government development policies. As such, its key objective is not control, but the efficient and economical delivery of goods and services guided by a solid set of transparency, ethics, and accountability principles. Members of the Organization for Economic Cooperation and Development are increasingly recognizing that modern public procurement is more about information, coordination, analysis, and management than regulation. Without this conceptual transformation, any technical solutions are likely to fail. The Mexican system would benefit from a fresh and critical review if this modern conception of procurement was adopted. The old control approach resulted in rules and requirements that add processes, not commensurate value, integrity, or transparency.

In other words, the procurement function should not be seen as an end itself. Success should not be defined merely by procedural compliance with complex internal controls. Rather, government spending should be viewed within the context of overall institutional objectives with a view to ensuring compliance with procurement rules and the successful and timely acquisition of the goods and services required to fulfill institutional objectives.

The World Bank report notes duplication stemming from a lack of coordination in the creation of procurement regulations, stating that the "present institutional structure for public procurement in Mexico permits various agencies to issue procurement regulations independently. This greatly increases the risk of inconsistencies, overlaps, or gaps, and no mechanism is available to coordinate the development of procurement regulations...so that all can be reconciled and better aligned with government policy." To help modernize procurement practices, the World Bank calls for the elimination of unnecessarily complex approval processes. It also places a premium on coordination, consistency and efficiency in public purchasing. The report also notes a lack of coordination between the budgeting and financial management systems and the procurement process, finding that "interfaces are missing that would allow both to share information needed for the procurement process and the budget and treasury management functions to operate smoothly. Currently, these processes do not interact adequately to support the effective management of fiscal resources."

The report calls for a systemic review of existing practices to bring them in line with the following objectives:

- incorporating a fresh approach guided by objectives of efficiency and better use of public resources rather than by control objectives;

- ensuring alignment of the system with the objectives of the government in relation to improving competitiveness and transparency;

- streamlining the system to provide for the necessary flexibility to adapt more easily to changing markets, procurement techniques, and needs;

- eliminating unnecessary processes that do not add substantial value or integrity to the system;

- promoting the standardization of processes and documentation throughout government agencies based on best practice;

- removing regulatory barriers to making use of the full potential of the government's electronic procurement system; and

- establishing appropriate regulation for intellectual and professional services of an intellectual nature.

While focused on Mexico's procurement practices, many of the observations in the World Bank's report have universal resonance. Its above-noted recommendations should serve as guidelines for all purchasing institutions that are serious about modernizing their procurement practices.

2 **Integrity Indicators**

Does your organization have the necessary safeguards in place to address procedural improprieties, including unfair advantage, conflict of interest and evaluation bias?

Maintaining the integrity of the procurement process is of paramount importance to protecting the public interest. The case studies in this section illustrate the need to establish clear and transparent practices to deal with ethical considerations and protect the procurement process from conflict of interest, unfair advantage and bias.

Judging Ethical Purchasing Dilemmas

Canada has a long history of high-profile spending scandals. Yet, below the surface of those high-profile cases lies an even deeper pool of largely unnoticed decisions dealing with ethical dilemmas in public purchasing. These reported decisions tend to focus on three recurring themes: (1) conflict of interest within institutions; (2) unfair bidder advantage; and (3) a lack of transparent ethics rules. This column surveys a small selection of cases from the author's *Ethics and Accountability* workshop materials and asks you to judge the ethical dilemmas for yourself.

1. Conflict of Interest Within the Institution

Purchasers should ensure that their evaluation decisions are made free from personal interest or bias. Conflict of interest arises within the purchasing institution when a decision-maker's ability to exercise impartial discretion in the public interest is compromised by that decision-maker's personal interests or where decision-makers apply an improper preference to certain suppliers.

The Ethical Dilemma
A municipal alderman owns an interest in a company that bids on a contract for the municipality. The alderman casts the deciding vote in favour of awarding the contract to that company. If you were the judge, would you:

   a)   order the alderman to surrender any profits back to the municipality; or

   b)   prohibit the municipality from carrying out the illegal contract?

The Decision

In its August 1893 decision in *Coughlin & Mayo v. Victoria (City)*, the British Columbia Supreme Court found that an alderman was in a conflict of interest because he owned an interest in a company and cast the deciding vote to award a contract to that company. The court noted that the alderman's personal interest could undermine his ability to properly discharge his public duties in the event that a contract dispute arose between the city and the supplier. The court found that the contract award was tainted with illegality and prohibited the city from carrying out the contract.

2. Unfair Bidder Advantage

Purchasers should ensure that bidders are not provided an unfair advantage during a tendering process. Bidder unfair advantage includes instances where a bidder has an "inside advantage" created through access to specific information or decision-makers to which other bidders do not have access.

The Ethical Dilemma

The Department of National Defence awards a contract for logistic and administrative support. After the contract is awarded, it discovers that a former government employee had participated in the preparation of the winning tender. The government decides to rescind the contract award and is sued by the terminated contractor. If you were the judge would you:

a)   award lost profit damages to the terminated contractor; or

b)   uphold the government's decision to terminate the contract?

The Decision

In its August 1995 decision in *LGS Group Inc. v. Canada (Attorney General)*, the Federal Court of Canada upheld a government decision to rescind a contract award on account of conflict of interest and unfair advantage. The contract was awarded and then rescinded when it was discovered that a former government employee had participated in the preparation of the winning bidder's tender.

3. Transparency of Ethics Rules

To better ensure that their evaluation decisions are transparent and defensible, purchasers should clearly define the circumstances that they consider to be an unfair advantage or conflict of interest.

The Ethical Dilemma

The Department of Health issues a tender call for a consumer research study regarding health warnings on tobacco products. The Department rejects a bidder for conflict of interest because he had worked for the tobacco industry in the prior three years. The rejected bidder challenges the disqualification. If you were on the judge would you:

1. uphold the disqualification since the rejected bidder's prior work for the tobacco industry reflects a potential bias that could impact the reliability of the contemplated research; or

2. award the rejected bidder damages for his lost profits due to the improper disqualification?

The Decision

In its March 2000 determination in *Re Luik*, the Canadian International Trade Tribunal found that the government had improperly rejected the complainant based on undisclosed conflict of interest rules. The Tribunal ordered the government to compensate the complainant for lost profit damages. As this case illustrates, purchasers should be clear in defining what constitutes a conflict of interest if they want to safely reject bidders on those grounds.

Future Considerations

Issues relating to ethics and accountability can have a significant impact on the government procurement process and on the public's confidence in that process. Government institutions should therefore adopt and enforce clear and transparent conflict of interest rules aimed at eliminating conflict of interest and prohibiting unfair bidder advantage. The lessons offered by existing case law can serve as a valuable source in the development of these rules.

Federal Court Says Conflict Rules Go Without Saying

Serco Facilities Management Inc. v. Defence Construction Canada
Federal Court of Appeal, 2008

In its December 2007 determination in *Serco Facilities Management Inc. v. Defence Construction Canada,* the Canadian International Trade Tribunal found that the government breached the *Agreement on Internal Trade* by failing to properly disclose its conflict of interest rules. The case dealt with a Defence Construction Canada ("DCC") invitation to tender for replacement windows and renovations at the Department of National Defence ("DND") base in Goose Bay. DCC rejected Serco's tender because Serco was already retained for the preparation of drawings, specifications, estimates and construction phase services for the project. DCC maintained that awarding the construction contracts to Serco would put Serco in a conflict of interest:

> Serco was serving as the DND design authority for the project in question ... and would be reviewing shop drawings and providing inspection and hand-over assistance. According to DCC, this meant that Serco, if awarded the contracts, would be not only performing the work but also overseeing and inspecting the project. DCC added that awarding a contract to any contractor who is known to be the design engineer of

record and thus has a more detailed knowledge of the requirements of the project, would also be unfair to other potential suppliers. For these reasons, DCC confirmed that it would not accept future bids submitted by Serco where Serco had been directly involved in either the design or inspection of the work.

While it agreed with the finding of a conflict of interest, the Tribunal upheld Serco's complaint because the government failed to expressly include conflict of interest rules in its tender call and concluded that they could not be implied.

However, in its May 2008 judgment, the Federal Court of Appeal overturned the Canadian International Trade Tribunal determination, finding that it was unnecessary to explicitly set out a prohibition against conflict of interest since that could be presumed to apply under the *Agreement on Internal Trade*:

> The absence of a conflict of interest or the right to reject a bid for that reason are not a requirement of the procurement, an evaluation criterion, or an evaluation methodology which, as contemplated in Article 506(6) of the AIT, must be clearly identified in the tender documents.

The court thereby upheld the federal government's implied right to reject tenders on the basis of conflict of interest and recognized that those conflict rules did not have to be expressly stated as evaluation criteria in order to be enforced. While the Federal Court of Appeal ultimately determined that the conflict of interest rules could be implied under the treaty, to avoid bid disputes government institutions should clearly disclose their conflict rules in their solicitation documents so that conflicted bidders are put on notice ahead of time about their ineligibility for award.

BPS Directive Code of Conduct

In 2010 the Ontario government enacted the Broader Public Sector Procurement Directive which sets out a number of mandatory governance requirements relating to the procurement practices of broader public sector institutions in the university, college, school board and health sectors. The Directive includes the obligation to establish an ethical code of conduct within these public institutions. Highlights from the Directive are reproduced below.

Ontario

Broader Public Sector Procurement Directive

7. Mandatory Requirements

7.1 Supply Chain Code of Ethics (Code)

The Code does not supersede codes of ethics that Organizations have in place, but supplements such codes with supply chain-specific standards of practice.

Organizations must formally adopt the Code in accordance with their governance processes. The policy intent is to establish that the conduct of all Members of an Organization involved with Supply Chain Activities must be in accordance with the Code.

The Code must be made available and visible to all Members of the Organization, as well as suppliers and other stakeholders involved with Supply Chain Activities.

Ontario Broader Public Sector (BPS) Supply Chain Code of Ethics

Goal: To ensure an ethical, professional and accountable BPS supply chain.

I. Personal Integrity and Professionalism

Individuals involved with Supply Chain Activities must act, and be seen to act, with integrity and professionalism. Honesty, care and due diligence must be integral to all Supply Chain Activities within and between BPS organizations, suppliers and other stakeholders. Respect must be demonstrated for each other and for the environment. Confidential information must be safeguarded. Participants must not engage in any activity that may create, or appear to create, a conflict of interest, such as accepting gifts or favours, providing preferential treatment, or publicly endorsing suppliers or products.

II. Accountability and Transparency

Supply Chain Activities must be open and accountable. In particular, contracting and purchasing activities must be fair, transparent and conducted with a view to obtaining the best value for public money. All participants must ensure that public sector resources are used in a responsible, efficient and effective manner.

III. Compliance and Continuous Improvement

Individuals involved with purchasing or other Supply Chain Activities must comply with this Code of Ethics and the laws of Canada and Ontario. Individuals should continuously work to improve supply chain policies and procedures, to improve their supply chain knowledge and skill levels, and to share leading practices.

…

7.2.24 Mandatory Requirement #24: Conflict of Interest

Organizations must monitor any conflict of interest that may arise as a result of the Members' of the Organization, advisors', external consultants', or suppliers' involvement with the Supply Chain Activities. Individuals involved with the Supply Chain Activities must declare actual or potential conflicts of interest. Where a conflict of interest arises, it must be evaluated and an appropriate mitigating action must be taken.

Ontario *Municipal Conflict of Interest Act*

Ontario's Municipal Conflict of Interest Act establishes statutory rules that prohibit elected municipal officials from becoming involved in official business in matters for which they have a personal interest. Sanctions for breaching this statute can include monetary penalties, the removal from public office and a ban against seeking re-election. Highlights from the Ontario municipal conflict of interest statute are set out below.

Ontario

Municipal Conflict of Interest Act

5.(1) Where a member, either on his or her own behalf or while acting for, by, with or through another, has any pecuniary interest, direct or indirect, in any matter and is, present at a meeting of the council or local board at which the matter is the subject of consideration, the member,

(a) shall, prior to any consideration of the matter at the meeting, disclose the interest and the general nature thereof;

(b) shall not take part in the discussion of, or vote on any question in respect of the matter; and

(c) shall not attempt in any way whether before, during or after the meeting to influence the voting of any such question.

(2) Where the meeting referred to in subsection (1) is not open to the public, in addition to complying with the requirements of that subsection, the member shall forthwith leave the meeting or the part of the meeting during which the matter is under consideration.

(3) Where the interest of a member has not been disclosed as required by subsection (1) by reason of the member's absence from the meeting referred to therein, the member shall disclose the interest and otherwise comply with subsection (1) at the first meeting of the council or local board, as the case may be, attended by the member after the meeting referred to in subsection (1).

…

10.(1) Subject to subsection (2), where the judge determines that a member or a former member while he or she was a member has contravened subsection 5(1), (2) or (3), the judge,

(a) shall, in the case of a member, declare the seat of the member vacant; and

(b) may disqualify the member or former member from being a member during a period thereafter of not more than seven years; and

(c) may, where the contravention has resulted in personal financial gain, require the member or former member to make restitution to the party suffering the loss, or, where such party is not readily ascertainable, to the municipality or local board of which he or she is a member or former member.

(2) Where the judge determines that a member or a former member while he or she was a member has contravened subsection 5(1), (2) or (3), if the judge finds that the contravention was committed through inadvertence or by reason of an error in judgment, the member is not subject to having his or her seat declared vacant and the member or former member is not subject to being disqualified as a member, as provided by subsection (1).

Former Councillor Banned From Re-election and Ordered to Pay $20,000 After Breaching Conflict Rules

Mondoux v. Tuchenhagen
Ontario Superior Court of Justice, 2010

In its December 2010 decision in *Mondoux v. Tuchenhagen*, the Ontario Superior Court of Justice found that an elected municipal official had breached the *Municipal Conflict of Interest Act* by participating in a council vote to approve a tendering process for the sale of property for which he intended to bid. The case dealt with vacant property that had been seized by the City of Thunder Bay due to tax arrears and was to be put up for sale by public tender. The respondent was, at the material time, an elected official who had served on the municipal council for twelve years. He took an interest in acquiring the property in question and ultimately submitted the winning bid. Rather than recusing himself from council's approval process, he participated in the council vote that authorized the city to proceed with the tendering process. A neighbour of the relevant property submitted the only other bid on the property and, after losing the bidding process, launched an application under the *Municipal Conflict of Interest Act* seeking a declaration that the councillor had breached the statute and seeking restitution for financial loss arising out of that breach.

In its decision, the court cited the relevant excerpts from the statute regarding the duty of municipal councillors to declare any financial interests in any proceedings before council and to recuse themselves from any such proceedings.

The court determined that the respondent knew he would be bidding on the property in question, should have disclosed this intention to council and should have recused himself from the vote when council approved the tendering process for the sale of the land in question.

After determining that the respondent had breached the statute by failing to follow the prescribed disclosure and recusal protocols, the court then considered whether the statutory breach could be excused as having being made through inadvertence or by reason of an error in judgment. The court concluded that it could not be excused on those grounds:

> I accept that Mr. Tuchenhagen was open with Realty Services Division about his interest in the property. However, I do not find that there was otherwise the requisite candour and complete frankness required of him in the circumstances. This is not to attribute ill motive to Mr. Tuchenhagen. However, Mr. Tuchenhagen had been a member of Council for almost 12 years. He would, or should, have been well aware of the need to avoid placing himself in a conflict of interest. If he had turned his mind to the question of conflict on this issue, one would reasonably expect him to have some uncertainty about his position. Just hours before attending the Committee of the Whole on July 21, 2008, he had made an appointment to view the property. If, notwithstanding the steps that he had taken, he did not consider the question of conflict, then it is reasonable to characterize his conduct as reckless or wilfully blind. Further, in my opinion, a reasonable and fair-minded elector, apprised of all the circumstances, would not accept that Mr. Tuchenhagen's attendance at the July 21, 2008 meeting of the Committee of the Whole amounted to an error in judgment on his part within the meaning of the MCIA.

After finding the respondent in breach of the statute, the court noted that the statute required that the councillor's seat be declared vacant. However, since the respondent was no longer serving on council, the court ordered that he be disqualified from holding municipal office for four years, which effectively barred him from running in the next election:

> Unlike subsection 10(1)(a), subsection 10(1)(b) is discretionary – a member who has contravened subsection 5(1) may be disqualified from being a member for not more than seven years. The issue is, how serious was the contravention. There is no evidence that Mr. Tuchenhagen acted in bad faith. The City suffered no loss. There was no policy prohibiting Mr. Tuchenhagen from bidding on real estate declared surplus to the City's needs. There was no interference with the public tender process. Mr. Tuchenhagen has given the City 12 years of public service. However, because the municipal election has just been held, any disqualification of less than the four-year term of the present Council would result in no sanction. It was Mr. Tuchenhagen's choice not to run in the most recent election. The only meaningful sanction that I can impose, because I cannot declare his seat vacant, is to disqualify Mr. Tuchenhagen from running in the next election. If I had been required to declare Mr. Tuchenhagen's seat vacant, I would have been disposed to impose a shorter disqualification as was done by Killeen J. in *Blake v. Watts*, 1973 CarswellOnt 372 (Co. Ct.), where he declared vacant the seat on Council of the respondent members and imposed a nominal two week disqualification. In the present case, there must be some consequence flowing from the contravention. I hold that a disqualification of four years would be fair and just in this case.

However, the court denied the applicant's request for damages for restitution, finding that the applicant had failed to prove that the respondent had made a profit from the transaction in question or had caused the applicant to suffer a financial loss.

As this case illustrates, the failure to adhere to statutory conflict of interest disclosure and recusal protocols can have significant consequences on elected officials. Where that conflict causes a loss to other affected parties, restitution may also be available as a legal sanction. In this instance, the former councillor was barred from running in the subsequent election. While no financial restitution was awarded, the former councillor was subsequently ordered to pay the applicant $16,750 in court fees plus $3,568 in related disbursements.

Former Public Servant Guilty
of Breaching Conflict Law in Land Sale
R. v. Kupfer
Manitoba Court of Queen's Bench, 2008

In its November 2007 judgment in *R. v. Kupfer*, the Manitoba Provincial Court found the accused guilty of violating a provision of *The Legislative Assembly and Executive Council Conflict of Interest Act*. The case involved a former senior public servant who, contrary to the one year cooling-off period prescribed under the statute, was found to have acted on behalf of a private company in a real estate transaction involving property that he had a prior involvement with when he had worked for the government.

As noted in the judgment, section 19.2 of Manitoba's *The Legislative Assembly and Executive Council Conflict of Interest Act* reads as follows:

> Where a minister or senior public servant acts for or advises the government or a Crown agency with respect to a matter in which the government or Crown agency has an interest, the minister or senior public servant shall not, for a period of one year following the date on which the minister or senior public servant leaves office, act for or on behalf of a person, partnership or unincorporated association or organization in relation to the matter.

The court found that in his prior official capacity as an Assistant Deputy Minister for the provincial government, the defendant had knowledge and involvement with the real estate in question:

> Treasury Board Minute 108/98 – item 8 dated March 17, 1998 authorized the sale of the property at 290 Drury Avenue. The Land Management Services appraisal was $625,000.00 comprising $435,520.00 in depreciated building value and $189,480.00 in land value in July 1997.

> Mr. Kupfer was involved in the decision making process in this regard. He was also involved in the process to determine if there were other departments or agencies capable or willing to take over the property. The Accommodation Division, headed by Mr. Kupfer declared the property surplus.

> From 1998 until 2004, there were 26 offers to purchase which for a variety of reasons were not accepted. In many instances, Mr. Kupfer was consulted about the offers. Mr. Kupfer was also consulted about others making use of the property, for example as a soccer pitch and as a filming sight. The inference to be drawn is that Mr. Kupfer was well aware of the property and the fact that it was difficult to sell it.

The court also noted the public policy significance of the conflict of interest law and the need to give it a broad interpretation:

> This conflict of interest law is important legislation. It is a code of ethics setting out appropriate standards of conduct to be followed by politicians and senior public servants. It is intended to enhance public confidence in the activities of politicians and senior public servants. It is intended to prevent doubts or suspicions arising from decisions made or actions taken by politicians or senior public servants (see: The Canadian Encyclopaedia and *Arbez v. Johnson* ((1998) 126 Man. R. 271)). As such, the legislation must be given a broad interpretation. This legislation is broader than merely requiring disclosure of certain interests. This legislation is broader than trying to prevent someone taking advantage of insider information. It is intended to do more than just prevent harm from taking place or damage being suffered. It is intended to set out a normative standard to which politicians and senior public officials should adhere.

The court then concluded that the defendant had, within one year of leaving office as Assistant Deputy Minister, acted for a third party in connection with the real estate in question:

> I am satisfied that Mr. Kupfer acted for 4914971 Manitoba Ltd. within one year of leaving the office of Assistant Deputy Minister with respect to the purchase by that company from the Government of 290 Drury.

> He acted for the company by delivering an offer. That may seem a trivial action; one that could be done by a courier, but it was an initial step in the process of acquiring the property. It saved time and expense.

> He acted for the company by having a conversation with the manager of land services and determined that the offer was going to be allowed to lapse. The manager stated that he was not revealing any confidential information but was providing information appropriately. There seems to be no dispute about this. However, after the information was received, an offer at an increased price was received by the Government. A phone call may be regarded as trivial but it is a step in the process. Moreover, Mr. Kupfer knew who to phone and what to say. He could manoeuvre within the bureaucracy. That is not trivial.

> Also, Mr. Kupfer had a telephone conversation with Mr. Kent to point out that the land description was in error and additional land must be included in the transfer documents. Mr. Kent agreed. This was significant.

> In this case, Mr. Kupfer's conduct violated section 19.2 and I find him guilty.

In its July 2008 decision, the Manitoba Court of Queen's Bench upheld the Provincial Court's judgment, finding that the phone call made to the government by the appellant during the bidding process breached the conflict of interest law:

> Did Kupfer act for the numbered company on its purchase? The phrase "act for" is used in both instances in relation to government and in relation to the numbered company. The use of the same phrase generally indicates a similar meaning. In relation to government, "act for" means perform an act from within or from outside of government. No doubt, Olson acted for the numbered company as president and negotiator on its purchase, but the numbered company was agent for Pioneer. Kupfer, a director of Pioneer, made a critical telephone call during the time referred to in the information. Pioneer had twice offered $250,000 for the property. It or its agent then submitted a low-ball offer of $200,000. Olson then instructed Kupfer to make a telephone call in order to ascertain whether there were any other offers, whether government might accept the low offer or whether it would have to make a higher offer in order to get the property. When Kupfer received the answer from Kent, the numbered company raised its offer above the initial $250,000 offers. It would be an understatement to say that Olson and Kupfer maximized their chance of getting the lie of the land by having Kupfer make the call to Kent, Kupfer's former colleague. In the context of the circumstances of this case, Kupfer, in making that call, performed an act that was prohibited under the section. There is no need to debate whether delivery of the offer or other minor actions are prohibited. That can be decided in another case. Having regard to the purpose of the legislation and perceptions of and protection of the public that are at the root of the section, that telephone call was sufficiently tied to the government's interest in 290 Drury and the scope of Kupfer's advice in relation to 290 Drury while employed by government that he was required to refrain from making that telephone call, and he committed a breach of the section when he made the call. That government suffered no loss is not relevant.

As this case illustrates, the post-employment use of inside information and internal contacts can compromise the integrity of the bidding process by giving some bidders an unfair advantage over other bidders. In some jurisdictions, statutory codes have been enacted to govern the activities of former public officials and prohibit the use of inside information for post-service personal gain. Where such restrictions are in effect, they can prohibit former public servants from using information obtained while within government to assist outside parties, including suppliers bidding on government contracts, in their dealings with government institutions. In jurisdictions where such statutory codes have not been enacted, purchasers should establish clear tendering rules to deal with these post-service conflict risks.

Inside Advantage Taints Tendering Process and Breaches Trade Treaty

Bureau d'études stratégiques et techniques en économique v. CIDA
Canadian International Trade Tribunal, 2007

Re Bluedrop Performance Learning Inc.
Canadian International Trade Tribunal, 2008

Inside advantage can prejudice the fairness of a procurement process and result in breaches of applicable trade treaties.

In its September 2007 determination in *Bureau d'études stratégiques et techniques en économique v. Canadian International Development Agency*, the Canadian International Trade Tribunal considered allegations of conflict of interest and bias in connection with the procurement of consulting services for an international local governance project. The complainant claimed that its competitor had an inside advantage because of access to government information obtained during its involvement in the planning stages of the project and that the government's prior relationship with the competitor during those planning stages biased the subsequent evaluation process.

With respect to the first allegation, the Tribunal agreed that the complainant's competitor had access to information that was not available to other bidders:

> In the Tribunal's opinion, it is clear from the evidence on the record that the contract winner had information in his possession that was not available to B.E.S.T.E. and the other bidders. The Tribunal notes that, within the context of the contract with CIDA to assist with the selection and award of the CSA contract for the LGM project, from February 3, 2006, to March 31, 2007, Mr. Courtemanche had access to information of which B.E.S.T.E. and the other bidders for the RFSP were deprived. More specifically, this was information common to both procurements, the one for the selection of the CSA and the one in issue here.

The Tribunal also noted that this access to inside information translated into a clear advantage during the evaluation process:

> It must be noted, for Requirements 10 and 11 of the RFSP, of the seven bidders, the contract winner received the most points. He received nearly all points or almost 50 percent more than the second-place bidder, while B.E.S.T.E. received very few points for these two requirements. The Tribunal cannot determine that the contract winner would not have received the most points for these two requirements had it not

been for the fact that he had access to the information of which the other bidders were deprived. According to the evidence on the record, however, it is reasonable to conclude that he appears to have obtained a clear advantage from it. The Tribunal therefore finds that the fact that B.E.S.T.E. was deprived of information relevant to the preparation of its bid, information that the contract winner had because of his mandate relating to the selection of the CSA, constitutes a breach of the AIT.

After concluding that the access to inside information resulted in a breach of the *Agreement on Internal Trade*, the Tribunal then considered allegations of favouritism flowing from the prior relationship between the contract winner and the government and whether that situation constituted a reasonable apprehension of bias. The Tribunal's analysis provides a good example of how the use of external advisors can result in downstream conflict of interest and undermine a procurement process:

> In this case, the Tribunal has closely studied the facts and, while it does not find there is *de facto* bias on the part of CIDA, it is of the opinion that, in applying the relevant test, there is indeed a reasonable apprehension of bias. Several factors support the Tribunal's reasoning in this regard. The mere fact that one of the evaluators had worked with Mr. Courtemanche in the past is not sufficient, in itself, to warrant a finding of reasonable apprehension of bias. Rather, it is the particular circumstances of this case that support this finding.

> First, the Tribunal notes that it was for the same overall project, namely, the LGM project for which Mr. Courtemanche provided his services to CIDA for the selection of the CSA. The evaluator of the contract at issue and Mr. Courtemanche were called upon to work closely on this project, no doubt since February 3, 2006, the start date of his contract. This working relationship began well before the date on which the bids for the contract at issue were opened. It is therefore inevitable that he knew Mr. Courtemanche professionally.

> Second, looking at the time frame, it can be seen that, because of his previous contracts with CIDA, Mr. Courtemanche had worked for the evaluator as early as August 2004. As the head of the evaluation team, this CIDA employee also sat on the selection committee for the CSA and the selection committee for the monitor/advisor. It seems, then, that the contract winner had worked for this CIDA employee starting in 2004, before becoming his colleague on the selection committee for the CSA, in 2006, and before finally being evaluated by him for the mandate of monitor/advisor later that same year.

Third, the Tribunal considers the key role played by the evaluator in question. Indeed, the head of the evaluation team for the monitor/ advisor contract is the Senior Project Officer of the Maghreb Program, in the Europe, Middle East and Maghreb Branch of CIDA. It is likely that, because that person was the head of the evaluation committee, that person's opinion and judgment had considerable weight, and it is reasonable to believe that that person may have influenced the other two members of the evaluation team. Moreover, the Tribunal notes that the evaluator in question is the one who awarded Mr. Courtemanche the most points.

In applying the criterion set out in *Committee for Justice and Liberty v. National Energy Board* and, in particular, in doing an overall analysis of the facts of the case, the Tribunal finds that there is a reasonable apprehension of bias. Indeed, the Tribunal determines that, in light of the facts, in all likelihood, an informed person, viewing the matter realistically and practically, and having thought the matter through, would conclude that the evaluator in question, and perhaps even the evaluation committee, whether consciously or unconsciously, would not decide fairly.

The Tribunal concluded that this prior relationship tainted the government's contract award process and cast "doubt on the impartiality of the evaluating committee in evaluating all the proposals of the bidders with regard to all the requirements." As this case illustrates, a finding of reasonable apprehension of bias can seriously undermine the defensibility of the government's evaluation process. As a remedy, the Tribunal gave the government the option of either cancelling the awarded contract, or conducting a re-evaluation with a new team of evaluators who were not involved in any way with the procurement process, and then compensating the complainant if its proposal turned out to be the highest score after that new evaluation.

In its September 2008 determination in *Re Bluedrop Performance Learning Inc.*, the Canadian International Trade Tribunal ordered the government to terminate a contract due to conflict of interest arising out of the involvement of a former employee in a tendering process.

The case dealt with a re-issued RFP for learning services for the Department of National Defence. The commanding officer who oversaw the development and release of the original RFP retired while the RFP was on the market. That RFP lapsed and was then reissued. In the interim, the former commanding officer was hired as vice-president of a firm that submitted a bid on the re-issued RFP. That firm was awarded the contract. The Tribunal summarized the material facts as follows:

The following facts are not in dispute:

- the former commanding officer was Commanding Officer of the G7 Branch of the CTC Headquarters during the drafting of RFP-1;

- the former commanding officer's subordinates had a direct role in drafting RFP-1;

- the former commanding officer maintained an overview of the RFP-1 project and provided technical advice for the preparation of RFP-1, as required;

- all members of the RFP-1 technical evaluation team worked within the G7 Branch of the CTC Headquarters under the former commanding officer;

- the former commanding officer participated at a bidders' conference relating to RFP-1 (which was held to provide prospective bidders with information on the proposed procurement) as the DND technical authority and would have been the designated technical authority for any contract awarded pursuant to RFP-1;

- some time after bid proposals had been received in respect of RFP-1, the former commanding officer retired from the Canadian Forces and was hired by Acron to serve as its Vice-President, Strategic Initiatives;

- on December 10, 2007, shortly after the former commanding officer's departure from DND, RFP-1 was allowed to expire without a contract having been awarded pursuant thereto; and

- RFP-2, which was issued on January 31, 2008, was essentially a re-tendering of DND's RFP-1 requirement.

A competing bidder challenged the contract award, alleging conflict of interest. In considering the detailed conflict of interest provisions in the tendering documents, the Tribunal determined that the government had a duty to look behind the winning bidder's "no conflict" misrepresentation and reject the bid. Since the Tribunal found that this failure to reject the bid compromised the integrity of the bidding process and violated the applicable trade treaty provisions, it ordered the government to terminate the contract or pay the complainant its lost profits.

As these examples illustrate, failing to address the risks created by inside advantage can significantly impact the integrity of an institution's procurement processes. Institutions should therefore ensure that their procurement practices include clear protocols for dealing with confidentiality considerations to guard against downstream issues that undermine the integrity of future competitions.

Court Awards Chrétien $200,000 in Bias Battle

The Right Honourable Jean Chrétien v.
The Honourable John H. Gomery
Federal Court of Canada, 2008

In December 2011, former Prime Minister Jean Chrétien was back in the news after the Federal Court awarded him $200,000 for legal costs incurred during a court battle over biased public remarks made by Justice Gomery during the Sponsorship Inquiry.

This case comment summarizes the original trial decision that led to the $200,000 legal costs award and illustrates why decision-makers should avoid making public comments during formal proceedings.

In its June 2008 judgment in *The Right Honourable Jean Chrétien v. The Honourable John H. Gomery*, the Federal Court of Canada struck down the Gomery Commission's findings relating to Jean Chrétien after concluding that Commissioner Gomery had shown bias against the former prime minister. The Federal Court criticized Gomery for granting media interviews, finding that Gomery made inappropriate statements during those interviews which gave the appearance that he was pre-judging his conclusions before hearing from all key witnesses.

The judgment renders the Commission's findings relating to Jean Chrétien's role in the Sponsorship Scandal null and void and serves as a compelling case study showing how improper comments made by decision-makers can undermine the appearance of fairness and impartiality in formal proceedings. This case has significant crossover relevance to tender evaluation teams since the "bias test" that was applied to Gomery was the same test that is applied to evaluation committee members when unsuccessful bidders allege bias in a contract award process.

In its first major finding, the court determined that the significance of the issues under investigation by the Commission entitled participants to a high degree of procedural fairness:

> [T]he potential damage that the findings of the Commission could have
> on the reputations of the parties involved in the investigation was of
> such serious consequence that a high degree of fairness was required.

In other words, even though the inquiry was not a formal court proceeding, participants were still entitled to "due process" standards and to be treated in an impartial manner.

The court also stated that "procedural fairness requires that decisions be made free from a reasonable apprehension of bias by an impartial decision-maker" and restated the often-cited test for determining the potential bias of a decision-maker:

> [T]he apprehension of bias must be a reasonable one, held by reasonable
> and right minded persons, applying themselves to the question and

> obtaining thereon the required information … [T]hat test is "what would an informed person, viewing the matter realistically and practically — and having thought the matter through — conclude. Would he think that it is more likely than not that [the decision-maker] whether consciously or unconsciously, would not decide fairly.

In applying the test, the court determined that the remarks made by Commissioner Gomery during and after the proceedings reflected a reasonable apprehension of bias against Chrétien:

> After reviewing the evidence placed before me on this issue, I am convinced that there is more than sufficient evidence to find that an informed person, viewing the matter realistically and practically and having thought the matter through would find a reasonable apprehension of bias on the part of the Commissioner. The comments made by the Commissioner, viewed cumulatively, not only indicate that he prejudged issues but also that the Commissioner was not impartial toward the Applicant.

By way of example, the court noted that Commissioner Gomery granted media interviews in December 2004 when the inquiry was in recess for the holidays. During those interviews he was quoted as saying that he was "coming to the same conclusion as (Auditor General) Sheila Fraser that this was a government program run in a catastrophically bad way."

The court found that these remarks were premature since the hearings had not yet been completed and the mandate of the Commission was to conduct an investigation of all levels of government before making any findings.

The court rejected the government's arguments in defence of the remarks:

> I cannot agree with the Attorney General that the Commissioner, after conducting only three of nine months of hearings, was in a position to confirm the findings of the Auditor General or to conclude that the Sponsorship Program was "run in a catastrophically bad way." …[T]he Commissioner was not in a position to conclude that the program was mismanaged before having heard from government officials of all levels who were set to testify. This is especially so given that the Commissioner ultimately concluded that the Sponsorship Program was run out of the Prime Minister's Office ….

The court found that such statements gave the improper impression that the Commission had "prejudged some of the very matters it was tasked to investigate before hearing all of the evidence."

The court also found that Gomery's reference to the "juicy stuff" that would be forthcoming in the testimony of senior government officials, including former prime minister Chrétien, was inappropriate. The court found that the comment bore "a pejorative connotation to which no witness ought to have been subjected." The court also found that Gomery made other statements that brought his impartiality in question.

The court took particular issue with Gomery's widely quoted "golf ball" comments wherein the Commissioner was quoted as saying: "It's such a disappointment that the Prime Minister would put his name on golf balls. That's really small-town cheap, you know, free golf balls." As the court concluded, the statements suggested a pre-determined bias against Chrétien:

> Not only was this remark a personal insult directed at the Applicant and his background, but it suggests that the Commissioner had come to the conclusion that the Applicant had acted improperly even before the Applicant appeared before the Commission to give his evidence.

At the time Gomery had defended his decision to grant media interviews:

> We have also seen over the last decades an increasing pressure for judges to come out of their ivory towers to establish some sort of a relationship with the media and to permit the media to have a better understanding of what it is that is taking place in the courtrooms or before commissions of inquiry of this kind.

> It was on the understanding of this evolution that led me to make – to grant certain interviews at the end of the year. I was told by representatives of the media that there was a desire to know a little bit better what was going on and what could be expected. It was in that context that these press interviews were granted.

The court disagreed with this rationale, finding that the media focus adversely impacted the fairness of the proceedings:

> I agree with the Applicant that the Commissioner became preoccupied with ensuring that the spotlight of the media remained on the Commission's inquiry, and he went to great lengths to ensure that the public's interest in the Commission did not wane. This preoccupation with the media outside the hearing room had a detrimental impact on the fairness of the proceedings …. [T]he media is not an appropriate forum in which a decision-maker is to become engaged while presiding over a commission of inquiry, a trial, or any other type of hearing or proceeding.

The court ultimately concluded that the remarks to the media gave rise to a reasonable apprehension of bias that compromised Gomery's conclusions as they related to Chrétien:

The nature of the comments made to the media are such that no reasonable person, looking realistically and practically at the issue, and thinking the matter through, could possibly conclude that the Commissioner would decide the issues fairly.

In setting aside the Commission's findings relating to Chrétien, the court provided a useful reminder to government decision-makers of the importance of maintaining impartiality.

Losing Bidder Cites Alleged "Body Shop" Comments in $250 Million Bias Claim

TPG Technology Consulting Ltd. v. Canada Federal Court of Canada, 2011

In its September 2011 decision in *TPG Technology Consulting Ltd. v. Canada*, the Federal Court of Canada dismissed an unsuccessful bidder's allegation of bias in a government evaluation process. The case dealt with a federal government procurement process valued at approximately $428 million for the acquisition of information technology engineering and technical support services.

An unsuccessful bidder launched an action seeking over $250 million in damages against the federal government. The losing bidder claimed that PPI Consulting Ltd. ("PPI"), the external consulting firm retained by the government to assist in the evaluation process, was biased against it and lowered its score during consensus scoring sessions. The plaintiff claimed that the consensus scoring had been arbitrarily applied by PPI, who they claimed had a pre-existing bias against them as a "body shop":

> TPG claims that PPI, the third party facilitator "had a manifest bias against awarding the contract to TPG and disparaged TPG as a 'body shop'" ....
> The evaluation consisted of a consensus score model whereby the five evaluators would meet to discuss their individual scores and then arrive at a consensus score. TPG alleges that these consensus scores were arbitrarily applied to unjustifiably reduce TPG's scores. Additionally, PPI maintained control over the evaluation record and at some point changes were made to the evaluation record that resulted in lower scores for TPG.
>
> The plaintiff alleged that the government had selected the consensus scoring method because its high subjectivity allowed personal biases to infiltrate the evaluation

To support its allegations, the plaintiff pointed to disparaging public remarks attributed to the president of PPI as evidence that bias had tainted the evaluation process. As the court noted:

The appropriateness and effectiveness of consensus method itself, specifically chosen by PWGSC in an effort to produce the fairest result by ensuring that evaluators are using a consistent understanding of the requirements, is questioned by TPG. During the hearing, counsel for TPG advanced the argument that PWGSC intentionally selected the consensus model, the most subjective model in their view, as a way to allow personal bias and preferences to infiltrate the process. The bias was one against "body shops" – TPG maintaining that Mr. Tibbo might have had a prejudice against small companies and "body shops" as Mr. Howard Grant, president of PPI was quoted in an industry publication in 2009, as speaking disparagingly of "body shops".

With respect to the consensus scoring sessions, the court noted that PPI presided over group discussions to address instances where the five evaluators had arrived at different scores. While the court noted that some errors occurred during PPI's tabulation of the consensus scores, it also cited affidavit evidence submitted by the individuals who were involved in the process who swore that, contrary to the plaintiff's allegations, they had not been influenced by anyone to alter the plaintiff's scores or manipulate the outcome of the evaluation:

> Mr. Tibbo admits that there was an error in the spreadsheet that he manually compiled on October 2, 2006. What he initially thought was a rounding error turned out to be a transposition error. This error, however, had no effect on the final technical result. Additionally, the final October 12 spreadsheet did not contain any human errors.

> Mr. Tibbo swears in his affidavit that at no time prior during or after was he approached by or influenced by anyone seeking to secure a particular outcome, nor did he witness any such activity. Similarly, Mr. Bartlett provided an affidavit testifying to the fairness and transparency of the evaluation process.

The court rejected the plaintiff's allegations of impropriety in the evaluation process, finding that the plaintiff failed to prove its theory of a tainted and biased evaluation:

> I am not satisfied that TPG is able to provide any evidence beyond mere speculation and conjecture to suggest that a trial is warranted to further flesh out this allegation. The theory that the scores changed is based on vague, second-hand information extracted in the course of a personal phone call interpreted with the most conspiratorial gloss. I am sure that TPG was disappointed with the results, and this disappointment has largely fuelled this litigation.

The court therefore dismissed the plaintiff's $250 million claim against the government. As this case illustrates, unsuccessful bidders who allege improprieties in an evaluation process bear the onus of proving their allegations. That said, purchasing institutions should note that public comments made by their officials and by their consultants can be used against them in legal challenges in an attempt to impugn the integrity of an evaluation process. Furthermore, purchasing institutions that employ consensus scoring should ensure that such processes are implemented with a high degree of diligence since: (i) scoring changes arising out of consensus scoring can be subject to a legal challenge; and (ii) tabulation errors arising out of such sessions, however innocuous and inadvertent, can be used against the institution in those legal proceedings.

3 Open Competition Requirements

Does your organization have the appropriate policies and procedures in place to comply with its open competition obligations and avoid trade treaty complaints based on inappropriate sole sourcing, unauthorized branding and biased specifications?

Open competition is a key pillar of public procurement and serves to promote both transparency and value-for-money. As the following case studies illustrate, bypassing or restricting open competition can subject an institution to public criticism, audit risk and legal challenge. Given the expanding network of trade treaties that recognize open competition, and given the increasing public expectation for probity and transparency in the procurement process, public institutions should ensure that they have the necessary protocols and procedures in place to meet their open competition requirements.

Energy Costs Surge as Ontario Phases Out Competitive Bids
Annual Report of the Auditor General of Ontario, 2011

In its 2011 annual report the Ontario Auditor General found that the provincial government's decision to phase out competitive bidding in favour of uncompetitive subsidized programs led to considerable increases in renewable energy costs. As the report noted, while Ontario's renewable energy program had initially utilized competitive RFP processes to procure hydro, wind, solar and bioenergy power, the province decided to phase out competition in order to subsidize local job creation and the promotion of a made-in Ontario "green industry." The

Auditor General recommended that the province revisit its renewable energy sourcing strategy with a view to balancing sustainability with reliable supply and value-for-money.

As the report noted, prior to implementing its highly subsidized "Feed-in-Tariff" ("FIT") program, the government had directed the Ontario Power Authority ("OPA") to phase out the competitive RFP approach in favour of a somewhat costlier Renewable Energy Standard Offer Program ("RESOP") that sourced supply from small scale operations at pre-set prices:

> [T]he complexity and cost of developing competitive RFPs was seen as favouring larger projects at the expense of smaller ones. To remove these barriers to small projects, the Minister issued a direction in 2006 to the OPA to develop a Renewable Energy Standard Offer Program (RESOP) that would offer smaller renewable energy projects a standard pricing regime while providing for simplified regulations, including eligibility and contracting. Prices under RESOP were about 16% to 40% higher than the competitive prices under the RFPs, as illustrated in Figure 8. The OPA indicated that RESOP would not be successful if the standard prices were not set high enough to attract investment in renewable energy projects. On the other hand, the OPA did acknowledge that the standard-offer process might have had some unintended consequences arising from an absence of the competitive tension that encourages innovative solutions, and it did ultimately result in high prices and oversubscription.

While the RESOP standard offer program was already resulting in higher prices when compared to the prices won through larger competitive RFPs, the government decided to accelerate and expand its renewable energy subsidy policy with the launch of its above-noted FIT program. As the Auditor General observed, the government decided to replace both its competitive RFP process and its standard offer RESOP program in favour of the costlier FIT program which was both heavily subsidized and required made-in-Ontario components. This added $4.4 billion in renewable energy costs over a twenty year period:

> Earlier procurement programs for renewable energy included competitive bidding and the Renewable Energy Standard Offer Program (RESOP), which were both very successful and achieved renewable generation targets in record time. In particular, RESOP received overwhelming responses. It was expected to develop 1,000 MW over 10 years, but it exceeded this target in a little more than one year. Although continuing the successful RESOP initiative was one option, the Minister directed the OPA to replace RESOP with a new Feed-in Tariff (FIT) program that was wider in scope, required made-in-Ontario components, and provided renewable energy generators with significantly more attractive contract prices than RESOP. These higher prices added about $4.4 billion in costs over the 20-year contract terms as compared to what would have been

incurred had RESOP prices for wind and solar power been maintained. The Ministry indicated that replacing RESOP with FIT successfully expedited its renewable energy program and promoted Ontario's domestic industry.

As the Auditor General noted, the government justified its more expensive energy sourcing strategy as an attempt to "create jobs and protect the environment." However, the report noted that the FIT program guaranteed renewable energy developers an 11 percent after-tax return on investment and found that no independent price-control protocols were established to measure the reasonableness of those energy costs. In fact, the Auditor General found that the Ontario Energy Board's traditional role of reviewing and approving energy prices was not extended to provide oversight over the FIT program. Instead, the Auditor General noted that the Ontario Power Authority would be conducting its own "in-house" review that would be "supported by consultants as needed" and that the government had "not decided whether to involve an independent third party in the review."

In conclusion the Auditor General found that the entire renewable energy program, and in particular the FIT subsidy program, significantly increased the cost of energy when compared to more traditional energy sources and that those higher energy costs had been locked in for periods of between twenty and forty years. Moving forward the Auditor General recommended that the government "conduct adequate analyses of the various renewable energy implementation alternatives so that decision-makers are able to give due consideration to cost, reliability, and sustainability." As this case study indicates, replacing competitive bidding with government-controlled subsidy programs can prove to be a costly policy decision with long term consequences to the taxpayer.

Trade Treaty Tsunami:
New Compliance Challenges for Government Procurement
By Rosslyn Young

Canada's steady current of trade treaty activity, both internationally and domestically, has been a driving force behind the standardization and expansion of open, public procurement at all levels of government. This steady tide of treaty developments has recently become a tsunami-sized source of new governance requirements.

The increasingly complex matrix of trade treaties operating within the Canadian public sector increases the challenges faced by purchasing professionals, both in their day to day transactions and in developing compliant policies and procedures.

While many trade treaties share common themes, such as open procurement and reciprocal non-discrimination, each trade treaty contains its own unique idiosyncrasies. Navigating the unique waters of the various treaties requires careful analysis of the seemingly murky requirements embodied in often opaque treaty language.

To ensure compliance and avoid challenges, public sector entities must ensure their policies and procedures comply with each separate trade treaty that applies to the particular institution.

By way of background, Canada joined global efforts to promote open, competitive and geographically neutral procurement in 1996 when it agreed, together with other member states of the World Trade Organization ("WTO"), to adhere to the procurement requirements set out in the *Agreement on Government Procurement* ("AGP"). Motivated by recognition that the collective buying power of government entities represented a significant portion of global economic activity, the AGP requires that the signatories guarantee fair and non- discriminatory procurement practices that allow suppliers from all member states to compete fairly for government contracts. It also requires that a dispute resolution mechanism be established so that suppliers can challenge allegedly unfair or discriminatory procurement practices. The WTO continues to advance open and competitive procurement practices globally, providing an international operating system that impacts trade and federal procurement within Canada.

On a smaller geographic scale, but no less important to Canadian trade, the *North American Free Trade Agreement* ("NAFTA") increased trade liberalization across the continent in 1994. Executed by Canada, the U.S. and Mexico, NAFTA only applies to the federal level; however, its impact on Canadian procurement has been significant. In addition to strengthening the already significant trade relationship across North America, the implementing legislation also created the Canadian International Trade Tribunal ("CITT") to provide an administrative dispute mechanism for suppliers.

While only federal procurements can be challenged at the CITT, its jurisprudence has had a lasting impact on shaping procurement practices across Canada more generally.

In the wake of these global and continental developments, Canada continues to successfully negotiate international trade treaties and is currently negotiating bilateral and multilateral agreements with countries in Asia, South America and Africa. Canada has also been actively pushing its agenda with respect to the negotiation of a Comprehensive Economic and Trade Agreement ("CETA") with the European Union. The ninth round of negotiations concluded in 2011 and the parties remained committed to finalizing a deal in 2012. According to the *Canada-European Union Joint Report: Towards a Comprehensive Economic Agreement*, a report jointly issued by Canada and the EU in March 2009,

> [A]ny agreement should substantially improve access to public procurement markets aiming to achieve full coverage of central and sub-central government procurement in all sectors, to ensure inter alia treatment no less favourable than that accorded to locally-established suppliers. Language on transparency should be added in order to provide insight into laws, regulations, procedures and practices, in a manner to provide business communities with easily accessible information on public procurement.

If this goal of securing commitments from Canada's provinces and territories with respect to broader public sector participation is integrated into the final version of the agreement, the impact will be felt by public sector entities across the country at all levels of government.

While international trade treaties are an important part of the public procurement landscape and will continue to increase the complexity of future compliance requirements, most public procurement professionals are already facing the tide of existing domestic treaty obligations. The most comprehensive domestic trade treaty is the *Agreement on the Internal Trade* ("AIT"), which covers the federal sector, all ten provinces, as well as the North West Territories and the Yukon, and includes the MASH (municipalities, academia, schools and hospitals) sectors.

The AIT requires specific procurement procedures, in addition to mandating non-discriminatory, geographically-neutral procurement for all captured entities and requiring open competitive procurement processes above the monetary thresholds. The AIT also includes a complex set of single and sole source exemptions, pursuant to which entities may legitimately run a procurement process that deviates from the prevailing standards. These exemptions form the basis of many purchasing policies within the Canadian public sector. The AIT continues to evolve and improve as a framework document for governing procurement across Canada.

The Eighth Protocol of Amendment expanded the government-to-government complaint process to also give suppliers the right to bring a complaint under the AIT. This expansion provides another stream for suppliers to challenge public sector procurement processes.

Domestically, the AIT is supplemented by various regional trade treaties that exist between two or more provinces. For example, the 2009 *Ontario-Quebec Trade and Cooperation Agreement* superseded and expanded the open procurement protocols that were initially established under the 1994 *Agreement on the Opening of Public Procurement between Ontario and Quebec.*

There has also been an increase in regional trade treaty agreements within Canada. The *Atlantic Procurement Agreement* ("APA"), which is between the four Atlantic Provinces and was originally entered into in 1996, was expanded in 2008 to increase access to provincial government purchasing by removing all forms of trade discrimination between the four provinces. The 2008 amendments also lowered the applicable tendering thresholds to increase opportunities for smaller businesses. Going further than other domestic trade treaties, the APA also requires some public sector entities to use a set of Standard Terms and Conditions for their procurement projects.

The other important regional treaty is the *New West Partnership Trade Agreement* ("NWPTA"). The NWPTA, which was signed by British Columbia, Alberta and Saskatchewan and came into effect on July 1, 2010, built on the prior *Trade, Investment and Labour Mobility Agreement* ("TILMA") that was originally only between B.C. and Alberta. The NWPTA provides for open competitive procurement practices and mandates non-discrimination between the three provincial parties. It also provides an avenue to challenge specific procurement processes: the three provinces are finalizing an interprovincial bid-dispute mechanism, which starts with a public procurement entity's local bid dispute procedures and escalates to a yet-to-be-established tri-party process for addressing bid disputes.

The relentless tide of domestic and international trade treaty developments will continue to draw Canadian procurement professionals into the increasingly complex waters of open public procurement. Rather than sailing these unchartered waters without assistance, to find safe passage, public institutions would be wise to seek the assistance of experienced procurement counsel. As is often the case with public procurement, proper advice can help ensure a safe voyage.

Over the Line: Considerations on Value and Thresholds in Public Procurement

By Rosslyn Young

Value-for-money and open competition are the twin policy pillars that define due diligence under the trade treaties for public institutions. Public tendering is the main vehicle through which these policy goals are accomplished. The threshold question facing Canadian public purchasing professionals on a daily basis is whether the contract value of the procurement calls for open competition. This article will examine the overlapping threshold requirements impacting Canadian public procurement under our various trade treaties and will also discuss how "procurement value" should be defined and calculated when applying those thresholds.

The first issue to consider is, "What is the appropriate threshold?" There are a number of overlapping trade treaties operating across Canada, ranging from the national *Agreement on Internal Trade* ("AIT") to regional treaties such the *New West Partnership Trade Agreement* and the *Atlantic Procurement Agreement*. Each of these treaties imposes different thresholds for open competition. Further, there are different thresholds for different categories of purchases, depending on whether the purchase is for goods, services or construction. Where a public institution is subject to more than one trade treaty, a careful analysis of these requirements is essential to ensure compliance.

The second issue to consider is, "What should be included in the calculation of 'procurement value'?" Again, definitions of "procurement value" vary across Canada depending on the governance matrix of trade treaties, directives and statutes that differ by region and sector. Broadly, the definition of procurement value is the total estimated value of a purchase, but what is included or excluded to calculate that value varies greatly. For example, the AIT excludes optional renewals of a contract when the main duration of the contact is at least a year in length, but the Ontario procurement directives, which apply to the provincial government and the broader public sector in Ontario, expressly *include* optional renewals within the definition of procurement value. Some definitions also provide further details as to what should be included in the calculation. For example, Ontario's *Management Board of Cabinet's Procurement Directive* includes a list of items that must be included in the calculation for the purposes of determining the appropriate threshold, which includes among other requirements, indirect payments by the government to successful suppliers and conferred value flowing from the government to suppliers.

Finally, public sector institutions must determine whether the opportunity constitutes a procurement process at all. In *Bell Nexxia Inc. v. The Commissioner of Corrections and Telus Integrated Communications Inc.*, a Federal Court of Appeal decision from 2002, the court held that the procurement of a telecom provider to supply telephone services in federal corrections facilities did not constitute a "procurement" for the purposes of the AIT. The telephone services were paid for by the inmates personally and accordingly there were no payments made by Corrections Services Canada to the service provider. The Court of Appeal decision overturned a prior Canadian International Trade Tribunal ("CITT") determination that had found that the RFP *did* constitute a procurement process. In rendering the decision, the Court of Appeal found that because Corrections Services Canada was not paying for the services, there was no "financial commitment" for the purposes of the definition of procurement value and therefore the tendering process was not subject to AIT and the jurisdiction of the CITT. While the *Bell Nexxia* decision found that the opportunity for a private company to make money through the public sector did not constitute procurement for the purposes of the AIT, many public sector institutions still opt to put such "concession" opportunities to public tender. Examples include the procurement of food service providers for cafeterias in government buildings or coffee kiosks on university campuses. Under these types of arrangements, the service provider pays the public sector for the opportunity to offer food services on public property. Another high-profile example of the public tendering of a revenue-generating opportunity was the public procurement process recently run by the Niagara Parks Commission to procure a service provider for the boat tour services in the Niagara Gorge, an opportunity that nets millions of dollars for the Ontario government annually and was recently awarded to a new supplier after a long-term untendered incumbency.

There are many considerations to weigh when deciding whether a public entity is required to put a contract opportunity to public tender. In order to ensure that public funds and resources are being managed efficiently, it is essential that procurement value be properly calculated according to the appropriate governance structure, that the correct internal and external thresholds are applied and that all public policy considerations are appropriately considered to determine whether, irrespective of the amounts being paid in public funds, the opportunity should be competed to better serve the public interest.

The Rise of Judicial Review

Case law developments in the area of judicial review have been quietly redefining the legal landscape in ways that could have a long-term impact on public procurement in Canada. This column surveys the significance of the judicial review remedy as a means of keeping government accountable for its contracting decisions.

The judicial review remedy has a long jurisprudential history. Its origins trace back to the 1600s when King James proclaimed special royal prerogatives which gave him unfettered decision making power. The courts took a different view. In 1611, England's Chief Justice, Sir Edward Coke, famously declared in the *Case of Proclamations*, that "the King hath no prerogatives but what the law of the land allows him." In finding that even the King was subject to the rule of law, Sir Edward Coke set a precedent that laid the foundation for our tradition of responsible government.

Today, in the realm of government procurement, we hear echoes of King James whenever public institutions purport to assert their "rights and privileges" and we see manifestations of Sir Edward Coke whenever the courts scrutinize government decisions. While in Canada most of these check-and-balance battles have been fought within the Contract A paradigm, the oversight role of the courts under the judicial review remedy is becoming increasingly important in its own right, no matter how the courts treat liabilities under the Contract A paradigm.

For some time, many assumed that government procurement decisions were beyond the scope of judicial review. While this assumption was always overstated (since it was based on largely extinct constitutional privileges inherited by ministers of the Crown from King James and his successors), it was rarely an issue in Canada since contract law had largely occupied the procurement field following the Supreme Court's seminal 1981 Contract A decision in *R. v. Ron Engineering*. While Contract A-based disputes have taken much of the attention when it comes to tendering claims, the judicial review remedy has quietly re-asserted its centuries-old grip over government decisions and has recently re-occupied the procurement field. For example, in its April 2009 decision in *Irving Shipbuilding Inc. v. Canada (Attorney General)*, the Federal Court of Appeal confirmed that judicial reviews can apply to government procurement decisions, noting that "the closer the connection between the procurement process and the exercise of statutory power, the greater the likelihood that the activities can be subject to judicial review."

In a judicial review application, a supplier asks the court to determine whether a procurement decision was fair and reasonable. If the court determines that the government contravened the procurement rules, it can order the government to revisit its decision. This remedy can apply even where no Contract A was created and is typically rendered much faster than a Contract A-based lost profits claim. This remedy can even apply to post-award contract administration decisions.

By way of example, in its February 2008 decision in *Wise v. Legal Services Society*, the British Columbia Supreme Court dealt with a case involving a legal aid lawyer whose contract was terminated by the Legal Services Society. The court determined that the termination decision was subject to judicial review. The court stated that "it has recently been recognized that 'commercial' decisions made by a statutory body may be subject to judicial review." To support this conclusion, the court noted that the institution exercised statutory powers, spent government funds and acted in an area of public interest. This describes most public institutions in Canada and should serve as a wake-up call to ensure the probity of contracting decisions.

With respect to tender evaluations, a successful judicial review application can require a public institution to revisit flawed contract award decisions. For example, in its August 2009 decision in *Bot Construction v. Ontario (Ministry of Transportation)*, the Ontario Divisional Court ordered the government to revisit an award made to a non-compliant bidder. The court determined that the Minister was conducting its highway construction procurement under the general statutory powers of the *Public Transportation and Highway Improvement Act* and that it was a matter of public interest that the exercise of those powers complied with the government's internal procurement directives. Since the government breached its internal procurement rules by awarding to a non-compliant bidder, it was ordered to revisit its award decision. While the specific ruling was later overturned by the Ontario Court of Appeal, the analysis advanced by the Divisional Court that led to the judicial review of the government decision has since been applied in other cases to scrutinize government conduct.

As these cases illustrate, the courts will continue to cast a watchful eye over government's procurement decisions in the post-*Tercon* era through the remedy of judicial review. Public institutions will therefore be well served to follow their procurement rules and not take false comfort in their reserved rights and privileges.

Court Reviews Reasonableness of City's Sole-Source Decision

Friends of Lansdowne Inc. v. Ottawa
Ontario Superior Court of Justice, 2011

In its July 2011 judgment in *Friends of Lansdowne Inc. v. Ottawa (City)*, the Ontario Superior Court of Justice rejected an application to quash a direct contract award made by Ottawa City Council. The case dealt with a sole-source agreement entered into by the city and the Ottawa Sports and Entertainment Group ("OSEG") for the redevelopment of Lansdowne Park. The application to quash the contract award was brought by a community group that was established in opposition to the city's decision to abandon a design competition for the award of the redevelopment contract.

The court cited the governing authorities with respect to the judicial review of government decisions and determined that it was not the role of the court to second-guess the merits of the policy decisions made by City Council in relation to Lansdowne Park.

In so stating, the court echoed the prior statements made by the motions judge during a related pre-trial disclosure hearing, where the motions judge summarized the debate behind the controversial sole-source decision.

In deciding whether to quash the contract award, the court considered whether the sole source decision was validly made in accordance with the relevant city bylaw. As the court noted, the city's purchasing bylaw required a competitive bidding process but also allowed the city to waive this requirement where there was an absence of competition for technical or other reasons and where only one supplier could provide the requirements:

> The City Manager's Report to City Council on September 2, 2009, which outlined the proposed LPP, also addressed the question of whether the City's Purchasing By-law required that there be a competitive bid process for this project. He advised Council that, pursuant to paragraph 22 of the City of Ottawa's Purchasing By-law, it was permissible for the City to waive the requirement for competitive bid solicitation for goods, services, and construction, and replace it with negotiations where there is an absence of competition for technical and other reasons and the goods, services, or construction can only be supplied by a particular supplier and no alternative exists.
>
> I accept the City's evidence that it was the understanding of City staff that the Ottawa Option Policy, which is a component of the Purchasing By-law and applies to unsolicited proposals received by the City, did not apply to the LPP, because it was a land development project. In any event, the City did in fact assemble an evaluation team and performed a detailed evaluation of the LPP, including an assessment of the merits and risks, the technical, commercial, managerial and financial capability and the benefits to the City. Based on the outcome of the detailed evaluation, it was determined that the LPP met the sole source criteria and did not require further competition. This is essentially the process required under the Ottawa Option Policy.
>
> City Council has decided that it wanted a project that would both revitalize Lansdowne Park and bring CFL football back to Ottawa. The proponents of the LPP argued that this proposal was the only one that could do both. The project includes, as an integral part thereof, the entry by the City into limited partnerships with OSEG to which OSEG will bring CFL and OHL franchises, both of which are said to be essential to the proposed agreement. These franchises will be owned by limited partnerships to which the City will be a party, and are said to be necessary to the business model which lies at the heart of the proposed project. City Council was entitled to accept this approach.

In coming to its conclusion, the court reviewed the relevant terms of the purchasing bylaw, which incorporated parts of the relevant trade treaty rules relating to direct contract awards:

The Purchasing By-Law provides as follows:

22(1) The requirement for competitive bids solicitation for goods, services and construction may be waived under joint authority of the appropriate Director and Supply Management and replaced with negotiations by the Director and Supply Management under the following circumstances:

[...]

(d) Where there is an absence of competition for technical or other reason and the goods, services or a construction can only be supplied by a particular supplier and no alternative exists,

[...]

(8) Any non-competitive contract that does not satisfy the provisions of subsection 22(1) is subject to the City Manager's approval.

[...]

25(2) Any procurement activity resulting from the receipt of an unsolicited proposal shall comply with the provisions of this by-law and the separate Ottawa Option Policy for unsolicited proposals as approved by City Council on October 23, 2002.

(3) A contract resulting from an unsolicited proposal shall be awarded on a non-competitive basis only when the procurement complies with the requirements of a non-competitive procurement.

While the court ultimately rejected the application for judicial review and thereby preserved the City Council's direct award decision, this case is significant in that the court actually reviewed the sole-source award to determine whether it complied with the purchasing bylaw and the open competition protocols that were incorporated into it from the relevant trade treaties. Since the courts have traditionally been reluctant to give standing to parties to challenge sole-source awards, this decision could reflect a potential area of expansion for the judicial review remedy in future years.

Improper Sole-Sourcing Breaches Treaty Rules

One of the principle commitments established in domestic and international procurement treaties is the obligation on public bodies to openly compete the award of contracts. Unless the situation fits into one of the legitimate treaty-recognized exceptions to open competition, bypassing open competition in situations where the contract value exceeds the applicable treaty threshold constitutes a breach of the procurement treaty.

By way of example, the *2011 UN Model Procurement Law*, which was updated to align with the major international trade treaties, provides some general guidelines for situations that may justify direct contract awards. Those circumstances include:

1. where the deliverables are only available from a single supplier or where the particular supplier has exclusive rights in respect of such deliverables and where no reasonable alternative exists;

2. where unforeseen urgency or a catastrophic event makes tendering proceedings or other alternatives impractical;

3. where for reasons of standardization or compatibility the public institution determines that it needs to procure additional deliverables from the original supplier; and

4. where the procuring entity determines that other methods of procurement are not appropriate for protecting the essential security interests of the state.

Within Canada, the domestic *Agreement on Internal Trade* establishes similar principles, recognizing that the circumstances for direct awards should be limited in scope and be subject to transparent rules. In keeping with the principles recognized by the *2011 UN Model Procurement Law*, the *Agreement on Internal Trade* recognizes exceptions to open tendering in situations where:

1. using a third-party vendor could nullify existing warranties;

2. proprietary rights require the use of a specific supplier;

3. the supply of a good or service is controlled by a statutory monopoly;

4. a situation of unforeseeable urgency arises;

5. the subject matter of the procurement is highly sensitive;

6. no suppliers respond to a properly issued tender call;

7. the procurement is for original works of art, for subscriptions to newspapers, magazines or other periodicals or for real property;

8. the procurement contract is with another public body, a non-profit organization or a philanthropic institution.

The federal government's treaty obligations, including those set out in the *Agreement on Internal Trade,* are subject to legal challenge before the Canadian International Trade Tribunal. In accordance with the treaty protocols operating at the federal level, prospective suppliers are provided notice by the federal government of an intended direct award through a publicly posted Advance Contract Award Notice. Suppliers who want to challenge the federal government's intended direct award can bring a challenge to the Tribunal.

The Tribunal's long history of direct award determinations offers useful case studies for other public institutions when considering the appropriate use of the *Agreement on Internal Trade*'s direct award exceptions. The body of case law clearly reflects the trade treaty bias in favour of open competition. In fact, apart from cases dealing with the use of exclusive intellectual property rights and with national security exceptions for certain military procurements, the federal government's attempts to rely on treaty exceptions to defend direct contract awards have been largely unsuccessful. As stated by the Tribunal in its *Re Cognos Inc.* determination, "competition is the norm under the trade agreements, with limited tendering procedures being the exception. The onus is on the government institutions to establish that the decision to choose a limited tendering procedure is permitted under the applicable trade agreements in the particular circumstances of the case."

To comply with the trade treaty transparency obligations, the government's rationale for a direct award should be clearly documented. By way of example, in its determination in *CMI Interlangues Inc. v. Canada (Department of Public Works and Government Services)*, the Canadian International Trade Tribunal found that the government breached its trade treaty obligations by issuing an advance contract award notice for language training services with inadequate information. It upheld the complaint of the potential supplier who was denied the opportunity to compete.

Even in the area of exclusive proprietary rights, where the federal government has enjoyed some success in defending its direct award decisions, the Tribunal has found that this *Agreement on Internal Trade* exception only applies where other competitively available products cannot meet the technical requirements. For example, in the case of *Information Builders (Canada) Inc. v. Department of Public Works and Government Services*, the Tribunal determined that the government failed to conduct an open competition. It ordered that the contract in question be put to tender. The case involved the acquisition of business intelligence software for use by the Department of Indian Affairs and Northern Development in remote First Nations communities. The government claimed that the uncertainty of communication links with those communities required the use of a "cubes" design. It directly awarded a contract to a supplier whose software complied with that specification. The Tribunal disagreed, finding that the government had mistakenly set out with a "predetermined solution rather than simply a required outcome." It ordered the government to abandon its direct award and proceed with an open competition.

As these cases illustrate, in order to comply with trade treaty duties, public institutions should ensure that their direct award decisions are subject to appropriate internal approvals and are clearly documented with rationales that properly fall within recognized treaty exceptions.

Branding Allowed Only as a Last Resort

Re Cognos Inc.
Canadian International Trade Tribunal, 2002

In February 2002 in *Re Cognos Inc.*, the Canadian International Trade Tribunal determined that the government was allowed to use branding in its specifications only as a last resort. The dispute dealt with a request for proposals for an online analytical processing platform. The complainant challenged the government's specifications, arguing that they improperly referred to a competitor's brand.

The Tribunal recognized that the *North American Free Trade Agreement* ("NAFTA") calls for performance-based specifications that incorporate recognized industry standards:

> The Tribunal notes that the fact that entities are responsible for determining their requirements does not relieve them from the obligation to ensure that the technical specifications that they prepare, adopt or apply do not have as a purpose or effect the creation of unnecessary obstacles to trade. Article 1007(2) of NAFTA is clear in this respect and stipulates that the technical specifications prescribed by entities must be specified in terms of performance criteria rather than design or descriptive characteristics and be based on international or recognized national standards, regulations and codes.

The Tribunal also found that NAFTA and the World Trade Organization's *Agreement on Government Procurement* permit "the use of a particular trademark or name, patent, design or type in preparing technical specifications only when there is no sufficiently precise or intelligible way of otherwise describing the procurement requirements." In other words, purchasing institutions that are subject to trade treaties should, as a general rule, use branded specifications only as a last resort. In this case, the specifications were found to violate the neutrality standards of the applicable treaties, so the Tribunal ordered the government to cancel, amend and reissue its RFP.

NAFTA Rules Open Door to Open-Source Software
John Chandioux Experts Conseils Inc. v. PWGSC
Federal Court of Appeal, 2004

The Federal Court of Appeal decision of *John Chandioux Experts Conseils Inc. v. Canada (Department of Public Works and Government Services)* represents a big win for open source software solutions in the ongoing battle for global market share and reflects the critical role played by trade treaties in removing barriers to open competition.

The dispute involved a Canadian federal government tender call for a turnkey system that could operate in Environment Canada's computer network and translate meteorological bulletins between English and French. The tender call specifications required the solution to operate "on personal computers devoted exclusively to this use in a Windows environment." The $1.2 million five-year deal was awarded to a bidder who proposed a LINUX system. While the award amount was relatively small, it set a big precedent for future competition. A competitor, who had bid a Windows system, challenged the contract award on the basis that the competition was limited to Windows solutions and that the contract had been awarded to a non-compliant bidder. Both the Canadian International Trade Tribunal and the Federal Court of Appeal rejected the complaint and upheld the federal government's contract award to the LINUX solution.

In its defence, the federal government maintained that it required a system that could operate in and be compatible with a Windows environment. However, this did not restrict the tender call to Microsoft Windows solutions since this "would have imposed a technical restriction contrary to the provisions of the trade agreements, which require performance-based specifications."

The relevant trade treaties, the *Agreement on Government Procurement* ("AGP"), the *North American Free Trade Agreement* ("NAFTA") and the *Agreement on Internal Trade* ("AIT"), impose a series of open procurement obligations on various levels of governments. Where applicable, these rules prohibit tender calls with product-based specifications that unnecessarily restrict competition. Instead, they require neutral specifications based on functional requirements. In some past cases, where unnecessarily narrow product-based specifications have been challenged at the Canadian International Trade Tribunal, such specifications have been overridden and interpreted to allow for "equivalent" alternate products that meet the underlying functional requirements.

In this case, the federal government relied on these principles to support an interpretation of the specifications that permitted an award to a LINUX solution that was compatible with the existing government network. The tribunal agreed. It held that the requirement in question called for "any system, Microsoft Windows or any other, that will operate in a Windows environment." The complaint launched by the Windows-based solution provider was therefore dismissed. The complainant appealed.

The Federal Court of Appeal also backed the contract award decision, reiterating the federal government's defence that a narrow interpretation that limited the field to Windows solutions would "create an unnecessary obstacle to trade contrary to paragraph 107(1) of the NAFTA, infringe subsection 107(3) which prohibits requiring a supplier to use or provide a product with a specific trade mark, and favour Microsoft Windows products contrary to paragraph 504(3)(b) of the AIT." The appeal was therefore dismissed and the government's contract award to the LINUX solution was preserved.

This case is significant on a number of levels. The decision reflects a trend towards an increasingly open playing field between competing software models and is therefore a big win for all open-source solution providers competing for a piece of the global software market.

The case also reflects a commitment on the part of the federal government to comply with its treaty obligations by fostering fair competition between alternative software models based on underlying functionality rather than product names. In other words, this case is an example of how the federal procurement system is working in accordance with Canada's international treaty commitments.

The aftershocks of this decision, while significant enough within the software industry, will likely be felt beyond the world of technology. As open competition becomes the ever-expanding norm in government procurement, trade treaty rules will continue to have a ripple effect that will be felt across all industries.

Trade Tribunal Finds Bias Buried in Technical Specifications

Halkin Tool Limited v. PWGSC
Canadian International Trade Tribunal, 2010

In its May 2010 determination in *Halkin Tool Limited v. Department of Public Works and Government Services*, the Canadian International Trade Tribunal determined that the government used biased specifications in a hydraulic press brake RFP. The Tribunal ordered the government to cancel its procurement process and redraft its RFP using specifications that complied with the applicable treaty rules.

In its determination, the Tribunal considered the technical details of the challenged specification and ultimately determined that they breached the relevant requirements by referring to a particular design or type, rather than referring to generic functionalities:

> Article 1007 of NAFTA provides as follows:
>
> ...
>
> 2. Each Party shall ensure that any technical specification prescribed by its entities is, where appropriate:

a. specified in terms of performance criteria rather than design or descriptive characteristics; and

b. based on international standards, national technical regulations, recognized national standards, or building codes.

3. Each Party shall ensure that the technical specifications prescribed by its entities do not require or refer to a particular trademark or name, patent, design or type, specific origin or producer or supplier unless there is no sufficiently precise or intelligible way of otherwise describing the procurement requirements and provided that, in such cases, words such as "or equivalent" are included in the tender documentation.

Halkin submitted that the mandatory requirements for the solicitation at issue were not specified in terms of performance criteria, but rather made reference to a particular design or type, namely, clevis-mounted hydraulic cylinders and centreline loading construction. PWSGC, on the other hand, submitted that the mandatory requirements support DND's legitimate operational requirements and are generic in nature and not specific to any particular design.

In the Tribunal's opinion, the requirements set out in mandatory technical specifications 2.1.2 and 2.1.17 refer to a particular design or type and cannot be construed as being generic in nature. It is clear to the Tribunal that, in making reference to clevis-mounted hydraulic cylinders and centreline loading construction, PWGSC was making reference to a design or to descriptive characteristics for the product that it was procuring rather than specifying the performance that it was seeking to achieve through the particular design, even if this type of design is well known in the industry.

In its GIR, PWGSC included a letter dated January 28, 2010, signed by a DND employee (a professional engineer) who was involved in establishing the technical specifications for the solicitation at issue in which the employee claims that the concepts of clevis-mounted hydraulic cylinders and centreline loading construction are not specific to any particular design. However, the Tribunal notes that, despite this claim, the letter includes the following passages: "…the use of the clevis mounting creates a superior design…" and "[t]he placement of the cylinders directly over the ram in the centre-line loading construction concept yields a simplified design... ." This only serves to reinforce the Tribunal's belief that the requirements set out in mandatory technical specifications 2.1.2 and 2.1.17 refer to a particular design or type.

By not including words such as "or equivalent" in these specifications, as required by Article 1007(3) of NAFTA and the similar provisions of the other applicable trade agreements, hydraulic press brakes based on other designs, which can potentially meet DND's operational requirements, are precluded from being considered by PWGSC. The Tribunal finds that such an omission creates or has the effect of creating an unnecessary obstacle to trade.

Therefore, in light of the foregoing, the Tribunal determines that Halkin's complaint, insofar as it relates to the improper formulation of the mandatory technical specifications, is valid.

In light of the above, the Tribunal determined that "not framing requirements in accordance with the applicable trade agreements represents a serious deficiency in the procurement process." As this case illustrates, the consideration of biased specifications will often be a complex assessment of facts requiring a close understanding of the relevant technical details. In these situations, qualified technical subject matters experts should be responsible for preparing defensible neutral specifications.

Saskatchewan Liable for Applying Hidden Local Preference Policy

Kencor Holdings Ltd. v. Saskatchewan
Saskatchewan Court of Queen's Bench, 1991

In its decision in *Kencor Holdings Ltd. v. Saskatchewan*, the Saskatchewan Queen's Bench held that the government could not rely on undisclosed criteria to bypass a low bidder. The case dealt with a tender call issued by the Government of Saskatchewan for the construction of a bridge. As the court's decision explains, Saskatchewan took the position that its general privilege clause allowed it to bypass the low bidder based on an undisclosed local preference policy:

> In the tender documentation the following privilege clause appears:
>
> 1200-1 . . .
>
> The Minister may refuse to accept any tender, waive defects or technicalities, or subject to Section 13 of the Highways Act accept any tender that he considers to be in the best interests of the Province.

Section 13 of *The Highways and Transportation Act*, R.S.S. 1978, c. H-3 reads:

> Where the minister deems it inexpedient to let the work to the lowest bidder, he shall report the matter to and obtain the authority of the Lieutenant Governor in Council before awarding the contract to any other than the lowest bidder.

According to the Government, the combination of these two clauses permitted it to decline the lowest bid and to approve the more expensive one.

The low bidder sued, arguing that these clauses did not give Saskatchewan the right to rely on undisclosed criteria, maintaining that "in the exercise of its discretion respecting tenders, the Government may not consider policy which is unknown to bidders." The court agreed, noting that there "was no indication in the tender documents that preference might be extended to Saskatchewan bidders, and the plaintiff was unaware of this possibility." The court found that in the interest of maintaining the integrity of the bidding process, evaluation factors should be clearly disclosed:

> To maintain the integrity of the tendering process it is imperative that the low, qualified bidder succeed. This is especially true in the public sector. If governments meddle in the process and deviate from the industry custom of accepting the low bid, competition will wane. The inevitable consequence will be higher costs to the taxpayer. Moreover, when governments, for reasons of patronage or otherwise, apply criteria unknown to the bidders, great injustice follows. Bidders, doomed in advance by secret standards, will waste large sums preparing futile bids. The plaintiff here for example, spent $23,000.00 on its abortive tender.

The plaintiff was awarded lost-profit damages due to the government's improper reliance on undisclosed selection criteria. As this case illustrates, whenever purchasers intend to rely on factors other than best price in making their contract award decisions, those factors should be clearly disclosed to all bidders. This case illustrates the following general principles that have been applied by the courts with respect to the disclosure of evaluation criteria:

1. A purchaser should not rely on undisclosed evaluation criteria when making a contract award in a formal bidding process.

2. A purchaser is typically not permitted to rely on a privilege clause to apply undisclosed criteria or hidden preferences.

3. In appropriate circumstances, undisclosed evaluation criteria can legitimately be applied under general evaluation categories or privilege clauses.

4. Evaluation preferences for factors other than price are typically permitted as long as they are properly disclosed to all bidders.

5. The failure to provide proper disclosure of evaluation criteria can constitute a breach of the purchaser's common law duties or applicable trade treaty obligations.

As a general rule, a purchaser should therefore strive for transparency and clarity in its evaluation criteria in order to enhance the defensibility of its evaluation process.

Local Preference in Public Purchasing: Risks and Recommendations

These recommendations are extracted from a whitepaper by Paul Emanuelli commissioned by the Ontario Public Buyers Association that was released in March 2009 to help inform the issue of Canadian content and local preference as it impacts public procurement in the Ontario municipal sector.

In the heat of the recent economic crisis, the issue of local preference (i.e. giving preferential treatment to local suppliers over other suppliers as a means of using public spending to create or protect local jobs) has re-emerged on the procurement landscape. In the midst of an anticipated increase in transfer funds to municipalities, municipal purchasing departments in Ontario are facing considerable pressure to adopt Buy Canadian policies and other local preference practices to help support local businesses and protect and create local jobs.

The Canadian Auto Workers Union ("CAW") has been at the forefront of this debate, calling for the implementation of Buy Canadian policies across the public sector. The CAW commissioned a legal opinion which claims that governments can legally adopt Buy Canadian policies, whether at the municipal, provincial or federal levels. While the legal opinion may, for the most part, be technically correct within its specific narrow context, an issue of this significance cannot be reduced to the narrow legal analysis of specific trade treaty provisions of the *Agreement on Internal Trade* ("AIT"). Rather, it must be framed within the broader legal and policy context within which the public procurement process operates. More specifically, the CAW's "Buy Canadian – Build Communities" campaign raises the following significant legal and policy concerns:

- **Narrowing Competition**: the CAW campaign advocates creating a preference to contractors based on their place of origin, citing narrow exceptions that permit Canadian content polices under limited circumstances while downplaying the letter and spirit of domestic and international trade rules that generally aim to remove protectionist barriers to competition;

- **Distinguishing Canadian Content from Local Preference:** the CAW's "Buy Canadian – Build Communities" campaign fails to adequately distinguish between Canadian content and local preferences, noting narrow exceptions that permit Canadian content while glossing over the general prohibition against local preferences and other restrictive specifications;

- **Implementation Risks:** the CAW campaign downplays the practical challenges posed in properly implementing a Canadian content policy, calling on governments to eventually enact legislation to establish clear rules while, in the interim, leaving municipalities to fend for themselves to navigate significant legal and policy risks in a legislative and policy vacuum;

- **Politicized Procurement:** the CAW campaign politicizes the public procurement process in the name of overriding public policy considerations but fails to adequately consider the significant risks created whenever "exceptional circumstances" are cited as a reason to bypass the established best practices of open, transparent and fair competition.

Narrowing Competition: Trade Treaties and Trade Wars

While it is technically true that the AIT contains narrow exceptions for Canadian content preferences, those exceptions run in stark contrast to the generally prevailing letter and spirit of international and domestic trade treaties that prohibit protectionist practices and promote open competition. The AIT is a domestic treaty so it is, by definition, largely silent on international matters. However, this is not the same as saying that the municipal sector conducts its procurement in a vacuum that makes it immune from international trade issues.

Recommendation 1:
Before a municipality adopts protectionist policies in favour of domestic or local suppliers or products, it should assess the potential impact on our domestic and local suppliers of retaliatory protectionist practices adopted by U.S. municipal institutions.

Blurring the Canadian Content Exception and Local Preference

The CAW's "Buy Canadian – Build Communities" campaign fails to clearly distinguish between permitted Canadian content policies and prohibited local preferences. The AIT Canadian content provisions referred to by the CAW are an exception to the general non-discriminatory rules contained in that treaty. These rules prohibit the adoption of local or other geographic preferences or other restrictive procurement specifications and call for general reciprocal non-discrimination across all Canadian suppliers and products. "Buying Canadian" does not translate into building your local community. It simply allows for a generic Canadian preference for all Canadian suppliers and products across all Canadian communities.

Recommendation 2:
Municipalities should respect the reciprocal non-discrimination rules in the AIT and should adopt clear policies against local supplier preferences or other biased specifications.

Recommendation 3:

Before adopting any Canadian content preferences, municipalities should consider how these policies would benefit their own ratepayers and the net effect of such policies on municipal expenditures and revenues (i.e. will the costs of a Canadian subsidy paid by local taxpayers to Canadian suppliers and products from other parts of Canada create more jobs and revenues within the municipality?).

Implementation Risks

A. Treaty Breaches

As a general rule the AIT prohibits the adoption of local preferences. Unless a municipality can justify that local preference under another recognized exception, adopting such preferences would put it in contravention of the treaty.

Recommendation 4

Public institutions that are subject to the AIT should govern their procurement practices in accordance with the requirements of that treaty. Any departure from the general standards of open procurement should: (a) be based on the established exceptions recognized by the treaty; (b) be based on decisions made at the appropriately senior levels within the organization; and (c) be properly documented to ensure accountability and transparency in the expenditure of public funds.

B. Potential Statutory Restrictions

The federal *Competition Act* and Ontario's *Discriminatory Business Practices Act* are often cited within purchasing circles as potential statutory restrictions that could prohibit the adoption of local preference policies. A preliminary review of the relevant statutory provisions indicates that the application of these statutes to bar the adoption of restrictive procurement specifications (such as local preferences) is far from clear.

Recommendation 5

Prior to adopting a local preference policy, a purchasing institution should seek a written opinion from the federal Competition Bureau to confirm what, if any, restrictions may be imposed on local preferences by the Competition Act.

Recommendation 6

Before it applies any local preference to its procurement, a purchasing institution should investigate the possible application of the Discriminatory Business Practices Act *by: (a) seeking clarification from the government department responsible for administering the statute; and (b) investigating the possibility of obtaining an advance judicial interpretation on the issue.*

C. The Common Law Risks (Vague and Hidden Preferences)

Unless it establishes precise and transparent rules that meet the strict legal fairness standards imposed by the common law of competitive bidding, a purchasing institution that implements Canadian content requirements or other local preferences faces considerable legal exposures when conducting a tendering process.

The legal opinion commissioned by the CAW recommends that legislation be enacted to create standard practices to address: (i) the rules for ascertaining Canadian content; (ii) the circumstances where sufficient competition will be deemed to exist in order to limit competition to Canadian suppliers only; and (iii) the reporting requirements that would apply to public institutions in relation to the implementation of a Canadian content policy. There is much work to be done to properly implement a Buy Canadian policy in a consistent, transparent and legally defensible manner. In the absence of such clear standards and evaluation criteria, municipalities face significant legal exposures during a tendering process if they seek to implement these policies.

Recommendation 7

Purchasing institutions should ensure that all of their contract award criteria meet the standards of clarity, transparency and objectivity required to ensure a legally defensible tendering process.

Politicizing the Procurement Process

Buy Canadian policies and other local preferences can lead to the politicization of the procurement process. Irrespective of the merits of the particular context or the merits of the particular public policy that is being pursued, taxpayers have every right to be wary whenever a competitive procurement process is bypassed and a contract is negotiated behind closed doors in the name of "the greater public interest." The track record of the Canadian public sector in this regard has been far from stellar and by some well documented indications, the situation may actually be deteriorating rather than improving. When spending decisions are made at the political level and "pressing public priorities" are used to justify "exceptions" to general procurement rules, the public interest can be seriously compromised.

To maintain the integrity of the bidding process, contract award decisions need to be based on the objective application of transparent evaluation criteria. The integrity of the process and quality of the outcome can become compromised when the decision-making becomes politicized, is open to the influence of lobbying activities or is otherwise based on factors other than the objective application of predetermined transparent criteria.

Recommendation 8

As a general rule, government contract award decisions should be based on clear, transparent and objective criteria that are applied free from political considerations or political interference.

Chapter 2:
PROJECT GOVERNANCE

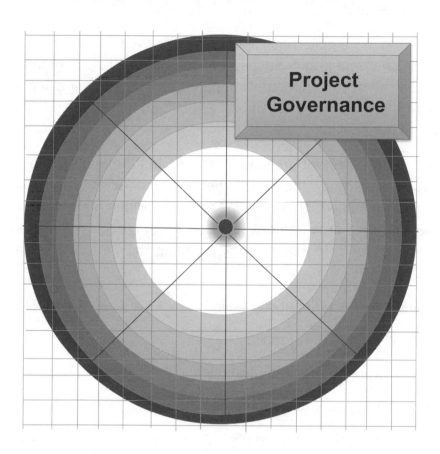

Introduction

Just as many downstream issues in the procurement cycle can be attributed to a lack of proper practices and procedures at the institutional level, many of the issues that arise on the transactional level can be attributed to a lack of proper planning at the project governance level. The following discussion summarizes some of the key project governance concepts that should be integrated into the planning of procurement projects. The subsequent case studies elaborate on the need to implement appropriate project approval and review processes. They also underscore the importance of clarifying roles and responsibilities within project teams and ensuring that project planning includes the clear definition of requirements and the proper selection of a tendering format.

Key Concepts for Major Procurements

This article is extracted from the Key Concepts in Major Procurements whitepaper written by Paul Emanuelli, which won the Best Practitioner Paper award at the 2006 International Symposium on Supply Chain Management.

Modern procurement is a complex interplay of rapidly evolving technological, commercial, administrative and legal trends. Domestically and internationally, procurement is a big deal. It is big business for private sector suppliers competing for contracts, it is increasingly critical to the functions of government and industry at all levels, and it plays a critical role in the quality of service delivery to the public.

As the significance of procurement projects increases, as the deals keep getting bigger and as the stakes keep getting higher, the need to get the job done right and the risks of failing to do so become more pronounced. The following article provides a number of key concepts for properly administering major procurement projects, offering critical insights that can benefit both public and private sector purchasers by directing their attention to the following five critical project areas:

1. identifying the role of legal counsel

2. addressing internal governance

3. developing proper plans and strategies

4. selecting the appropriate procurement format

5. focusing on critical project details.

These critical areas are discussed below.

1. The Role of Legal Counsel

In effectively managed major procurement projects, the role of legal counsel is more pronounced when compared with typical procurement. In major projects the legal issues are broader and more multi-faceted and the role of legal counsel is more integral to the ongoing planning and implementation of the project.

To empower effective procurement, legal counsel must serve as an embedded member of a broader multidisciplinary project team that typically includes:

- program-area clients responsible for project completion;

- internal and external procurement advisors;

- external arm's-length monitors also known as "Fairness Commissioners";

- internal and external business and technical experts; and

- other legal counsel who provide issue-specific advice.

In addition to providing the core commercial and procurement advice necessary to enable informed decision-making by the project team, counsel to major procurement projects must also provide or coordinate the provision of other critical legal advice which often includes:

- industry-specific advice focusing on distinct and specialized matters relevant to the specific industry;

- employment and labour relations advice, particularly where the project impacts in-house workers in a unionized setting;

- confidentiality and privacy advice where the project involves the handling of personal information or other confidential information such as sensitive business information;

- intellectual property law advice where the project includes the creation or transfer of intellectual property between the institution and the supplier; and

- litigation advice where the project is subject to actual or potential litigation.

To be effective, legal counsel must also understand and operate within the client's complex environment and be sensitive to the internal governance issues that can significantly impact the project.

2. Internal Governance

With respect to managing internal governance, the following four factors are critical to a project's success:

- identifying the organization's internal approvals roadmap;

- establishing a clear decision-making framework;

- identifying roles and responsibilities within the organization; and

- distinguishing between the internal and external audience.

(i) Internal Approvals Roadmap

A key component of empowered procurement is the identification of the client organization's internal approvals roadmap. Understanding the client's internal approval process and confirming the internal approvals obtained for the specific project can help shape the representations made to the supplier community during the procurement process and can help guide the team in its selection of the appropriate procurement format.

(ii) Decision-Making Framework

A clear internal governance and decision-making framework is another key component of empowered procurement. This framework can only be effectively established where all necessary internal stakeholders are identified at the outset of a project. Once those stakeholders are identified, a governance and decision-making framework can be tailored to provide direction to the team during all phases of the project.

(iii) Roles and Responsibilities

Identifying the roles and responsibilities of the various players on the multidisciplinary project team is another critical ingredient for successful projects. To guard against role overlap and accountability gaps, roles and responsibilities should be clearly and accurately identified and communicated at the outset of a project.

(iv) Distinguishing Internal and External Audience

The project team should be aware of both its internal and external audience and should clearly delineate between the documentation prepared for each. Only those details that are relevant to the competitive procurement process and to the performance of the contract should be disclosed to the external supplier community. To promote clear and concise external communications, internal matters should be left to the internal audience.

3. Plans and Strategies

Distinguishing process from purpose, developing thorough business plans and designing well-tailored procurement strategies are three critical strategic components of a successful procurement project. Legal counsel can provide crucial strategic and tactical advice to the project team to assist in the development of these critical project components.

(i) Distinguishing Process From Purpose

Distinguishing process from purpose is a critical key to effectively managing major procurement projects. An effective project team identifies and separates the means from the ends, tailoring its procurement documentation to clearly delineate between:

- the procurement process rules that lead to the selection of a preferred service provider; and

- the objectives that should be achieved under the contract once awarded.

(ii) Developing a Business Plan

A critical cornerstone of a successful major procurement is the development of a clear, concise and thorough business plan that identifies the objectives of the project. A flawed business plan can lead to significant deficiencies and delays in downstream implementation. A business plan should therefore be developed and approved at the outset of an initiative to serve as a reference point for all subsequent phases of the project.

(iii) Designing a Procurement Strategy

Once a business plan is established, the project team should develop a customized procurement strategy tailored to the specific objectives of the particular project. A critical component of a procurement strategy is the identification of appropriate procurement formats and processes. Legal advice is critical to informing the development of a sound strategy.

4. Selecting the Appropriate Procurement Format

The selection of a procurement format should be a conscious, informed and transparent decision that clearly identifies whether the particular competitive procurement process will be conducted under a binding bidding format or a negotiated format. Once a format is selected, mid-process paradigm shifts between binding tendering models and negotiated models should generally be avoided.

As stated in the United Nations Commission on International Trade Law's implementation guide to the 1994 *Model Law on Procurement of Goods, Construction and Services*, the suitability of each tendering format will depend on the particular circumstances:

> [T]hree procedures for selecting the successful proposal are provided so as to enable the procuring entity…to utilize a procedure that best suits the particular requirements and circumstances of each given case. The choice of a particular selection procedure is largely dependent on the type of service being procured and the main factors that will be taken into account in the selection process, in particular, whether the procuring entity wishes to hold negotiations with suppliers and contractors, and if so, at which stage in the selection process.

A legally binding tendering process, such as the no-negotiation RFP format, generally allows little latitude for post-close changes to the *pro forma* contact terms in the tender call. While some of the specific transactional details will be incorporated from the selected bidder's tender (e.g., price, specific products, personnel, etc.), the general performance terms originally set out in the tender call should remain materially unaltered.

To be viable, this approach calls for a predetermined certainty of terms and for the existence of standardized and broadly accepted industry practices. The absence of these factors tends to work against the feasibility of using a no-negotiation tender call format.

To be compatible with the restrictions of a no-negotiation format, the *pro forma* agreement should:

1. include all of the general governing terms and conditions;

2. incorporate all of the purchaser's business and technical requirements;

3. enable bidding based on the same set of common assumptions regarding performance terms and conditions; and

4. enable contract formation without recourse to any post-bidding negotiations that materially change the terms contained in the tender call.

While the procurement of simple goods and services can often be performed utilizing a take-it-or-leave-it no-negotiation model, the complexity of a major procurement project typically calls for a more flexible procurement format that permits negotiations between the institution and selected service provider.

5. Critical Project Details

In addition to calling for the development of clear business plans and sound procurement strategies, effective project management also calls for an attention to critical project details. These critical details typically include:

- meeting disclosure duties;

- reconciling requirements;

- coordinating concurrent drafting;

- achieving horizontal document integration;

- tailoring a legal agreement; and

- developing a negotiating strategy.

(i) Disclosure Duties

In an open, competitive procurement process, the purchasing institution should disclose the following material information:

- a clear description of the project deliverables;

- all material information that could impact the supplier's decision to bid and the amount that it bids;

- the evaluation criteria that will inform the selection of a preferred supplier; and

- the process rules that will govern the execution of a contract with the preferred supplier.

As illustrated in a number of reported legal decisions, the failure to provide this material information can have a significant adverse impact on the competitive process and on subsequent project performance.

(ii) Reconciling Requirements

Purchasers should clearly distinguish between those threshold requirements that determine a supplier's eligibility for award, those requirements that govern the ranking and selection of competing suppliers and those requirements that will govern the performance of the awarded contract. Organizing project requirements into these three distinct categories is critical to an effective procurement project and to a properly tailored contract.

(iii) Coordinating Concurrent Drafting

Complex procurements often involve the concurrent drafting of different components of an RFP document by different members of the multidisciplinary project team. This calls for a careful coordination of overall document development to ensure coherence and consistency in structure, content and terminology.

The project team should ensure the proper integration of the core components of the RFP including the description of the project requirements, the evaluation criteria and the pricing information.

(iv) Tailoring the Legal Agreement

The legal agreements created in major procurements tend to be complex and multi-tiered documents that must be tailored to properly fit the particular project. The extent to which the legal agreement and related contract documents are prepared in final form prior to the release of an RFP will depend on the specific situation and will be impacted by:

- the type of procurement format that is being utilized; and

- the extent to which competing service providers are expected to present unique and distinct approaches to the contemplated contract.

(v) Developing a Negotiating Strategy

Prior to the release of a negotiated RFP, the project team should develop a comprehensive negotiating strategy that:

- identifies roles, responsibilities and decision-makers to ensure that the bargaining team has recourse to a prompt issue-response and decision-making support structure;

- includes comprehensive briefing materials to help inform the bargaining team and decision-makers during negotiations; and

- anticipates and addresses issues that are likely to arise during the contract negotiation process in order to minimize improvisational responses to supplier-raised issues.

Concluding Comments – Legal Counsel a Key Player in Your Project Team

The complex and multi-faceted nature of major procurement projects requires legal counsel to play an intensive role in the project team. By integrating into that team and understanding the broader context within which these projects operate, legal counsel can be a key contributor to the success of a major project. To increase their chances of success, project organizers would be wise to retain this key player at the early stages of their major initiatives.

Approval and Review Process Flow

Does your organization's project process flow avoid approval bottlenecks and effectively integrate key subject matter experts into the early stages of project planning?

Establishing proper approval and review processes is one of the crucial conditions for ensuring the timely administration of the tendering process. As the following case studies illustrate, misalignments between internal approvals and external commitments can create significant liability for an institution. At the same time, organizations should guard against creating approval bottlenecks that cause gridlock and undermine broader institutional operations.

Nova Scotia and Newfoundland Liable For Internal Approval Mishaps

Canship Ltd. v. Newfoundland and Labrador Newfoundland and Labrador Supreme Court, 2005

Founders Square Ltd. v. Nova Scotia Nova Scotia Court of Appeal, 2001

Establishing clear contract approval and award protocols is essential to good governance in the procurement process. The following cases provide examples of how legal liability can turn on the failure to proper manage this key aspect of internal governance. The first example deals with an improper contract award that was made without first obtaining the necessary internal approvals. The second deals with a situation where an institution failed to follow up with proper paperwork to document a senior-level commitment to enter into a long-term contract. Both cases underscore the importance of properly lining up internal governance with the external commitments made to suppliers.

The decision of the Newfoundland and Labrador Supreme Court in *Canship Ltd. v. Newfoundland and Labrador (Minister of Works, Services and Transportation)* illustrates the risks of not aligning an institution's internal approvals with its external awards. The case dealt with a tender call for the provision of a container ocean vessel. Minutes before the expiry of the tenders, the government sent the plaintiff bidder a Letter of Acceptance. Within thirty minutes of sending the letter, the government attempted to rescind the award, taking the position that the letter had been issued without the required internal Treasury Board approvals. The court rejected this argument, noting that non-compliance with internal approvals did not give the government the right to cancel the contract award, particularly since the individual who made the award knew he was proceeding without internal approvals and had assumed that they would be obtained. As the court stated:

> In these circumstances I find there was no error on the part of the Government Purchasing Agency in sending the Letter of Acceptance to Canship. The Agency intended to communicate to Canship that it was the successful bidder and would be requested to enter into a formal contract. I accept that Mr. Baker knew the Letter should not go out before the Department received the authorization of Treasury Board to award to the higher bidder. I am satisfied, however, that he expected to have received this authorization by the telephone call to Treasury Board shortly before 2:00 p.m. I conclude the premature issuing of the Letter by the Purchasing Agency resulted from Mr. Baker's not being sufficiently explicit in his instructions to the Agency that the Letter should be held, from his not allowing sufficient time to request an extension of the Tender Validity Period in the event Treasury Board approval was not forthcoming, and from his not contacting the Agency or ensuring he would be available to Mr. Cahill before 2:00 p.m. once he realized Treasury Board approval would not be routinely granted.

The court awarded the plaintiff damages for breach of the improperly rescinded contract.

As illustrated in the Nova Scotia Court of Appeal decision in *Founders Square Ltd. v. Nova Scotia (Attorney General)*, the failure to properly document commitments made by a senior officials can cause significant downstream issues when new management takes over an organization. By way of background, the Nova Scotia government had purchased a number of derelict buildings near the Nova Scotia Legislative Assembly and planned to demolish them to build a central government office facility. However, the government came under pressure from heritage groups who lobbied to preserve the buildings. After striking a Cabinet Committee to address the issue, the Premier announced that Founders Square, a developer who was already in the area undertaking other projects, would restore the buildings. As part of the arrangement, the government would lease 25 percent of the restored space for 30 years to help amortize the costs. The paperwork setting out this arrangement was not completed. Instead, the matter was redirected to the Department of Government Services and it imposed a standard five-year letter lease on Founders Square. When a new Premier took over, the government relied on the letter lease to support a new policy direction and cancel the project. The developer sued. The court ordered the government to honour its original 30-year commitment. This case underscores the importance of having a clear internal approval and award process and of ensuring that contracts are documented to properly reflect the arrangements agreed to between the parties.

As these cases illustrate, institutions should maintain proper internal approval protocols and be careful to ensure that: (a) the commitments made to external suppliers properly align with those approvals; and (b) those commitments are clearly documented for future reference by decision-makers.

Stimulus Spending Rush Leads to Flawed Approval Process
Annual Report of the Auditor General of Ontario, 2010

In its 2010 annual report, the Ontario Auditor General found significant flaws in how the provincial government approved its funding for stimulus spending projects. The report noted that the province failed to allocate sufficient time and staff resources to the approval of thousands of funding requests and that it failed to properly prioritize those requests. The Auditor General also found that the government failed to document the rationale behind funding approval decisions and that this lack of transparency undermined the ability to properly protect against the politicization of the spending decisions.

The Auditor General's report reviewed three separate programs that administered $3.9 billion in federal-provincial stimulus spending. The report raised significant concerns over the volume of applications received and the time constraints under which the Ministry of Energy and Infrastructure ("MEI") approved those applications:

> With respect to the grant-application and application-assessment processes, we noted that:
>
> - MEI placed no limit on the number of applications that municipalities with populations of more than 100,000 could submit under ISF, the largest of the three infrastructure programs. This provided an incentive to submit large numbers of applications in hopes of getting as many of them approved as possible. For example, four municipalities submitted a total of almost 1,100 applications, accounting for 40% of the applications submitted by the 421 Ontario municipalities for this program.
>
> - Due to the tight deadlines, the time allotted for the provincial review of ISF applications was in most cases just one to two days. In one instance, we noted that a key component of the provincial review for 56 projects worth an estimated $585 million was carried out in just four hours. In our view, it would not have been possible to conduct the necessary review work within such a tight time frame.
>
> - Applicants were not required to prioritize their infrastructure needs, and none did in their applications, making it more difficult to assess the benefits of the proposed projects and make informed

funding decisions. One municipality submitted 150 applications valued at $408 million, and received approvals for 15 projects worth $194 million. From our visit to this municipality, we noted that 11 of the approved projects, valued at $121.7 million, were ranked at or near the bottom of the municipality's own priority list, while other, higher-ranked eligible projects were not approved.

- We noted that technical experts were generally not involved in assessing the applications even though thorough analysis by such experts would have helped assess the reasonableness of project cost estimates and identify those unlikely to meet the two-year completion deadline.

The report found that the government was unrealistic in expecting that projects that were approved for funding in 2009 could all be completed within the 2010 construction season. As the Auditor General noted, many of the projects encountered significant downstream issues attributed to, among other things, project size and complexity. The report found a lack of contingency planning for typical delays relating to weather conditions, soil conditions, permit approvals and land ownership issues.

The Auditor General also found significant deficiencies in how the government documented the criteria and decision-making process behind the selection of specific projects. As the report noted, after civil servants completed their rushed review process, the final funding decisions were made at the political level in a non-transparent and undocumented fashion:

> After assessment and review by civil servants in the appropriate ministries, applications were submitted to the office of Ontario's Minister of Energy and Infrastructure and to his federal counterpart for final review and approval. With respect to this process, we noted that there was a general lack of documentation to support the decisions regarding which projects got approved, and which did not.

> In some cases, ministers' offices approved projects that civil servants had earlier deemed ineligible or about which they had flagged concerns. We found little documentation to indicate how, or even if, the civil servants' concerns had been addressed prior to approvals being granted. Without such documentation, there is a heightened risk that the Ministry would be unable to demonstrate that the awarding of projects was open, fair, and transparent, or that political considerations did not come into play. In this regard, the results of our review of a sample of projects by electoral riding indicated there were no discernible patterns. Nevertheless, such approval decisions should be clearly documented and justified to ensure transparency and accountability in spending public money.

While the Auditor General's report found no apparent preference given to specific electoral ridings, it noted that provincial staff were "not in a position to confirm whether a particular project was added or removed by the provincial or federal minister." As the Ontario stimulus spending initiative illustrates, to better ensure public confidence in spending decisions, government institutions should implement proper planning and approval protocols for the funding of public projects.

World Bank Recommends Modernizing Moldova's Procurement System
Procurement Assessment Report for Moldova, 2010

In its June 2010 procurement review of Moldova, the World Bank recommended that the government phase out the role of the central Public Procurement Agency ("PPA") in reviewing and approving government contract awards under the Public Procurement Law ("PPL") so that the decentralized government agencies could more effectively govern their own procurement processes. As noted by the World Bank in its report, maintaining a centralized review and approval process in an otherwise decentralized procurement system undermines the independence of government agencies, creates duplication, increases inherent conflicts and results in approval bottlenecks:

> Since the enactment of the PPL in April 2007, the review and approval of award recommendations and contracts are still centralized and remain with the PPA, even though the conduct of public procurement was decentralized to public entities. The current centralized review and approval process has the following shortcomings:
>
> i.   The process results in shifting the responsibility and accountability of public entities to the PPA. In a fully decentralized public procurement systems, public entities are responsible and held accountable for their actions in conducting public procurement. In other words, approval of contracts by an authority like the PPA is not an internationally accepted practice, especially in member states of the EU, which Moldova aspires to be part of. In this practice, the decision is taken out of hands of the purchaser and given to an entity that has no technical expertise in conducting individual procurements and currently is answerable to no one. Complaints are made to the PPA (which now makes the ultimate decision in procurement) against actions taken by public entities that no longer have control of the ultimate decision.
>
> ii.   The process is considered a potential conflict of responsibilities because the PPA is also responsible for handling complaints

related to those cases which have already been reviewed and approved by the PPA. PPA's dual responsibility in approving the procurement decisions and also in resolving the complaints related to decision-making process and thus becomes both defendant and judge. Although the complaint review department of the PPA is a functionally independent unit within the PPA, it is not administratively independent from other units, and this apparent conflict in responsibilities may impose constraints in its freedom of action when handling complaints.

iii.   The process consumes most of the PPA's limited staff time and resources. The PPA reviews and approves about 23,000 contracts per year (more than 100 contracts per day), which means that it is simply unable to address the issues required to make a proper decision. The PPA can add very little value to the procurement process. If the public entity responsible for the procurement process is incapable of making the final decision in an informed way over a period of months based on technical input, then the value added by a centralized procurement decision that takes only minutes is uncertain. The approval process sometimes simply causes delays in some of the procurement transactions. It is getting much harder for the PPA to keep up with its current workload and responsibilities with the existing number of staff. The international practice is that the central public procurement agency focuses on preparation of secondary legislation, capacity building and similar functions where it can add more value in improving the whole public procurement system instead of dealing with individual procurement transactions.

In its report, the World Bank recommended that Moldova consider an immediate termination of the Public Procurement Authority's central review and approval role. This would bring its system in line with more modernized procurement regimes that have decentralized procurement functions and have left the monitoring of bidding activities by government agencies to the supplier community:

> What modern systems of procurement have done (even in those civil law countries which originally championed the centralized control approach, such as France, Belgium, Italy, and Germany) is to turn bidders into free policemen. Since they are closest to the procurement process and have a direct financial interest in the outcome, they are in the best position to identify and bring to the attention of the authorities any perceived breaches of the rules. In this way, only cases where wrongdoing is

suspected need to be "controlled," thereby avoiding centralized approval where it is not needed and concentrating the focus and resources on those instances where there is real cause for concern.

The World Bank's review recommendations serve as useful guidelines for other jurisdictions that are seeking to update the allocation of roles and responsibilities within their procurement systems while avoiding bureaucratic gridlock.

(5)   Proper Roles and Responsibilities

Does your organization's project governance process establish a project governance framework that clearly documents roles and responsibilities in order to avoid role overlaps and accountability gaps?

Selecting the right team composition and establishing clear roles and responsibilities is a crucial element for ensuring project success. The following case studies illustrate the importance of ensuring that project teams are empowered with a proper governance framework and that they are supported with the appropriate technical expertise to meet the institution's due diligence duties.

Alberta Auditor General Calls for Better Project Governance
November 2011 Report of the Auditor General of Alberta

In its November 2011 report, the Alberta Auditor General found that the project launched by Alberta Innovates – Technology Futures ("Technology Futures") to address internal business inefficiencies lacked a proper project governance structure. While the provincial body was established to facilitate the commercial use of technology and encourage an entrepreneurial culture in Alberta, the Auditor General's report found it wanting with respect to its own project governance. It made a series of useful recommendations to help address those problems.

The Auditor General noted that a prior attempt to implement an information management system by Technology Future's predecessor, Alberta Research Council, had resulted in a significant project failure. As the Auditor General stated, "In 2004, the former Alberta Research Council began building a new information management system. The project was not completed and ARC wrote-off $2.2 million in project costs consisting of $1.4 million in consulting fees and $800,000 in licensing costs."

To address its "significant business inefficiencies," Technology Futures launched a new corporation information systems ("CIS") initiative. While it decided to contract out the implementation of the project, the Auditor General noted that this did not remove the ultimate accountability of Technology Futures for ensuring the successful completion of the project. As the Auditor General stated, "Although functions were outsourced to third parties, the Corporation remains accountable for successful completion of the project. In our June 5, 2009 management letter to ARC, we pointed out that the lack of systems development processes could and did contribute to the previous project's failure."

The Auditor General noted that Technology Futures had failed to implement the project governance policies and processes established by its predecessor in the wake of the prior project failure. Instead, Technology Futures had retained an external project manager. However, the Auditor General noted that external consultants are no substitute for ensuring proper internal project governance:

> In response to our June 5, 2009 management letter, the former ARC had developed policies and processes following termination of the previous Management Information Systems project. When we assessed the current project, those policies and processes were not available; rather, the Corporation relied on the skills of the Project Manager. Management advised us that they would rely on an implementation partner to provide a structured project management process. However, the Corporation still needs to implement project management policies, processes and standards to supplement the implementation partner's controls. Part of the reason for the failure of the previous management information system project in the former ARC, was due to not having the proper internal resources to support and monitor the contracted resource.

The Auditor General found that the dependency on external advisors to run mission-critical projects places an organization at significant risk and that this risk should be managed thorough the implementation of proper project governance structures. As the Auditor General stated, the "role of project governance is to provide a decision-making framework that is logical, robust and repeatable to govern an organization's capital investment. A lack of project governance could result in the Corporation implementing an inadequate corporate information system or incurring significant financial losses."

To help reduce the risk of another project failure, the Auditor General called for clear project management policies and procedures, an oversight structure, defined roles and responsibilities, clearly defined objectives and clear performance measures:

> We recommend that Alberta Innovates — Technology Futures improve its governance practices for the Corporate Information Systems project, by:

- establishing formal project management policies, processes, standards and controls for the Corporate Information System project

- establishing a project steering committee comprised of key stakeholders

- documenting and communicating the roles and responsibilities for all stakeholders, including the steering committee, board sub-committee and project sponsors

- updating the business case to set out the project's objectives that enables the steering committee to monitor and measure the project's progress

- formally assessing the impact of the project on other strategic business initiatives and periodically updating the assessment.

The Auditor General also warned that the failure to adhere to these recommendations could place the institution at significant risk.

While the Alberta Auditor General's recommendations were aimed at a specific institution and specific project, other institutions would be wise to take those guidelines into account and establish proper project governance frameworks before embarking on their own major projects.

Fairness Consultants No Substitute for Internal Due Diligence

As the deals keep getting bigger and the stakes keep getting higher, the risks of project failure become more pronounced. With spending scandals putting a spotlight on government procurement, public institutions are under increasing pressure to ensure that their contract awards are fair and transparent. Back in 2005 Justice Bellamy's Toronto Computer Leasing and Toronto External Contracts Inquiries Report ("the Bellamy Report") recommended the use of fairness consultants for major projects, noting that "the use of fairness commissioners is an important emerging risk mitigation tool aimed at strengthening both the reality and perception of integrity in public procurement." In some circles, particularly within some larger more well-resourced government institutions, fairness consultants are viewed as adding value by bringing greater project transparency. However, while a fairness consultant's "sign off" can be useful to government ministers at press conferences when announcing high-profile contract awards, public institutions should not assume that they can simply outsource their project accountability to these private contractors. Ultimately, it is the public institution that remains accountable for the project outcome. Careful consideration should therefore be given to overall project requirements before deciding to hire a fairness consultant. The following discussion canvasses five critical considerations that can help inform that decision.

1. Assessing the Value of Adding Another Consultant

High-value, high-profile, complex and controversial projects are the primary candidates for fairness consultants. However, given the additional cost, time and complexity that a fairness consultant adds to a project through additional consulting fees and additional layers of inputs, reviews and approvals, a public institution should give careful regard to value-for-money and project efficiency before deciding to add yet another consultant to an already complex project.

2. Comparing Unlicensed Consultants to Licensed Professionals

Where the decision to retain a fairness consultant has been made, the institution should think very critically about the qualifications of the individual in question since fairness consultants are unregulated and unlicensed and come with no independent professional certification or governing body. They are not qualified to provide legal advice or to provide the technical expertise offered by other licensed professionals such as engineers, architects and accountants. Where advice is required in any of these specialized areas, the institution should retain the services of the appropriate licensed professional, rather than assuming that the fairness consultant can perform double duty and provide that input as well.

3. Balancing "Independent Oversight" Against Institutional Risk

The Bellamy Report recommends that the fairness consultant have a degree of independence from the project team. As the report states, "for complex projects, fairness commissioners are usually independent, external third parties, typically in the form of consultants." However, public institutions should be aware that giving a consultant the title of "fairness commissioner," "fairness auditor" or "fairness monitor" does not provide formal independence or impartiality, bestow any special legal status or require the consultant to perform the "fairness" function to any predetermined standard. Unlike a lawyer, whose advice can be provided on a confidential solicitor-client basis, the fairness consultant's input and observations are not privileged. The fairness consultant can be required to testify against the institution if a losing bidder launches legal proceedings. Further, unlike a court or tribunal, there is no due process guaranteed for the purchasing institution with respect to the "findings" of the fairness consultant. Since situations of fairness consultants "going rogue" on their own clients are not unprecedented, institutions should think very carefully before running the risk of empowering an unregulated, unlicensed consultant with unfettered influence over their mission-critical projects.

4. Defining the Mandate and Assessing "Sign Off" Value

Where the decision to retain a fairness consultant has been made, the purchasing organization should clearly define the role of this consultant at the outset of the project. As the Bellamy

Report notes, one of the key functions of a fairness consultant is to oversee the fairness of the evaluation process. However, there is a significant risk of scope drift when a fairness consultant's role is not clearly defined or properly adhered to. Carefully defining this role is a critical preliminary detail that should be addressed during the initial planning stages of the project.

Furthermore, a fairness commissioner's "sign off" provides no guarantee that the project will be shielded from further scrutiny. By way of example, a fairness report did not prevent the Alberta Auditor General from conducting its own review, as documented in its April 2010 audit report, of the Alberta Schools Alternative Procurement project. The Auditor General's review revisited the conclusions arrived at by the fairness consultant to confirm whether the project team had actually met its due diligence standard. In addition to revisiting how the government conducted its procurement process, the Auditor General also investigated the role of the fairness consultant, reviewing high level committee meeting minutes to determine whether the project had obtained the interim fairness reports and fairness "sign off" on the evaluation criteria as contemplated by the project protocols:

> A Fairness Auditor was engaged to observe procurement processes and report on adherence to the fairness principles contained in the *Management Framework: Procurement Process*. The Fairness Auditor's interim and final reports concluded that the fairness principles were complied with.
>
> We tested conclusions contained in the Fairness Auditor's report. We:
>
> - interviewed selected individuals involved in the administration of tender processes
>
> - interviewed individuals involved in scoring submissions
>
> - examined correspondence with organizations who obtained the RFQ, or were invited to submit a proposal for the RFP
>
> - examined evidence to determine that RFQ and RFP scoring plans were developed and approved prior to the close of submissions
>
> - reviewed training materials provided to individuals scoring submissions
>
> - examined minutes of Deputy Minister Steering Committee meetings for evidence of interim reporting by the fairness auditor and approval of scoring plans.

While the Auditor General, after conducting its own detailed review, ultimately concurred with the fairness consultant's conclusions, the report underscores the fact that fairness consultant's "sign off" provides no guarantee against further scrutiny by public auditors, unsuccessful suppliers or the courts. It therefore remains critical that a project team ensure that it is meeting its own due diligence obligations and not rely on a third-party attestation as an assurance that it has protected itself from further scrutiny or legal liability.

5. Ensuring Self-Sufficiency and Self-Governance

As the Bellamy Report notes, a fairness consultant "should be seen as an adjunct to the procurement process, not as a substitute for the procedures, policies, and conduct of staff that show commitment to fairness and transparency in procurement." At the end of the day, it is the public institution that is ultimately responsible for both the fairness of the process and the success of the project. While the process must be fair and must be seen to be fair, these fairness and transparency considerations must be balanced against other critical objectives including getting value-for-money for the taxpayer within reasonable timeframes and navigating a tendering terrain that is full of legal risk. Before hiring a fairness consultant, public institutions should therefore ask themselves whether that would be time and money better spent focusing on the proper resourcing of their project teams to ensure that their organization meets the due diligence standards for which it will ultimately be held accountable.

Supreme Court Makes Engineers Accountable for Drafting Specs

Edgeworth Construction Ltd. v. N.D. Lea & Associates Supreme Court of Canada, 1993

In its decision in *Edgeworth Construction Ltd. v. N.D. Lea & Associates*, the Supreme Court of Canada found that the engineers who were retained to assist the government in the preparation of tender call specifications owed a duty of care to prospective bidders. As the Supreme Court stated:

> The engineers undertook to provide information (the tender package) for use by a definable group of persons with whom it did not have any contractual relationship. The purpose of supplying the information was to allow tenderers to prepare a price to be submitted. The engineers knew this. The plaintiff contractor was one of the tenderers. It relied on the information prepared by the engineers in preparing its bid. Its reliance upon the engineers' work was reasonable. It alleges it suffered loss as a consequence. These facts establish a *prima facie* cause of action against the engineering firm.

While the Supreme Court considered policy arguments against applying a direct duty of care to the engineers because this would undermine the certainty of contract terms between the respective parties, it ultimately rejected those arguments and found that the engineers owed a duty to prospective bidders. As the Supreme Court explained:

Many professionals in a wide variety of callings and circumstances assume duties toward persons other than those with whom they have contracted, and are held liable in tort for their proper discharge. Typically, the additional risks are reflected in the price of the contract. Alternatively, disclaimers of responsibility to third parties may be issued.

The Supreme Court also stated that a prejudiced bidder's recourse for design defects in a tender call should not be limited to contract-based claims against the institution that issued the tender call:

> The proposition that the only correct way to bring a claim for design defects is by suing the owner in contract, who then may claim over against the design professional, is similarly suspect. The result, in a case such as this, would be that the contractor would not be able to claim against anyone for design defects. Since the province as owner has excluded its responsibility for design defects under the contract, the contractor could not recover against it.

The Supreme Court supported this conclusion by noting that not applying such a duty to the government-retained engineers would compel each bidder to retain its own engineers in order to assess the situation, a time consuming and duplicative practice that would be commercially impractical and would increase project costs. As the Supreme Court noted:

> One important policy consideration weighs against the engineering firm. If the engineering firm is correct, then contractors bidding on construction contracts will be obliged to do their own engineering. In the typically short period allowed for the filing of tenders — in this case about two weeks — the contractor would be obliged, at the very least, to conduct a thorough professional review of the accuracy of the engineering design and information, work which in this case took over two years. The task would be difficult, if not impossible. Moreover, each tendering contractor would be obliged to hire its own engineers and repeat a process already undertaken by the owner. The result would be that the engineering for the job would be done not just once, by the engineers hired by the owner, but a number of times. This duplication of effort would doubtless be reflected in higher bid prices, and ultimately, a greater cost to the public which ultimately bears the cost of road construction.

The Supreme Court therefore held that applying a duty to engineers preparing tender call specifications fell within commercial realities and allocated accountability accordingly.

External Engineers Owe Bidders Duty of Care

Cardinal Construction Ltd. v. Brockville
Ontario High Court of Justice, 1984

In its decision in *Cardinal Construction Ltd. v. Brockville (City)*, the Ontario High Court of Justice held that the owner's external engineers owed a duty to care to bidders to ensure the accuracy of the information disclosed in a tender call. The case dealt with a contract for the reconstruction of sewers and water mains in the City of Brockville, Ontario. Performance issues arose. The contractor sued, alleging that the city and its advisors had failed to properly disclose relevant information in relation to the project. The contractor maintained that "cable" markings on the relevant diagrams failed to properly highlight potential issues regarding the presence of a concrete duct structure and the complications that this could present in performing the work. The court agreed.

As this case illustrates, an owner is typically under a duty to disclose material information about the contemplated contract to all bidders. The failure to do so can create liabilities, give rise to litigation and cause significant problems in contract performance.

In fact, the institution issuing the tender call can be found liable for failing to meet its disclosure duties, even when the information is prepared by its external advisors. In this case the court also held that engineers preparing tender call documents for construction projects have a "responsibility to ensure that the information in the tender documents is correct and complete" and that the engineer "must disclose in the tender documents all material information in his possession in order to enable the contractor to prepare a proper bid." The court also articulated the following rules for engineers who are advising owners in the preparation of a tender call:

> (a)   The engineer (Kostuch) who prepares tender documents owes a duty of care to tenderers, for whose use the documents are prepared, who are expected to rely upon the information contained therein.

> (b)   The duty is to exercise reasonable care that the information presented in the tender documents reflects with reasonable accuracy the nature of the work and its factual components, so as to enable the contractor to prepare a proper bid.

> (c)   If the engineer has not verified specific information presented, he has a duty to inform bidders in clear terms that he does not vouch for its accuracy so as to put the bidder on notice that he must himself investigate the doubtful element.

> (d)   Whether or not Kostuch had a duty to provide information about the nature of the Bell installation, once having undertaken to give information

about it, Kostuch had a duty to bidders to do so with reasonable care
because it knew the information would be relied upon.

(e)   Having learned during the tender period that the Bell installation
was concrete duct structure, and neither cable nor conduit, Kostuch had
a duty to bidders to inform them of the true fact.

While these principles were articulated in the context of the engineer's responsibilities in
relation to the construction industry, they provide guidance across all industries with respect
to the potential disclosure duties owed by an owner and its advisors during a tendering
process. Owners and their external advisors should therefore remember the Cardinal Rule
and ensure that they disclose material information about the tendered contract that could
impact a bidder's decision to bid or influence the amount that the bidder quotes in its tender.
The failure to do so can give rise to significant post-award disputes and legal claims.

Municipality Liable For Pre-Bid Verbal Spec Change

George Robson Construction (Weston) Ltd. v. Hamilton-Wentworth Ontario Superior Court of Justice, 2001

In its decision in *George Robson Construction (Weston) Ltd. v. Hamilton-Wentworth (Regional
Municipality)*, the Ontario Superior Court of Justice found that the written disclaimers in a
tender call did not protect the owner from the verbal misrepresentations it made to the
plaintiff bidder. The case involved a construction project for the installation of a sewer pipe
under a highway. A dispute arose over whether the contract was restricted to concrete pipe
liner or also allowed for less costly steel pipe liner. The bidder claimed that the owner had
verbally confirmed that the steel liner was acceptable and that it had calculated its price in
accordance with that representation. The court found that the bidder was prejudiced by the
owner's inaccurate verbal representation:

I find that Benner would not have submitted the plaintiffs' bid without
Szigeti's representation. Benner had finely tuned his bid, which depended
on his use of 750 mm steel as a liner because its outside diameter
would allow him to use the machine he planned to use.

The court also held that the disclaimer contained in the owner's tender call did not protect it
from this verbal misrepresentation:

The defendant is not entitled to rely on the written provisions in the
document entitled "Instructions to Bidders", in the face of the explicit
representations made by Szigeti.

Lord Denning said the following on this issue in *Mendelssohn v. Normand Ltd.*, [1969] 2 All E.R. 1215, [1970] 1 Q.B. 177 (C.A.) at pp. 183-84:

> There are many cases in the books when a man has made, by word of mouth, a promise or a representation of fact, on which the other party acts by entering into the contract. In all such cases the man is not allowed to repudiate his representation by reference to a printed condition, see *Couchman v. Hill* [1947] K.B. 554; *Curtis v. Chemical Cleaning and Dyeing Co.* [1951] 1 K.B. 805; and *Harling v. Eddy* [1951] 2 K.B. 739; nor is he allowed to go back on his promise by reliance on a written clause, see *City and Westminster Properties (1934) Ltd v. Mudd* [1959] Ch. 129, 145 by Harman J. The reason is because the oral promise or representation has a decisive influence on the transaction — it is the very thing which induces the other to contract — and it would be most unjust to allow the maker to go back on it. The printed condition is rejected because it is repugnant to the express oral promise or representation.

In addition to the representation by Szigeti the defendant knew, before accepting the plaintiffs' tender, that the plaintiffs had tendered the detail relating to Addendum #6 using steel as opposed to concrete. Therefore, the defendant is estopped from later invoking written provisions in the "Instructions to Bidders" with respect to this particular detail.

Notwithstanding the tender call disclaimer, the court found the owner liable due to the inaccurate verbal representation and awarded the prejudiced contractor $222,000 in damages. In light of the conflicting evidence at trial with respect to whether the verbal representations were ever actually made, this case underscores the need to formalize pre-bidding communications with bidders and ensure that all such communications are reduced to written form to ensure equal access to all bidders and to reduce the risk of future misunderstandings and disagreements.

While this decision was ultimately reversed by the Ontario Court of Appeal and sent for a retrial, it serves as a reminder of the importance of establishing clear communication protocols within a project team to avoid downstream disputes with contractors over project scope and specifications.

6 Clear Requirements and Formats

Do your organization's project planning protocols mandate the preparation of clear requirements and the selection of appropriate tendering formats?

Establishing clear requirements and selecting appropriate tendering formats are two of the core planning components of any properly governed procurement project. The following case studies focus on the importance of clearly defining and scoping requirements and of selecting the appropriate tendering format for the particular project.

Imprecise Requirements Cause Delays and Overruns in Banking Project Report of the Auditor General of Alberta, April 2010

In its April 2010 report, the Alberta Auditor General found that an information technology initiative launched by the Alberta Treasury Branch ("ATB") to update its banking and financial systems was "significantly over budget and behind schedule." The report identified deficiencies in project governance, particularly as they related to the proper planning of project requirements and timelines, as the key causes of the project problems. It made a series of recommendations that serve as useful benchmarks for other institutions seeking to implement proper project planning.

The Auditor General found that ATB underestimated the risks and complexities of the major technology transformation initiative. It found that ATB failed to: (i) make key business decisions relating to project scope prior to launching the initiative; (ii) put a proper governance structure in place to manage the vendors retained to implement the project; and (iii) establish an adequate reporting structure up to its board of directors. As the report noted:

> The Core project is significantly over budget and behind schedule. ATB's Core project governance processes were inadequate; management did not identify or resolve the key issues that caused the significant delays and cost increases. A primary cause has been unsatisfactory project management.

> We found that ATB management significantly misjudged the following:

- risks associated with being one of the first financial institutions in North America to implement the SAP solution

- the work required to customize the SAP solution for the North American banking market place complexities to successfully implement the Core project, and the skills and resources required to manage it.

As of December 2009, ATB had spent $145 million on the Core project. However, the project scope and significant business process decisions had not been finalized. Significant project change requests remained outstanding. The project design continues to evolve and ATB has not yet finished the design validation.

As part of the functional design phase (or blueprint phase), ATB identified 278 business processes that must be documented and validated by the line of business representatives on the project. As of December 2009, only 89 of the business processes had been completed and approved. There had also been 400 project change requests up to December 2009. As of January 2010, there were still 85 change requests that had not been resolved.

ATB hired two major vendors; SAP and Accenture, to assist ATB implement the Core project. ATB needed to carefully manage such a relationship between the three parties to ensure that there was no abdication of responsibility through the diffusion of responsibility.

ATB's contractual arrangements with SAP and Accenture did not set fixed limits on time and materials to be invoiced. The contractual arrangements did not include incentives or penalties that would have shared the project's risks amongst the three parties.

Management's performance reports to ATB's Board of Directors have not been sufficiently detailed to allow for meaningful comparisons of the actual project results to the original project plan. In particular, the matching of actual and budgeted project costs to predefined project outputs has not been clear.

The Auditor General made a series of recommendations aimed at addressing the project's deficiencies and avoiding further delays and cost overruns, including the introduction of proper control measures and clear project requirements.

Moving forward, the Auditor General's recommended that ATB "resolve pending business decisions," "lock down the project's scope" and develop a new project plan with a "realistic schedule and budget to complete the project." As this case study illustrates, the success of a project can be seriously undermined by the failure to set clear requirements and set down realistic and measureable timeframes during project planning. The fact that these remedial measures were recommended after the initial project expenditure of $145 million serves as a clear warning sign to all institutions of the importance of conducting proper project planning prior to initiating project implementation.

Over-Scoped Specs Trigger Bid Shopping Battles

Stanco Projects Ltd. v. British Columbia
British Columbia Court of Appeal, 2006

CMH Construction Ltd. v. Victoria
Newfoundland and Labrador Supreme Court, 2010

As recent cases have shown, the improper drafting of specifications can lead to downstream legal entanglements during the procurement process. The following examples highlight the importance of properly scoping specifications so they line up with budget limits.

In its decision in *Stanco Projects Ltd. v. British Columbia (Ministry of Water, Land and Air Protection)*, the British Columbia Supreme Court found the government liable for bid shopping due to post-bidding price reduction negotiations conducted by the provincial government after all of the bids came in over budget. The case involved a tender call for a water system upgrade project at Cypress Bowl Provincial Park. The project contemplated the installation of two water tanks but after the tenders were opened a decision was made to proceed with just one tank due to budget constraints. The tender call did not contemplate the severance of the contract and failed to ask for separate pricing for each tank. The low bidder was asked by the government's external advisors to provide a lower single tank price under an improvised post-bidding process that was referred to as an "Offer of Credit." The government wanted the low bidder to offer a pro-rated one tank price based on the original two-tank price. However, due to the loss of volume discount, the low bidder was not prepared to offer the same unit pricing on a one tank project that it had offered on a two tank project.

One of the low bidder's competitors was told the low bidder's price and was allowed to submit a follow-up bid for the single tank. When it found out that other bidders were re-bidding, the plaintiff refused to engage in any further price discussions. The contract was ultimately awarded to one of the low bidder's competitors. The low bidder filed a lawsuit for its lost profits. The trial court recognized that the law of tenders prohibits purchasers from seeking irrevocable bids and then engaging in post-bidding price reduction negotiations. As the court stated, this type of bid manipulation "is repugnant conduct which has no legitimate place in the proper operation of the tendering paradigm". The court awarded the low bidder lost profit damages. This decision was subsequently upheld by the British Columbia Court of Appeal. As this case illustrates, the formal tendering process does not permit the safe re-scoping of project specifications after the receipt of binding bids.

The decision of the Newfoundland and Labrador Supreme Court in *CMH Construction Ltd. v. Victoria (Town)* offers a similar cautionary tale. The municipality received a single over-budget bid for its Victoria Municipal Centre renovation project. It then re-scoped the project, dividing it into three separate contracts and directly awarded those contracts to other suppliers. The original low bidder sued. In finding the municipality liable for bid shopping, the court was highly critical of the municipality's initial specifications. The court found that those specifications were unrealistic in light of the project budget and that this unrealistic project scoping had caused the over-budget bid situation:

> Victoria clearly has the right to set the terms of its tender call. Victoria also has the right not to award the work or to reject CMH's bid in reliance on the privilege clause if it cannot afford the bid cost. However, in so doing, it must treat compliant bidders, with which it has formed a Contract A, fairly. Fair treatment in this case involves a recognition that budgetary concerns do not relieve an owner from its obligation to treat bidders fairly, and that its reasons for not awarding the work are subject to judicial review (see *Rockwood* and *Crown Paving*). In reviewing the circumstances leading to Victoria's reason for rejecting CMH's bid, it is clear that CMH's bid exceeded the project budget because Victoria provided specifications in the Tender call which did not realistically permit a bidder to bid within the project budget. In this case, Victoria set Tender specifications for the work and materials far in excess of what its budget could cover.

The court also found that the municipality's post-bid solution of dividing up the original project while the original bid remained valid and seeking follow-up bids from other contractors constituted bid shopping and breached the duty of fairness owed to the original bidder.

As these cases illustrates, budgetary constraints do not give purchasers free licence to safely engage in post-bid improvisations, scope re-adjustments and parallel bidding processes. Before going to tender, purchasers should therefore ensure that their project specifications are properly scoped to fall within their budget limits or select flexible tendering formats that permit post-bid price adjustments.

Ontario Auditor Finds P3 Hospital Costs $200 Million Extra in Financing
Annual Report of the Auditor General of Ontario, 2008

In its 2008 annual report, the Ontario Auditor General found that the use of a public-private partnership format ("P3") for the construction of the William Osler Health Centre ("WOHC") resulted in $200 million in additional costs to the taxpayer. In its report, the Auditor General recommended that institutions conduct a value-for-money analysis prior to utilizing the P3 approach to procurement.

As the Auditor General's report explains, the P3 financing model can be used by public institutions to shift project administration costs to contractors and extend the timeframe for paying for the infrastructure works:

> Generally, P3s are contractual agreements between government and the private sector by which private-sector businesses provide assets and deliver services, and the various partners share the responsibilities and business risks. In the case of a hospital agreement, the private sector partners would typically be responsible for the design costs, the construction costs, and the financing (and possibly the ongoing facility capital maintenance costs as well). The hospital would then repay the partners through a series of payments over the long term. Governments enter into P3s because they provide an opportunity to transfer risks to the private sector, allow both sectors to focus on what they do best, and accelerate investment to help bridge the gap between the need for public infrastructure and the government's financial capacity.

While the P3 model may have its benefits in the appropriate circumstances, in the WOHC hospital construction project the Auditor General found that the decision to use the P3 format had been imposed by the provincial government with insufficient consideration of its cost-effectiveness:

> We noted that WOHC had invested much time and effort in planning and delivering the new hospital project. However, WOHC did not have the option of choosing which procurement approach to follow. Rather, it was the government of the day that decided to follow the public-private partnership (P3) approach. We noted that, before this decision was made, the costs and benefits of alternative procurement approaches, including traditional procurement, were not adequately assessed. This, along with a number of other issues we had with respect to this first P3 project at WOHC, led us to conclude that the all-in cost could well have been lower had the hospital and the related non-clinical services been procured under the traditional approach, rather than the P3 approach implemented in this case.

The Auditor General noted that the province could have borrowed funds to finance the project at a more preferable interest rate at considerable savings to the taxpayer. In fact, had more traditional government-obtained financing been utilized, the "savings would be approximately $200 million over the term of the project's P3 arrangement." Unfortunately, the Auditor General found that the hospital "had not considered the impact of these savings in its comparison of the traditional procurement approach with the P3 project."

The Auditor General also noted that using the P3 format significantly increased the cost of external advisors and that those expenses were not factored into the consideration of the cost-effectiveness of the P3 format:

> WOHC and the Ministry engaged approximately 60 legal, technical, financial, and other consultants at a total cost of approximately $34 million. About $28 million of these costs related to the work associated with the new P3 approach, yet they were not included in the P3 cost. While acknowledging that additional professional services will be required given the newness of the P3 process, we still believe a significant portion of the professional costs relating to the P3 arrangement should have been included in the cost comparison.

Furthermore, the Auditor General found that in many instances the project failed to follow appropriate procurement protocols when those external advisors were retained:

> Over 40% of the advisers in our sample were single sourced. In addition, many consulting assignments were open-ended, without pre-established budgets or a ceiling price. We acknowledge that this was in part due to the arrangement being a pilot and to the uncertainty regarding the exact requirements of the various aspects of the project.

In its report, the Auditor General warned institutions that are considering the more complex P3 procurement format to realistically assess the total cost of the P3 approach when compared to more traditional financing and tendering formats. It advised that this "assessment should be carried out early in the process" as part of initial business case. As this case study illustrates, the selection of an appropriate tendering format is a critical component of proper project planning.

Alberta Auditor Calls for
More Transparency in Use of P3 Procurements
Report of the Auditor General of Alberta, April 2010

In its April 2010 report, the Alberta Auditor General reviewed the Alberta Schools Alternative Procurement Project ("ASAP 1"), a pilot project launched to determine whether the public private partnership ("P3") procurement model could be used to quickly build a large number of schools while also ensuring value-for-money to taxpayers. While the report determined that "the processes used for ASAP 1 resulted in a fair and open procurement" it also found that the project team "did not publish a report to inform Albertans how value-for-money was achieved." The Auditor General called for greater transparency when using a P3 approach to public procurement.

The Auditor General found that the ASAP 1 P3 initiative failed to follow the *Management Framework: Procurement Process* guidelines established by the Alberta Departments of Treasury Board and Infrastructure, which called for the creation and release of a value-for-money report upon the award of a P3 contract:

> The Management Framework: Procurement Process provides guidance on information that should be disclosed in a Value for Money Report and information that should remain confidential to avoid compromising the competitive process.
>
> To ensure that the P3 process is transparent, the framework states that a Value for Money Report be prepared, and published upon signing the P3 contract, to inform Albertans about how value for money was achieved. The Report should include the following content:
>
> - project background, objectives and alternatives (typically traditional delivery and P3 delivery)
>
> - a description of the selection process, short-listed proponents, preferred proponent, milestone dates, advisors (financial, engineering, process, fairness as applicable), and selection costs
>
> - a summary of the key terms of the Project Agreement
>
> - a financial summary including NPV lifecycle cost comparison, performance payment requirements and accounting treatment
>
> - any material scope changes to the project during the procurement
>
> - summary of the risk profile/allocation
>
> - innovations and creativity provided

As the above list reflects, a value-for-money report calls for the disclosure of material information about the entire procurement process. The ability to effectively provide this post-award report therefore requires an institution to establish the appropriate project governance protocols before it initiates its competition. In other words, downstream transparency obligations must be met at the planning stage of a major project.

Given the P3's relatively complex project financing arrangements and its multi-stage bidding and award protocols, the Auditor General recommends that the purchasing institution engage in a comparative analysis to justify the use of this format rather than more traditional and less complex procurement formats. The report also calls for the preparation of a business case to document the expected advantages of utilizing the P3 approach:

A P3 may be considered instead of traditional forms of infrastructure acquisition and maintenance where there is a reasonable expectation that the P3 can provide greater value for money through a combination of risk transfer, earlier project delivery, and lower initial capital and ongoing maintenance and cyclical renewal costs.

Departments prepare a business case to determine the procurement alternative that can provide the best value for money. The quantitative analysis compares the estimated costs of a traditional alternative — the Public Sector Comparator — to other viable alternatives, one of which is a P3.

As this recommendation illustrates, given its increased cost and complexity, institutions should test their assumptions before concluding that the P3 financing and tendering model is the appropriate approach to any particular project.

As with any other type of open public procurement, institutions that are employing a P3 model should ensure that their competitive bidding process adheres to the defensibility principles of open and fair competition. As the Auditor General stated in its report:

To ensure that the procurement process is fair and consistent, the following principles are used as guidelines throughout the process:

- all interested parties, respondents and proponents have the same opportunity made available to access information

- the information made available to interested parties, respondents and proponents is sufficient to ensure that they have the opportunity to fully understand the opportunity

- all interested parties, respondents and proponents have reasonable access to the opportunity

- the criteria established in the invitation documents truly reflect the needs and objectives in respect of the project

- the evaluation criteria and the evaluation process are established prior to the evaluation of submissions

- the evaluation criteria, RFQ/RFP, and evaluation processes are internally consistent

- the pre-established evaluation criteria and evaluation processes are followed

- the evaluation criteria and process are consistently applied to all submissions.

The Auditor General's transparency recommendations provide a useful roadmap to help ensure the defensibility of all procurement competitions, irrespective of the specific type of tendering format that is selected by the institution.

Vague Tendering Rules Increase Risk of Lost-Profit Awards

Canadian Logistics Systems Ltd. v. Canadian National Transportations Ltd. British Columbia Supreme Court, 2000

The British Columbia Supreme Court decision in *Canadian Logistics Systems Ltd. v. Canadian National Transportations Ltd.* underscores the inherent risk of ambiguously drafted tendering rules. In this case, the purchasing institution initiated a process that it referred to as a Request for Information and Pricing ("RFIP") for motor vehicle inspection services. A losing respondent sued for lost profits, claiming that it had submitted a legally binding tender and that the evaluation had not been conducted appropriately. The defendant countered by claiming that it never intended to initiate a binding Contract A bidding process. However, the court determined that the legally ambiguous RFIP had in fact created a Contract A bidding process. It awarded the bidder lost profits due to the flawed evaluation and award process.

Among other things, the purchaser was found have been deliberately disruptive during the plaintiff's demonstration session and had repeatedly interrupted with questions that prevented the plaintiff from properly making its presentation. The court also found problems with the purchaser's pricing calculations and found that the purchaser improperly permitted a competing bidder to repair its bid after the bid deadline. In describing the process, the court stated that it was "left with the distinct impression that what occurred here at best amounts to the workings of ineptitude and bias and at worst, the workings of *mala fides* on the part of the Evaluation Committee."

In its defence the purchaser claimed that it had intended to enter into a flexible tendering format that permitted dialogue between the parties and that it had never intended to create Contract A and be bound by those rigid tendering protocols:

> CN submits that here the terms of the RFIP, coupled with the process itself (including vendor presentations), indicated that it was well understood by all parties there would be an interaction between the vendors and CN following the opening of the bids. Since the RFIP had no irrevocability clause and no privilege clause, CN submits that it was clear it did not intend to enter into a competitive bidding process subject to the same

constraints as a request for quotation or an invitation to tender. Rather CN submits it was clear that it wished to have a flexible, open process in which it could seek the best practices and the best overall price/quality combination.

The court disagreed and relied on the absence of clear negotiation protocols within the tendering documents as a key factor for reading in an intention to create a legally binding Contract A bidding process.

While in many other instances the courts have relied on the absence of bid irrevocability as a telltale sign of a non-Contract A bidding process, in this case the ambiguity of the tendering rules left room for interpretation and for a finding of liability against the purchasing entity under the Contract A protocols even though there was no express requirement for irrevocable bids. This case therefore serves as a clear warning to purchasers to avoid the legal grey zones between the Contract A bidding protocols and more flexible non-binding tendering formats. A clear decision regarding the legal operating rules should be made during the planning stages of a project. Where institutions want to employ more flexible and lower-risk tendering protocols, they should ensure that their process rules: (a) are properly drafted to avoid triggering the Contract A tendering rules; (b) enable post-bidding rectifications and negotiations; and (c) permit the safe termination of unsuccessful negotiations and cancellation of the competition. As this case illustrates, the failure to properly integrate these legal protocols into tendering documents can leave institutions liable for significant lost profit claims.

Chapter 3:
FORMS AND FORMATS

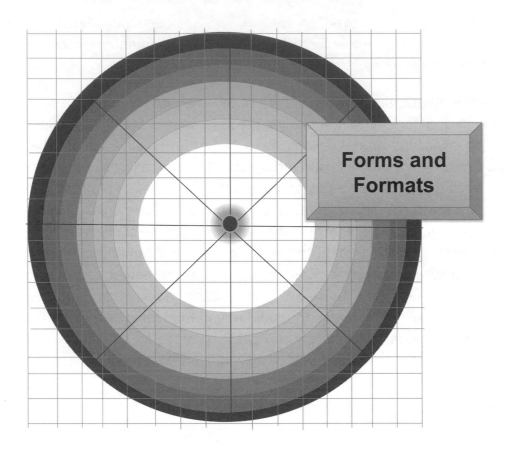

Introduction

Given the complexities of the modern procurement landscape, organizations can no longer limit themselves to one or two tendering formats. To meet their due diligence duties and accelerate their tendering cycles, purchasing institutions should deploy a full range of forms and formats. The following case studies consider the range of options available to institutions and highlight the importance of ensuring that standard template content is kept up-to-date to address the latest legal developments. They also illustrate the importance of ensuring that there is a broad organizational awareness of the legal risks and restrictions created by using certain tendering formats.

Does your organization use a broad range of tendering formats based on domestic and international best practices?

To meet the challenges of the procurement cycle, organizations need to diversify their procurement playbooks. The following section highlights recent international developments relating to the use of different tendering formats, providing an analysis of the use of these different competitive bidding formats within the Canadian legal context. It also highlights emerging international trends in the use of prequalification procedures and framework agreements.

UN Model Procurement Law – December 2011 Resolution

In December 2011, the General Assembly of the United Nations adopted the new Model Law on Public Procurement *which replaces and updates the prior 1994 version of the model law. The UN resolution is reproduced below.*

United Nations

Resolution adopted by the General Assembly

[on the report of the Sixth Committee (A/66/471)]

66/95. United Nations Commission on International Trade Law Model Law on Public Procurement

The General Assembly,

Recalling its resolution 2205 (XXI) of 17 December 1966, by which it established the United Nations Commission on International Trade Law with the purpose of furthering the progressive harmonization and unification of the law of international trade in the interests of all peoples, in particular those of developing countries,

Noting that procurement constitutes a significant portion of public expenditure in most States,

Recalling its resolution 49/54 of 9 December 1994 recommending the use of the United Nations Commission on International Trade Law Model Law on Procurement of Goods, Construction and Services,

Observing that the 1994 Model Law, which has become an important international benchmark in procurement law reform, sets out procedures aimed at achieving competition, transparency, fairness, economy and efficiency in the procurement process,

Observing also that, despite the widely recognized value of the 1994 Model Law, new issues and practices have arisen since its adoption that have justified revision of the text,

Recognizing that at its thirty-seventh session, in 2004, the Commission agreed that the 1994 Model Law would benefit from being updated to reflect new practices, in particular those resulting from the use of electronic communications in public procurement, and the experience gained in the use of the 1994 Model Law as a basis for law reform, not departing, however, from the basic principles behind it and not modifying the provisions whose usefulness had been proved,

Noting that the revisions to the 1994 Model Law were the subject of due deliberation and extensive consultations with Governments and interested international organizations, and that thus it can be expected that the revised Model Law, to be called the "United Nations Commission on International Trade Law Model Law on Public Procurement", would be acceptable to States with different legal, social and economic systems,

Noting also that the revised Model Law is expected to contribute significantly to the establishment of a harmonized and modern legal framework for public procurement that promotes economy, efficiency and competition in procurement and, at the same time, fosters integrity, confidence, fairness and transparency in the procurement process,

Convinced that the revised Model Law will significantly assist all States, in particular developing countries and countries with economies in transition, in enhancing their existing procurement laws and formulating procurement laws where none presently exist, and will lead to the development of harmonious international economic relations and increased economic development,

1.   *Expresses its appreciation* to the United Nations Commission on International Trade Law for developing and adopting the draft United Nations Commission on International Trade Law Model Law on Public Procurement;

2.   *Requests* the Secretary-General to transmit the text of the Model Law to Governments and other interested bodies;

3.   *Recommends* that all States use the Model Law in assessing their legal regimes for public procurement and give favourable consideration to the Model Law when they enact or revise their laws;

4.   *Calls for* closer cooperation and coordination among the Commission and other international organs and organizations, including regional organizations, active in the field of procurement law reform, in order to avoid undesirable duplication of efforts and inconsistent, incoherent or conflicting results in the modernization and harmonization of public procurement law;

5.   *Endorses* the efforts and initiatives of the secretariat of the Commission aimed at increasing the coordination of, and cooperation on, legal activities concerned with public procurement reform.

82nd plenary meeting
9 December 2011

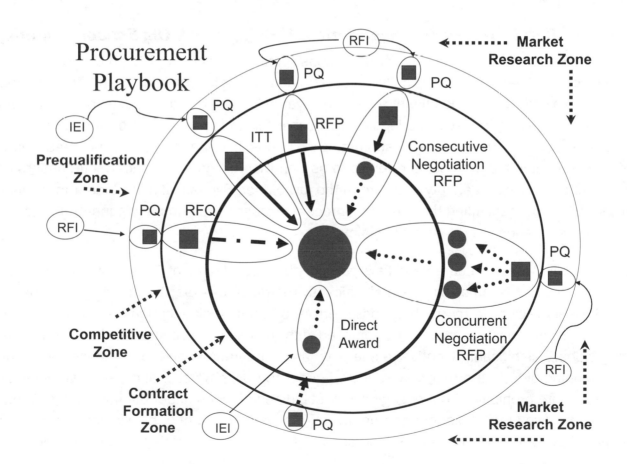

Leveraging International Standards to Build Your Procurement Playbook

While many public sector institutions are under treaty obligations that call for open public procurement, those treaties generally do not prescribe the method for conducting open competitions. However, in December 2011 the General Assembly of the Nations adopted the newly revised 2011 edition of the United Nations Commission on International Trade Law *Model Law on Public Procurement* ("UN Model Procurement Law"). The new UN Model Procurement Law recognizes that public institutions can meet their mandates for open transparent procurement and value-for-money by utilizing a wide range of procurement formats, protocols and procedures.

The new model law provides useful guidance for updating an institution's procurement playbook. The following discussion surveys the main competitive tendering formats recognized under the new UN Model Procurement Law: the Invitation to Tender, the Request for Proposal and the Request for Quotation. It also makes recommendations on how the UN protocols can be adapted and enhanced for practical implementation within the complex operating system of Canadian tendering law.

The Invitation to Tender/No-Negotiation RFP: High-Risk Old-School Tendering

The Invitation to Tender is often used for construction projects and for the acquisition of certain commodities. Price is typically the determining factor for contract award. The Invitation to Tender typically adds a significant additional layer of legal risk and formality to the tendering process by requiring that bids be legally irrevocable for a predefined period and by requiring bidders to guarantee their pricing by submitting bid bonds. In Canada, the legal process created by this irrevocable bid protocol is referred to as Contract A. Under Contract A, purchasers are subject to an implied legal duty to award to the low bidder. Bypassing a low bidder in favour of another bidder or cancelling the tendering process exposes the purchasing institution to "bid shopping" allegations and lost profit claims.

While the UN Model Procurement Law permits the acceptance of bids that contain minor variations, the Canadian courts have significantly restricted this discretion, finding purchasers liable for "bid repair" for correcting pricing errors or seeking clarifications and awarding lost profits when purchasers breach their implied duty to reject non-compliant bids. This gives losing bidders significant incentive to sue purchasing institutions and to challenge the validity of the winning bid. Furthermore, as reflected under the UN protocols and Canadian case law, purchasers are prohibited from engaging in post-bid negotiations under the Invitation to Tender format. This gives losing bidders another avenue to claim lost profits by alleging that post-bid changes, however minor, constituted bid shopping, bid repair or unfair process infractions.

The UN Model Procurement Law also states that, when an Invitation to Tender is used, all bids should be publicly opened. However, this public opening protocol is not broadly utilized in

Canada. In fact, public openings help facilitate bid manipulation by allowing a bidder to attend at the deadline with two envelopes, one with a competitive bid and another with an inflated bid that can be submitted if, through good fortune or prior collusion, no other bidder shows up to submit a competing offer. For these and other reasons, public openings are being phased out of Canadian public sector purchasing notwithstanding the UN protocol.

While listed under the UN Model Procurement Law as an RFP format, the No-Negotiation RFP is essentially the same format as the Invitation to Tender. Like the Invitation to Tender format, bidder pricing in No-Negotiation RFPs is irrevocable, contract terms are non-negotiable and tender compliance protocols prohibit the acceptance of bids that contain irregularities. Like the Invitation to Tender, the No-Negotiation RFP typically operates within the Contract A process rules that make the purchasing institution vulnerable to bidder lost profit claims. The key distinction between the Invitation to Tender and the No-Negotiation RFP is that the Invitation to Tender ranks suppliers based on the lowest price, whereas the No-Negotiation RFP combines price and non-price factors to rank suppliers based on the highest score. Given its inherent restrictions, the No-Negotiation RFP continues to lose market share as a viable tendering option since it has little to offer when compared against: (a) the relative simplicity of the low-bid Invitation to Tender; (b) the flexibility of lower risk negotiated RFPs; and (c) the simplicity and speed of lower risk RFQ formats.

While the Invitation to Tender continues to enjoy widespread use in the construction sector for medium-complexity projects, the *UN Model Legislative Provisions on Privately Financed Infrastructure Projects* provide a set of protocols that complement the new UN Model Procurement Law and recognize the use of flexible negotiated RFP formats when dealing with complex infrastructure-related construction projects. These model legislative provisions reflect a move within the construction industry away from their traditional tendering formats and towards the flexible formats used by many other industries that never adopted the No-Negotiation RFP or Invitation to Tender formats in the first place.

Negotiated RFPs: Fine-Tuning Flexible Low-Risk Open Competition

From the standpoint of facilitating flexible low-risk procurements, one of the significant enhancements contained in the 2011 edition of the UN Model Procurement Law is the expanded scope contemplated for negotiated RFP formats. Under the prior 1994 edition of the model law, the Invitation to Tender was the assumed default format for the procurement of goods and construction and RFPs were the default format for the procurement of services. The 2011 UN Model Procurement Law dispenses with these restrictive assumptions, opening up the use of all types of formats to all types of acquisitions, thereby giving institutions a complete range of options to choose from for each procurement project. This development will help accelerate the expanding adoption of negotiated RFP formats for goods, services and construction by institutions seeking to avoid the risks and restrictions of the Invitation to Tender and No-Negotiation RFP formats. Under the UN Model Procurement Law, Negotiated RFPs come in two standard models: the Consecutive Negotiation RFP and the Concurrent Negotiation/BAFO RFP.

The Consecutive Negotiation RFP format ranks proposals based on price and non-price factors and then allows the purchasing institution to run an accelerated negotiation process with the single top-ranked proponent. Within Canadian procurement circles, this approach is often referred to as the "Rank-and-Run RFP." As the UN Model Procurement Law contemplates, where it becomes apparent that the parties cannot come to terms, the Consecutive Negotiation RFP allows the purchaser to run down the rankings to negotiate with the next-ranked proponent. To supplement the UN model rules, it is useful to incorporate a pre-established timeframe for negotiations within the RFP negotiation protocols. This helps keep competitive pressure on the top-ranked proponent who must either close the deal or risk losing the deal to the next-ranked competitor. It also enhances the transparency of the process since everyone knows the timeframes for negotiations when they submit their proposals.

The Concurrent Negotiation/BAFO RFP allows the purchasing institution to enter into parallel discussions with multiple short-listed proponents. The UN Model Procurement Law contemplates that the purchaser invite at least three proponents into concurrent dialogues before providing each of those proponents an opportunity to submit its best-and-final-offer ("BAFO"). The final ranking is based on these final offers and under the UN Model rules the award goes to the final top-ranked proponent without any further negotiations.

To streamline and simplify the approach contemplated by the UN protocols, institutions should consider employing a "dual track" approach that reduces the number of short-listed proponents from three to two. This allows for a more manageable two-proponent process while maintaining competitive pressures through concurrent negotiations. Furthermore, to avoid getting bogged down in contractual legalities, the process rules should be crafted so that the dialogue between the parties focuses on the business issues during the concurrent negotiations. This way, rather than covering the legal issues with multiple concurrent proponents prior to the best-and-final-offer rankings, the purchasing institution can finalize contract terms with the single top-ranked proponent using the same contract finalization protocols recognized under the Consecutive Negotiation/Rank-and-Run RFP format. This helps bring greater speed and efficiency to the procurement process while enabling concurrent dialogues at the initial stages of the competition.

Another notable enhancement that can be introduced into the negotiated RFP formats is the addition of a rectification period during the threshold screening stage of the evaluation process. This allows the purchasing institution to avoid the trap of tender compliance disputes by allowing each proponent the opportunity to rectify their respective list of deficiencies. If properly structured with transparent and equally applied protocols, this approach encourages greater competition and avoids the unfortunate and common occurrence of being legally compelled to reject an otherwise superior proposal over a relatively minor irregularity.

The Request for Quotation ("RFQ"): Keeping it Simple

The RFQ, which can be used for a broad range of standard goods and services, is gaining increasing traction as a simple low-risk alternative to the high-risk and highly complex Invitation to Tender/No-Negotiation RFP formats. At minimum, institutions should consider deploying two types of RFQs: Invitational RFQs and Open RFQs.

Invitational RFQs can be created using simplified offer and acceptance protocols, often by way of email correspondence, with basic price-based evaluation rules and streamlined purchase order contract terms. As noted in the UN Model Procurement Law, the RFQ format is particularly effective for contracts valued under the trade treaty thresholds, where fully open competition is not required but where a minimum of three suppliers are invited to submit quotes to better ensure that the contract pricing is reasonable and that value-for-money is being obtained.

RFQs can also be scaled out for use beyond the three quote invitational protocol contemplated by the UN Model Procurement Law. Open RFQs can be used for publicly posted solicitations for contracts valued over the treaty thresholds. This provides a more simplified and lower risk alternative to the Invitation to Tender format in situations where price is the determining factor. Furthermore, Open RFQs can be enhanced with evaluation protocols that incorporate price and non-price factors, thereby providing purchasing institutions with an alternative to the higher-risk No-Negotiation RFP in situations where non-price factors will inform the rankings and negotiations are not required.

Leveraging International Standards For Accelerated Tendering

As illustrated by this survey of the UN Model Procurement Law's competitive bidding formats, institutions can leverage international practices to develop flexible streamlined tendering formats that enable open competition while accelerating the tendering cycle.

Building Your Bargaining Binder
By Marilyn Brown

The bargaining binder is a critical tool in the negotiation and contract-finalization stage of a negotiated procurement process. The content of a bargaining binder will differ from one project to another, but the basic structure is relatively consistent. Essentially, the bargaining binder is a consolidation of the documents and background materials that will be relied upon by the members of the negotiating team in one well-organized and professional-looking package. This article is designed to take you through the steps of developing your bargaining binder.

Binder Basics

The first step in preparing for the negotiation process is identifying your negotiating team. The negotiating team will include individuals directly involved in the negotiations and those who will provide assistance in the background. For the purposes of building your bargaining binder, determine which team members will be at the bargaining table. These individuals will all need a copy of the binder in front of them during the negotiation sessions, and should, as a team, determine the contents of the bargaining binder. To start the process, prepare a draft table of contents for the bargaining binder and include the basic documents you will need to refer to in the negotiation sessions. Examples include the main body of the procurement document, the preferred proponent's proposal, and the template agreement that was included in the procurement document. Be sure that the version of the procurement document included in your bargaining binder is the final posted version updated to reflect any changes made through addenda, and include a consolidation of all questions and answers from addenda, organized according to subject matter for ease of reference.

Critical Content

In addition to these basic documents, the bargaining binder should contain negotiation protocols. The protocols should include:

- the ground rules for the negotiations, as established in the procurement document, such as rules governing communications and confidentiality, and the timeframe for negotiations;

- documentation of your negotiating team structure and the roles and responsibilities of team members; and

- an approvals roadmap setting out the steps for obtaining the necessary approvals for the finalization and execution of the contract.

Your binder should also include a summary of high-level strategic and tactical considerations. To the extent possible, the negotiating team should attempt to anticipate and plan for issues likely to be raised by the proponent, and should include a clause-by-clause and schedule-by-schedule breakdown of the contract components, noting anticipated issues and prepared responses, and identifying the team member that will take the lead for each component of the contract. Any documented authority for the procurement and/or the negotiation stage of the process, such as recommendations to enter into negotiations approved by a Council or Board, should be included in your bargaining binder for reference.

Professional Presentation

The importance of first impressions should never be underestimated, and simple presentation strategies will immediately set a professional tone for the negotiations and convey to the proponent that your team is well prepared and serious about the process. Ensure that the content of your bargaining binder is put together in a professional-looking package – a plain black binder is always a good choice – and is well organized with a table of contents and relevant tabs, so documents can be located quickly and easily. In advance of negotiations, provide a copy of the binder to each team member so they can familiarize themselves with the layout and make any additional notes. Prior to the first negotiating session, determine where each team member will sit at the bargaining table in order to ensure optimal team seating for eye contact and other non-verbal communication. At the sessions, each team member should have a copy of the bargaining binder in front of them at the table. During the negotiations, all members of the team will be able to quickly locate and refer to documents in their binders, without fumbling through loose documents struggling to locate the relevant information.

Nimble Negotiators

Having taken the step of incorporating negotiated RFP formats into their procurement playbook, many organizations remain wary of and unsure how to prepare for the negotiation process. By building a complete and well-organized bargaining binder, you will have thoroughly prepared for negotiations by assembling your negotiating team, developing your negotiating strategy, finalizing your protocols, reviewing the relevant documents and assembling your materials. At this point, your team will feel more confident about walking into the room, taking your seats at the bargaining table and successfully negotiating the deal.

Using Prequalifications to Narrow the Playing Field

Prequalification processes have long been recognized as an effective means of bringing efficiency to a procurement process. As noted in the implementation guide for the 1994 *UN Model Procurement Law on Procurement of Goods, Construction and Services*:

> Prequalification proceedings are intended to eliminate, early in the procurement proceedings, suppliers or contractors that are not suitably qualified to perform the contract. Such a procedure may be particularly useful for the purchase of complex or high-value goods, construction or services, and may even be advisable for purchases that are of a relatively low value but involve a very specialized nature. The reason for this is that the evaluation and comparison of tenders, proposals and offers in those cases is much more complicated, costly and time-consuming.

The new 2011 UN Model Procurement Law recognizes a number of criteria that purchasing institutions can consider when screening suppliers to determine their eligibility to compete for a contract. Those criteria include:

- professional and technical qualifications and competence;

- financial resources, including financial solvency;

- good standing with respect to the payment of taxes; and

- a clean record with respect to any history of criminal offences relating to professional conduct or any history of misrepresenting qualifications.

Under the UN Model Procurement Law, a public institution must disclose its prequalification criteria and is entitled to disqualify suppliers on the basis of material misrepresentations. The Prequalification documentation must be provided without charge except for the cost of printing, and such documentation should include instructions, the main terms and conditions of any contemplated contract, the information that suppliers should submit to demonstrate their qualifications, the rules regarding the submission of qualifications and the provision of adequate time to allow for responses. The Prequalification rules also require public institutions to adhere to the same types of general transparency rules relating to supplier clarification requests, the disclosure of evaluation criteria and procedures, and the acceptance of only qualified suppliers as would apply to an Invitation to Tender process. To enhanced the UN protocols within the Canadian context, a Prequalification process should be refined to address many of the problems recognized in a "one-shot" Invitation to Tender process by expressly permitting suppliers follow-up opportunities to rectify shortcomings and become eligible for the subsequent competitive phase. This can result in fewer disqualifications and greater competition.

Since preparing submissions for complex projects can be a costly endeavour, a Prequalification should be considered in major projects to pre-screen suppliers. This allows the purchasing institution to avoid the unfortunate situation of having to disqualifying a bidder on a threshold requirement after that bidder incurred considerable expense preparing a complete submission. Following the Prequalification stage, shortlisted suppliers can be invited to respond to any solicitation format, which allows the purchasing institution to defer the decision with respect to format selection until it has a better idea regarding the composition of the competing supplier pool. This flexibility presents significant advantages to a public institution since it does not need to plan for every potential variation of supplier solutions based on the hypothetical participation of all suppliers. The Prequalification therefore helps facilitate greater efficiency for both purchasers and suppliers.

Leveraging Downstream Efficiencies With Framework Agreements

In situations involving multiple relatively small contracts for the same type of good or service, it may not be efficient or cost-effective to initiate a new open procurement process each time that particular good or service is required. As recognized by the new UN Model Procurement Law, in these circumstances a Framework Agreement can serve as a useful tool to reduce duplication by establishing a roster of qualified suppliers for expedited, invitational second-stage competitions.

A Framework Agreement involves the pre-screening of suppliers based on predetermined qualification criteria. Each pre-screened supplier enters into a master standing agreement with the purchasing institution, thereby establishing the general terms and conditions that will govern any future work assignments. As specific needs arise, those prequalified suppliers can be called upon in a relatively short timeframe to perform discrete work assignments awarded pursuant to invitational second-stage selection processes.

The UN Model Procurement Law recognizes two types of framework arrangements. Under Closed Framework Agreements, a finite number of suppliers are prequalified for a predetermined amount of time to compete for second-stage assignments. Under Open Framework Agreements, new suppliers can apply to enter onto the roster at any time during the term of the arrangement. The relevant provisions from the UN Model Procurement Law for both types of Framework Agreements are set out below.

United Nations

UN Model Procurement Law

Article 32
Conditions for use of a framework agreement procedure

1. A procuring entity may engage in a framework agreement procedure in accordance with chapter VII of this Law where it determines that:

    (a) The need for the subject matter of the procurement is expected to arise on an indefinite or repeated basis during a given period of time; or

    (b) By virtue of the nature of the subject matter of the procurement, the need for that subject matter may arise on an urgent basis during a given period of time.

2. The procuring entity shall include in the record required under article 25 of this Law a statement of the reasons and circumstances upon which it relied to justify the use of a framework agreement procedure and the type of framework agreement selected.

...

Chapter VII. Framework agreement procedures

Article 58
Award of a closed framework agreement

1. The procuring entity shall award a closed framework agreement:

    (a) By means of open-tendering proceedings, in accordance with provisions of chapter III of this Law, except to the extent that those provisions are derogated from in this chapter; or

    (b) By means of other procurement methods, in accordance with the relevant provisions of chapters II, IV and V of this Law, except to the extent that those provisions are derogated from in this chapter.

2. The provisions of this Law regulating pre-qualification and the contents of the solicitation in the context of the procurement methods referred to in paragraph 1 of

this article shall apply mutatis mutandis to the information to be provided to suppliers or contractors when first soliciting their participation in a closed framework agreement procedure. The procuring entity shall in addition specify at that stage:

(a) That the procurement will be conducted as a framework agreement procedure, leading to a closed framework agreement;

(b) Whether the framework agreement is to be concluded with one or more than one supplier or contractor;

(c) If the framework agreement will be concluded with more than one supplier or contractor, any minimum or maximum limit on the number of suppliers or contractors that will be parties thereto;

(d) The form, terms and conditions of the framework agreement in accordance with article 59 of this Law.

3.   The provisions of article 22 of this Law shall apply mutatis mutandis to the award of a closed framework agreement.

Article 59
Requirements for closed framework agreements

1.   A closed framework agreement shall be concluded in writing and shall set out:

(a) The duration of the framework agreement, which shall not exceed the maximum duration established by the procurement regulations;

(b) The description of the subject matter of the procurement and all other terms and conditions of the procurement established when the framework agreement is concluded;

(c) To the extent that they are known, estimates of the terms and conditions of the procurement that cannot be established with sufficient precision when the framework agreement is concluded;

(d) Whether, in a closed framework agreement concluded with more than one supplier or contractor, there will be a second-stage competition to award a procurement contract under the framework agreement and, if so:

  (i) A statement of the terms and conditions of the procurement that are to be established or refined through second-stage competition;

  (ii) The procedures for and the anticipated frequency of any second-stage competition, and envisaged deadlines for presenting second-stage submissions;

(iii)   The procedures and criteria to be applied during the second-stage competition, including the relative weight of such criteria and the manner in which they will be applied, in accordance with articles 10 and 11 of this Law. If the relative weights of the evaluation criteria may be varied during the second-stage competition, the framework agreement shall specify the permissible range;

(e)   Whether the award of a procurement contract under the framework agreement will be to the lowest-priced or to the most advantageous submission; and

(f)   The manner in which the procurement contract will be awarded.

2.   A closed framework agreement with more than one supplier or contractor shall be concluded as one agreement between all parties unless:

(a)   The procuring entity determines that it is in the interests of a party to the framework agreement that a separate agreement with any supplier or contractor party be concluded;

(b)   The procuring entity includes in the record required under article 25 of this Law a statement of the reasons and circumstances on which it relied to justify the conclusion of separate agreements; and

(c)   Any variation in the terms and conditions of the separate agreements for a given procurement is minor and concerns only those provisions that justify the conclusion of separate agreements.

3.   The framework agreement shall contain, in addition to information specified elsewhere in this article, all information necessary to allow the effective operation of the framework agreement, including information on how the agreement and notifications of forthcoming procurement contracts thereunder can be accessed and appropriate information regarding connection, where applicable.

Article 60
Establishment of an open framework agreement

1.   The procuring entity shall establish and maintain an open framework agreement online.

2.   The procuring entity shall solicit participation in the open framework agreement by causing an invitation to become a party to the open framework agreement to be published following the requirements of article 33 of this Law.

3.   The invitation to become a party to the open framework agreement shall include the following information:

(a) The name and address of the procuring entity establishing and maintaining the open framework agreement and the name and address of any other procuring entities that will have the right to award procurement contracts under the framework agreement;

(b) That the procurement will be conducted as a framework agreement procedure leading to an open framework agreement;

(c) The language (or languages) of the open framework agreement and all information about the operation of the agreement, including how the agreement and notifications of forthcoming procurement contracts thereunder can be accessed and appropriate information regarding connection;

(d) The terms and conditions for suppliers or contractors to be admitted to the open framework agreement, including:

   (i) A declaration pursuant to article 8 of this Law;

   [(ii) If any maximum limit on the number of suppliers or contractors that are parties to the open framework agreement is imposed in accordance with paragraph 7 of this article, the relevant number and the criteria and procedure, in conformity with paragraph 7 of this article, that will be followed in selecting it;]

   (iii) Instructions for preparing and presenting the indicative submissions necessary to become a party to the open framework agreement, including the currency or currencies and the language (or languages) to be used, as well as the criteria and procedures to be used for ascertaining the qualifications of suppliers or contractors and any documentary evidence or other information that must be presented by suppliers or contractors to demonstrate their qualifications in conformity with article 9 of this Law;

   (iv) An explicit statement that suppliers or contractors may apply to become parties to the framework agreement at any time during the period of its operation by presenting indicative submissions, subject to any maximum limit on the number of suppliers or contractors and any declaration made pursuant to article 8 of this Law;

(e) Other terms and conditions of the open framework agreement, including all information required to be set out in the open framework agreement in accordance with article 61 of this Law;

(f) References to this Law, the procurement regulations and other laws and regulations directly pertinent to the procurement proceedings, including those applicable to procurement involving classified information, and the place where those laws and regulations may be found;

(g) The name, functional title and address of one or more officers or employees of the procuring entity who are authorized to communicate directly with and to receive communications directly from suppliers or contractors in connection with the procurement proceedings without the intervention of an intermediary.

4. Suppliers or contractors may apply to become a party or parties to the framework agreement at any time during its operation by presenting indicative submissions to the procuring entity in compliance with the requirements of the invitation to become a party to the open framework agreement.

5. The procuring entity shall examine all indicative submissions received during the period of operation of the framework agreement within a maximum of … working days [the enacting State specifies the maximum period of time], in accordance with the procedures set out in the invitation to become a party to the open framework agreement.

6. The framework agreement shall be concluded with all qualified suppliers or contractors that presented submissions unless their submissions have been rejected on the grounds specified in the invitation to become a party to the open framework agreement.

[7. The procuring entity may impose a maximum limit on the number of parties to the open framework agreement only to the extent that capacity limitations in its communications system so require, and shall select the suppliers or contractors to be parties to the open framework agreement in a non-discriminatory manner. The procuring entity shall include in the record required under article 25 of this Law a statement of the reasons and circumstances upon which it relied to justify the imposition of such a maximum limit.]

8. The procuring entity shall promptly notify the suppliers or contractors whether they have become parties to the framework agreement and of the reasons for the rejection of their indicative submissions if they have not.

Article 61
Requirements for open framework agreements

1. An open framework agreement shall provide for second-stage competition for the award of a procurement contract under the agreement and shall include:

(a) The duration of the framework agreement;

(b) The description of the subject matter of the procurement and all other terms and conditions of the procurement known when the open framework agreement is established;

(c)   Any terms and conditions of the procurement that may be refined through second-stage competition;

(d)   The procedures and the anticipated frequency of second-stage competition;

(e)   Whether the award of procurement contracts under the framework agreement will be to the lowest-priced or the most advantageous submission;

(f)   The procedures and criteria to be applied during the second-stage competition, including the relative weight of the evaluation criteria and the manner in which they will be applied, in accordance with articles 10 and 11 of this Law. If the relative weights of the evaluation criteria may be varied during second-stage competition, the framework agreement shall specify the permissible range.

2.   The procuring entity shall, during the entire period of operation of the open framework agreement, republish at least annually the invitation to become a party to the open framework agreement and shall in addition ensure unrestricted, direct and full access to the terms and conditions of the framework agreement and to any other necessary information relevant to its operation.

Article 62
Second stage of a framework agreement procedure

1.   Any procurement contract under a framework agreement shall be awarded in accordance with the terms and conditions of the framework agreement and the provisions of this article.

2.   A procurement contract under a framework agreement may be awarded only to a supplier or contractor that is a party to the framework agreement.

3.   The provisions of article 22 of this Law, except for paragraph 2, shall apply to the acceptance of the successful submission under a framework agreement without second-stage competition.

4.   In a closed framework agreement with second-stage competition and in an open framework agreement, the following procedures shall apply to the award of a procurement contract:

(a)   The procuring entity shall issue a written invitation to present submissions, simultaneously to:

(i)   Each supplier or contractor party to the framework agreement; or

(ii)   Only to those suppliers or contractors parties to the framework agreement then capable of meeting the needs of that procuring entity in the subject matter of the procurement, provided that at the same time notice of the second-stage competition is given to all parties to the framework agreement so that they have the opportunity to participate in the second-stage competition;

(b)   The invitation to present submissions shall include the following information:

(i)   A restatement of the existing terms and conditions of the framework agreement to be included in the anticipated procurement contract, a statement of the terms and conditions of the procurement that are to be subject to second-stage competition and further detail regarding those terms and conditions, where necessary;

(ii)   A restatement of the procedures and criteria for the award of the anticipated procurement contract, including their relative weight and the manner of their application;

(iii)   Instructions for preparing submissions;

(iv)   The manner, place and deadline for presenting submissions;

(v)   If suppliers or contractors are permitted to present submissions for only a portion of the subject matter of the procurement, a description of the portion or portions for which submissions may be presented;

(vi)   The manner in which the submission price is to be formulated and expressed, including a statement as to whether the price is to cover elements other than the cost of the subject matter of the procurement itself, such as any applicable transportation and insurance charges, customs duties and taxes;

(vii) Reference to this Law, the procurement regulations and other laws and regulations directly pertinent to the procurement proceedings, including those applicable to procurement involving classified information, and the place where those laws and regulations may be found;

(viii) The name, functional title and address of one or more officers or employees of the procuring entity who are authorized to communicate directly with and to receive communications directly from suppliers or contractors in connection with the second-stage competition without the intervention of an intermediary;

(ix)   Notice of the right provided under article 64 of this Law to challenge or appeal decisions or actions taken by the procuring entity that are allegedly not in compliance with the provisions of this Law, together with information about the duration of the applicable standstill period and, if none will apply, a statement to that effect and the reasons therefor;

    (x)   Any formalities that will be required once a successful submission has been accepted for a procurement contract to enter into force, including, where applicable, the execution of a written procurement contract pursuant to article 22 of this Law;

    (xi)   Any other requirements established by the procuring entity in conformity with this Law and the procurement regulations relating to the preparation and presentation of submissions and to other aspects of the second-stage competition;

(c) The procuring entity shall evaluate all submissions received and determine the successful submission in accordance with the evaluation criteria and the procedures set out in the invitation to present submissions;

(d) The procuring entity shall accept the successful submission in accordance with article 22 of this Law.

Article 63
Changes during the operation of a framework agreement

During the operation of a framework agreement, no change shall be allowed to the description of the subject matter of the procurement. Changes to other terms and conditions of the procurement, including to the criteria (and their relative weight and the manner of their application) and procedures for the award of the anticipated procurement contract, may occur only to the extent expressly permitted in the framework agreement.

8 **Template Content**

Do your organization's standard template terms comply with the expanding body of red-tape regulations flowing out of treaties, statutes, directives, good governance guidelines and case law developments?

As regulatory requirements and case law developments reshape the tendering landscape, organizations are under unprecedented pressure to overhaul the content of their tendering templates. Institutions should critically assess whether their existing templates can adequately withstand the rigours of the modern tendering process since, as the following case studies illustrate, traditional privilege clauses and liability disclaimers may not provide adequate protection from legal liability.

Privilege Clauses Don't Cure Non-Compliant Bids

In a formal binding bidding process, a purchaser is under a duty to reject non-compliant tenders. As the Supreme Court of Canada noted in its 2000 decision in *Martel Building Ltd. v. Canada*, this implied duty to reject non-compliant tenders is one of the cornerstones of a formal binding bidding process since:

> [I]t would make little sense to expose oneself to the risks associated with the tendering process if the tender calling authority was "allowed, in effect, to circumscribe this process and accept a non-compliant bid".

If a tender is non-compliant, the bidder is deemed to have failed to meet the basic requirements necessary to be eligible for contract award. The purchaser owes compliant bidders a duty to reject the non-compliant tender.

For example, in its January 2001 decision in *Johnson's Construction Ltd. v. Newfoundland*, the Newfoundland Supreme Court found that the omission of a line-item in a bidder's rate bid form rendered its tender non-compliant and that this non-compliance could not be saved by the purchaser's privilege clause.

The case dealt with a tender call for the construction of a water system. The plaintiff, an unsuccessful bidder, challenged the contract award, alleging that its competitor's tender was non-compliant. The case turned on whether the amount left blank for the "supply and installation of thaw cable" could actually be incorporated into another line-item in the rate bid form or whether it was an oversight that rendered the selected tender non-compliant.

While Newfoundland relied on its privilege clause as a basis for accepting the tender, the court noted that the Supreme Court of Canada placed significant constraints on the exercise of such reserved rights, particularly in instances involving non-compliant tenders:

> In *M.J.B. Enterprises Ltd. v. Defence Construction (1951) Limited*, [1999] 1 S.C.R. 619, the Supreme Court of Canada considered the effect of the statement commonly found in tender documents, "the lowest or any tender shall not necessarily be accepted", which is comparable to article 10 of the Instructions to Bidders in the tender at issue. The clause is generally referred to as "the privilege clause".

> Speaking for the Court, Iacobucci J. began with a review of the proper approach to the privilege clause ... he concluded that the privilege clause does not permit the acceptance of a non-compliant bid. Rather, he found "that the privilege clause is compatible with the obligation to accept only a compliant bid".

The court therefore held that the purchaser's right to exercise its privilege clause is limited to the pool of compliant tenders and does not extend beyond those tenders to allow discretion with respect to non-compliant tenders:

> The general principles with respect to the tendering process set out by the Supreme Court of Canada in the *M.J.B. Enterprises* case would apply to the tender at issue before this Court. The fundamental aspects of the tendering processes were similar. On this basis, I conclude that the owner had an obligation to all those submitting tenders to accept only a compliant tender. The privilege clause could not be relied upon to override this obligation. It follows that, if the Newfound Construction tender was non-compliant, the owner was required to reject it and award the contract to one of the other bidders.

The court then turned its attention to whether the impugned tender was compliant and concluded that the omission in question rendered the tender non-compliant. Since the privilege clause could not save the tender and render it legally capable of acceptance, the court concluded that Newfoundland should have rejected the tender. As this case illustrates, purchasers risk potential legal challenges with costly outcomes when they decide to award a contract to a non-compliant bidder and then rely on a privilege clause to shield them from liability.

Supreme Court of Canada Strikes Down Tender Disclaimer and Awards $3.3 Million in Damages

Tercon Contractors Ltd. v. British Columbia Supreme Court of Canada, 2010

In its February 2010 decision in *Tercon Contractors Ltd. v. British Columbia*, the Supreme Court of Canada struck down a liability disclaimer and held that the British Columbia government liable for $3.3 million in lost profit damages for awarding to a non-compliant bidder.

The case involved a tender call for the construction of a gravel highway in the Nass Valley of British Columbia. The tender call rules clearly prohibited joint venture bids. Notwithstanding this rule, the government awarded the contract to a low bid submitted by a joint venture. One of the unsuccessful bidders sued, alleging that the contract was awarded to a non-compliant competitor. While the awarded contract was styled to reflect only one of the two joint venture parties as the prime contractor, the trial court saw through the government's attempted bid repair. The government was found to be in breach of its tendering law duties.

The trial court then considered the applicability of the following limitation of liability provision contained in the tender call:

> Except as expressly and specifically permitted in these Instructions to Proponents, no Proponent shall have any claim for any compensation

of any kind whatsoever, as a result of participating in this RFP, and by submitting a proposal each proponent shall be deemed to have agreed that it has no claim.

The trial court noted that the courts have discretion to limit the enforceability of such exclusionary clauses: (a) within the tendering context due to policy considerations; and (b) more generally under contract law based on doctrines such as fundamental breach, unconscionability, unfairness and unreasonableness. The trial court concluded that it would not allow the government to shield its conduct behind the exclusionary clause contained in the tender call.

To allow purchasers to avoid their fairness duties in formal tendering processes by relying on limitation of liability provisions seemed to fly in the face of the more nuanced treatment of privilege clauses in prior decisions. For example, in its April 1999 decision in *M.J.B. Enterprises Ltd. v. Defence Construction (1951) Ltd.*, the Supreme Court of Canada had limited the scope of the privilege clause (which typically reserves the right to "reject any and all tenders, low bid not necessarily accepted") by finding that it did not permit the purchaser to accept non-compliant bids. *M.J.B* confirmed that the purchaser's discretion is typically limited to the pool of compliant bids and tempered by its overarching duty to act fairly and in good faith, which protects the integrity of the bidding process and safeguards the rights of compliant bidders.

However, in an alarming decision released in 2007, the British Columbia Court of Appeal reversed the trial judge's ruling. Its decision purported to allow a purchaser to receive binding bids under a formal bidding process and to then bypass fairness obligations and judicial scrutiny by using a broad limitation of liability provision. This judicial "hands off" approach was at odds with the traditional role of the court as protector of the integrity of the bidding process. It left the law of tenders in a state of uncertainty since it was unclear how the balanced approach to reserved rights and implied duties reflected in the *M.J.B.* decision could be reconciled with the "anything goes" approach from the British Columbia Court of Appeal's *Tercon* reversal.

In its controversial, February 2010 five-to-four split decision, the Supreme Court of Canada restored the trial judgment, struck down the liability disclaimer and found the British Columbia government liable for $3.3 million in damages. With future lost profit claims hanging in the balance, the level of protection offered to purchasing institutions under their tender disclaimers remains highly untested and unclear.

Supreme Court *Tercon* Verdict Sparks Mass Recall on Tendering Templates

The Supreme Court of Canada's split decision in *Tercon Contractors v. British Columbia* has revealed a potentially fatal design defect in the tendering templates used by countless purchasing institutions across Canada. The decision – which saw the Supreme Court confirm a $3.3 million trial judgment against the British Columbia government and steamroll over the liability disclaimer contained in the government's RFP – graphically illustrates the risks of using high-risk Contract A-based procurement formats. This column explains why these overly complicated tendering templates should be immediately recalled and retrofitted with simplified, low risk formats.

For years the purchasing profession has counted on the legal provisions in its tendering templates for protection against the hazards of the procurement highway. We've counted on privilege clauses to serve as the seatbelts of the bidding process, protecting us in collisions with aggressive bidders. We've deployed disclaimers as airbags, cushioning us from legal liability when we stray from strict process paths. With a false sense of security, many institutions have been setting new speed records for their procurement cycles and blurring the boundaries of lawful evaluation processes. Unfortunately, as *Tercon* illustrates, these privilege clauses and liability disclaimers contain potentially fatal design defects, offering limited protection in litigation rollovers.

Using the highly legalistic Contract A bidding system, purchasing institutions have been building bigger and bulkier procurement vehicles for decades. Rigid, risky and resource draining formats like the Invitation to Tender and the No-Negotiations RFP have rolled off the assembly lines in unprecedented numbers, leaving us choking on red tape emissions. Whether they have us idling in never-ending drafting and evaluation meetings, swerving around unrelenting procedural potholes or jammed in endless litigation gridlock, these resource-guzzling templates have turned the procurement superhighway into a purchasing scrap yard. Complex formats are too top-heavy to sustain the uncertainties of the current tendering terrain. In the post-*Tercon* era, aerodynamic simplicity is the new state of the art. We need to re-engineer our production lines and retrofit our template designs with user-friendly, flexible, low-risk formats.

For starters, the litigation-prone Invitation to Tender should be phased out of production. While we may want to keep a few in the garage for use in those exceptional circumstances when we have sufficient resources to run high-maintenance processes, the majority of our trips down "low-bid lane" should be on simplified Request for Quotation frameworks. When properly designed, RFQs offer transparent price competition without the built-in litigation risk of the Invitation to Tender. In a properly structured RFQ, all parties waive their right to sue over process irregularities and price is binding once a contract is awarded. Instead of requiring bid security, institutions can enforce other remedies when bidders fail to honour their quotes, such as disqualification from the current process and barring from future processes. These procedural sanctions give the simplified RFQ a great deal of traction for obtaining price certainty from competing suppliers while also avoiding the legal complications of Contract A.

Most no-negotiation RFP formats have an inherent design flaw: they are built on the high risk, resource draining Invitation to Tender framework. While these RFPs are often sold as offering greater flexibility, this feature is highly overrated since non-price evaluation criteria are the only distinguishing feature compared to the standard Invitation to Tender. These RFPs lack the low risk versatility found in the flexible RFPs that are designed to outmanoeuvre the uncertainties of the Contract A landscape. As the UN Model Procurement Law recognizes, no-negotiation RFPs are only appropriate for buying simple standard services. They are ill-equipped for procurements that require purchasers to kick the tires and engage in creative dialogue with prospective suppliers.

With so many fresh procurement pileups visible in the rearview mirror, purchasing institutions can no longer afford to employ a strategy of denial. To avoid totaling their next tender, institutions should steer a safe course through the post-*Tercon* procurement cycle by recalling their outdated tendering formats and conducting a rapid template retrofit. Once they complete this overhaul by phasing out the Invitation to Tender in favour of the non-binding Request for Quotation and re-engineering their RFPs onto flexible frameworks, institutions will be in a much better position to face the hazards of the procurement highway. Until then, buyers should beware of what's lurking under the hood of their current fleet of tendering templates.

The Architecture and Anatomy of Template Design

While the UN Model Procurement Law recognizes a diverse range of tendering formats and sets out governing protocols that serve as guidelines for the use of those formats, to operationalize those procurement methods, purchasing institutions must develop their own tendering templates and tailor them to their specific legal systems and institutional requirements. The increasingly complex legal landscape calls for the deployment of professionally designed and drafted documents. The following discussion addresses the dual aspects of proper template design: template architecture and template anatomy.

Architectural Concepts

One of the critical features that distinguishes state-of-the-art tendering templates from antiquated purchasing documents is the incorporation of proper design features based on the principles of modularization. Every solicitation document can be modularized into four core content categories: (i) a description of requirements that sets out what the institution wants to buy; (ii) performance terms that will govern payment and performance under the awarded contract; (iii) evaluation criteria that will determine which supplier will be selected for contract award; and (iv) tendering process rules that set out the process protocols from the time the opportunity is issued through to the contract award and debriefing stages. Many templates lack this clean four-pillar architecture, which creates incalculable inefficiencies in the drafting process and significant downstream interpretive risks. Professionally designed templates incorporate this four-pillar strategy so that the different components interoperate while allowing project teams to draft different components concurrently prior to final assembly. This helps maximize the use of limited drafting time. Adopting a four-pillar architecture across your entire suite of tendering documents also enables the creation of standard content modules, such as evaluation criteria, pricing structures and scoring formulas, that can be re-used seamlessly from one procurement to the next irrespective of the particular format being used.

Core Anatomy of Tendering Terms

No matter which type of tendering document you are using, there are certain core requirements that are universal to all solicitation documents and should be included as base provisions. These core provisions include clauses covering the following:

- placeholders for users to insert a brief description of the requirements;

- placeholders for the inclusion of the terms and conditions that will govern the performance of the contract;

- placeholders for the purchasing institution's disclosure of material information;

- placeholders for the insertion of key dates, along with tender submission protocols;

- interpretive provisions setting out the hierarchy between electronic and physical submissions as well as statements regarding any applicable trade treaties;

- provisions addressing the applicability of any public access laws and the related notices and consents regarding the use of bidder information;

- confidentiality, conflict of interest and inappropriate conduct protocols to protect the integrity of the bidding process and prohibit lobbying, collusion, contacting the media, insider advantage, bypassing official contacts or any other conduct that could prejudice the process, as well as the appropriate disqualification and bidder barring provisions for bidders who breach these protocols;

- provisions governing supplier questions, the release of pre-bid addenda and other pre-bid communications between the purchasing institution and the supplier

- standard evaluation process provisions setting out the stages of the procurement process from the screening of threshold requirements to the assessment of ranking criteria, along with placeholders for the inclusion of project-specific evaluation factors;

- selection protocols governing the formalization of a legal agreement with the top-ranked supplier;

- notice and de-briefing protocols for informing unsuccessful suppliers and providing them with an opportunity for a post-process debriefing;

- bid dispute protocols as may be required by applicable trade treaties;

- legal disclaimers confirming no guarantee of work volumes or contract exclusivity;

- legal disclaimers stating that suppliers bear their own costs, that their submissions will not be returned, that information provided in the solicitation documents is only an estimate and that bidders bear the onus of making their own pre-bid inquiries;

- process protocols requiring that suppliers follow the process rules with appropriate disqualification provisions for non-compliance;

- protocols for the pre-bid amendment and withdrawal of submissions;

- tender cancellation protocols; and

- the relevant forms that suppliers will be required to execute in order to make valid submissions.

In addition to this basic anatomy, tendering templates also call for specialized provisions that are particular to the specific type of procurement format, which would include bid irrevocability and bid bond protocols along with the appropriate reserved rights and privileges for the Invitation to Tender and No-Negotiation RFP formats, and "no claims" covenants, rectification processes and, where applicable, negotiation protocols for the other tendering formats.

Professional Design

While this list is by no means exhaustive, it provides a benchmark against which you can measure the content of your existing tendering templates in order to determine whether you can get by with some minor spot repairs or whether it's time for a template overhaul. As purchasing professionals know, it's hard to keep things simple when it comes to tendering templates. It takes experience and precision to balance the complexity of the tendering process with the need to maintain simplicity and ease of use for end-client departments. Purchasing institutions should therefore select the right design team when assigning someone to tool up their procurement playbook.

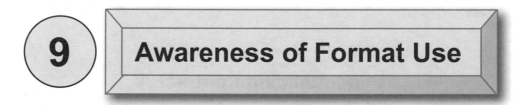

9 | Awareness of Format Use

Does your organization have a clear understanding of the legal liabilities created by certain tendering formats and is it properly avoiding the risks of bid repair, unfair process and bid shopping claims?

To properly manage legal exposures, purchasing institutions should ensure that there is a proper awareness across their organization of the legal duties created by different tendering formats. Since Contract A formats create a significant layer of additional legal risks and restrictions, institutions should carefully control when and how those formats are used. The following discussion summarizes the implied duties that apply under Contract A tendering. The subsequent case studies illustrate how these implied duties impact bid validity, restrict any post-bid corrections or changes and create significant exposures for purchasing institutions.

Mapping the Five Implied Duties

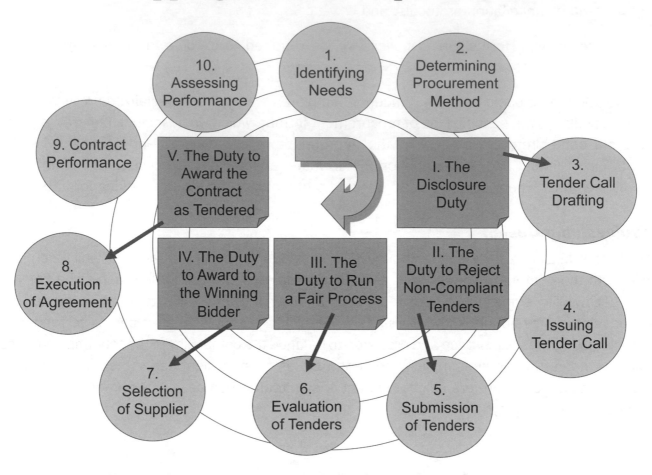

Understanding Contract A
By Rosslyn Young

There is a wide body of case law from courts across Canada recognizing that, in certain circumstances and depending on the terms of the procurement document, a competitive procurement process can give rise to "Contract A," a binding process-contract between compliant bidders and a purchasing entity. The leading case that first recognized the existence of Contract A was a 1981 Supreme Court of Canada case called *Ontario v. Ron Engineering*. *Ron Engineering* recognized that when a bidder submits a compliant tender in response to an irrevocable tender call, Contract A is created and exists during the tendering process until the purchasing entity and the successful bidder execute the performance contract.

In 1999, the Supreme Court refined the Contract A legal analysis in its *MJB v. Defence Construction* decision by creating a four-part test to be applied when determining Contract A bid disputes. The *MJB* analysis includes four questions:

1. Was Contract A created?

2. What are the terms of Contract A?

3. Was there a breach of Contract A?

4. Are there any damages flowing from the breach of Contract A?

Courts will look at a number of different factors to determine if the purchasing entity and the bidders intended to create a contractual relationship; however, the primary factor is the irrevocability of the bids, which may also include the requirement to submit bid security. The jurisprudence in Canada also recognizes that there are five implied terms of Contract A:

1. The disclosure duty
Purchasing entities are under an obligation to disclose all material information relating to the procurement opportunity and the resulting contract that will affect either the bidders' decision to submit a bid or their pricing. Further, public sector entities are under a similar obligation to disclose how bids will be evaluated.

2. The duty to reject non-compliant tenders
Under Contract A, the public sector entity must reject non-compliant bids.

3. The duty to run a fair process
Another implied duty of the purchasing entity under Contract A is the duty to run a fair process, which includes the duty to follow the established evaluation rules and to avoid bias and conflicts of interest.

4. The duty to award to the winning bidder
In a Contract A procurement process, a public sector entity also has an implied duty to award the contract to the best bid. This may be the lowest bid in an invitation to tender or the highest-scoring bid in a formal RFP process.

5. The duty to award the contract as tendered
In a formal Contract A procurement process, the contract that is signed by both parties, must be materially unaltered from the contract that is issued with the solicitation document. Negotiations or changes to the contract as part of the process of selecting the top-ranked proponent could constitute "bid shopping," "bid repair" and unfair process challenges.

When purchasing institutions choose a Contract A format, all parties involved in the procurement project must be aware of all of the contractual duties and obligations that bind the institution in order to avoid potentially costly legal risk.

Formalities Can Be Fatal to Validity of Low Bids

R. Litz & Sons Co. v. Manitoba Hydro
Manitoba Court of Queen's Bench, 2006

Steelmac Ltd. v. Nova Scotia
Nova Scotia Supreme Court, 2007

The failure to adhere to tendering formalities can be fatal to a low bidder's eligibility for contract award.

For example, in its decision in *R. Litz & Sons Co. v. Manitoba Hydro*, the Manitoba Court of Queen's Bench considered the issue of tender compliance in a case dealing with three Manitoba Hydro tender calls for heavy equipment contractors. The dispute dealt with the rejection of all three tenders submitted by the plaintiff bidder. In each instance, the rejected bidder had proposed alternatives to the tender call requirements. In all three instances, the court found that these proposed alternatives constituted counter-offers that rendered the tenders non-compliant. The court explained its reasoning:

> It would be unfair to other bidders ... to give effect to a bid on a 60-ton crane where a 65-ton unit is prescribed in the RFQ or a conventional crane where a hydraulic crane is sought because other bidders might reasonably have offered the lesser equipment at a lower price. They might, in turn, have filed bids offering even lesser equipment at especially low prices .... [E]ven a lay person would say that its bids are counter-offers. I therefore find that the bids in question were neither strictly compliant nor substantially compliant. They were counter-offers.

Manitoba Hydro's decision to reject the tenders was therefore upheld and the bidder's action was dismissed.

In its decision in *Steelmac Ltd. v. Nova Scotia (Attorney General)*, the Nova Scotia Supreme Court also upheld the government's decision to reject a low bidder's tender for non-compliance. The case involved a tender call for the installation of concrete slab reinforcements for two high schools. The low bidder was rejected after it submitted the wrong tender submission forms with its bid. The bidder sued, arguing that its low bid should have been accepted.

As the court noted, the tender call prescribed the use of a "Bid Form" that contained the requisite legal representations necessary to create a legally binding bid. However, the court found that the bidder mistakenly used a set of "RFQ" forms which were contained in the tender call for other administrative purposes and lacked the necessary legal formalities to create a binding bid:

The "Bid Form" requires the bidder to agree that it "Determined the quality and quantity of materials required; investigated the location and determined the source of supply of the materials required; investigated labour conditions; and has arranged for continuous prosecution of the work herein described." No such assurance is contained in the RFQ form.

In the "Bid Form" the bidder agrees to be "bound by the award of contract and if awarded the contract on this bid to execute the required contract within ten (10) days after notice of the award." No such assurance is contained in the RFQ form.

Finally, in the "Bid Form" the "undersigned declares that the bid is made without connection with any other persons submitting bids for the same work and is in all respects fair and without collusion or fraud." No such assurance is contained in the RFQ form.

While the bidder maintained that the tender was substantially compliant notwithstanding the use of the RFQ forms, the court disagreed, noting that the "commitments made by use of the 'Bid Form' are clear, unequivocal, and potentially enforceable." The court therefore concluded that "by using the RFQ forms to submit its two bids, Steelmac was not compliant with the tender instructions and therefore in the circumstances the Province was acting correctly when it rejected the two bids." As these cases illustrate, being the low bidder is no guarantee of contract award if the bidding paperwork is not properly executed.

Bidders Lose Major Projects Over "Minor" Irregularities

Aquicon Construction Co. v. Vaughan
Ontario Superior Court of Justice, 2003

Smith Bros. and Wilson (B.C.) Ltd. v. BC Hydro
British Columbia Supreme Court, 1997

Seemingly "minor" bid irregularities can prove fatal to bid compliance and contract awards. As the following cases illustrate, these small tendering irregularities can produce large and costly consequences for unsuccessful bidders.

In its decision in *Aquicon Construction Co. v. Vaughan (City)*, the Ontario Superior Court of Justice upheld the strict enforcement of the tendering rules and the rejection of the low bid. The case involved a tender call for the construction of a community centre. The low bidder lost a $39 million deal due to a technical irregularity in the rate bid form.

The relevant tender call rule stated that "all strikeouts, erasures or overwriting must be initialled by an authorized person executing the bid." The bidder's president signed the bid form, but did not attend the closing. Another authorized representative attended the closing. That other representative filled in some outstanding pricing information, amended one of the line-item numbers, adjusted the total price and submitted the tender. It was the low bid. The city rejected the tender since the representative who made the final amendments was not listed on the bid form as an authorized person. The court considered the bidder's signing process and acknowledged that it fell within industry practices:

> [A]dditions and changes are customarily made to the contents of the bid form by someone other than the corporate officer who signed on behalf of the bidding general contractor. It is common industry practice for the person who signs the bid on behalf of the corporate bidder to be someone other than the person who completes the bid form and attends the bid closing. Information is supplied to the bidder within the last few moments prior to the bid closing because of the competitive nature of the construction industry.

However, the court ultimately found that the express tender call rules prevailed over any implied industry practices and decided that the city was within its rights when it rejected the tender. This case shows how small details can have a big impact on the outcome of a bidding process and how a bidder's non-compliance for even minor irregularities can cause it to lose not only a large deal but also the resulting lawsuit. Given the risk, the need for clearly written rules and adherence to those rules is paramount.

The British Columbia Supreme Court decision in *Smith Bros. and Wilson (B.C.) Ltd. v. British Columbia Hydro and Power Authority* illustrates how procedural requirements can also prove fatal to a bid. The case involved a public utility tender call for a plant replacement and construction project at Stave Falls, British Columbia. The plaintiff's $13 million low bid was rejected because it was submitted at 11:01 a.m. when the tender submission deadline was 11:00 a.m. The contract went to a bidder whose bid was $304,000 higher but whose tender was submitted minutes before the deadline. The late low bidder sued and took issue with the accuracy of the time recording at the submission location.

The court closely scrutinized evidence regarding the accuracy of the purchaser's time-keeping and time-stamping functions and ultimately held that that the bidder's tender had been properly rejected. This case illustrates how strictly procedural requirements can be enforced in order to reject a tender for non-compliance. In the particular instance, a $13 million deal was lost due to a bid that was rejected for being less than a minute late.

As these cases illustrate, bidders should take great caution with their bids since even minor errors can result in costly consequences.

Variations Can Undermine Bid Validity

The following cases illustrate how a bidder's insertion of variations in its tender documents can undermine the compliance of its bid and prove fatal to its subsequent legal challenges.

In its 1991 decision in *St. Lawrence Cement Inc. v. Ontario (Minister of Transportation)*, the Ontario Court (General Division) held that the complainant's tender was non-compliant because the tender rates did not correspond with the instructions provided to bidders in a pre-close addenda. As the court stated:

> The applicant proposed that the unit prices be changed on the job site. I reject that suggestion. To do so would be unfair to other bidders and contrary to the manual.
>
> In my view the Ministry had the right to reject an improper bid ... [T]he applicant got the addendum, understood it, and tried to comply with it. At one stage Mr. Ostrander, Dufferin's representative, said; "We made a mistake". I think that says it all.

The bidder's alternative pricing proposal took it outside of the tender call rules. This mistake proved fatal to its attempts to have its disqualification quashed by the court.

Similarly, in its 1995 decision in *Altoba Development Ltd. v. SaskPower*, the Saskatchewan Court of Queen's Bench upheld the purchaser's decision to reject the plaintiff bidder's tender once it became apparent that the bidder did not intend to perform the dam repair contract in accordance with the specifications set out in the tender call. As the court held:

> [The bidder] informed those in attendance at the bid clarification meeting that he did not intend to perform the work according to the specifications, but rather as he proposed, by using the hydroblast method for concrete demolition. Thus, the plaintiff's tender was not...in accordance with the terms of the call for tenders with the result that...the plaintiff's claim must fail.

The bidder's failure to accept the tender call terms proved fatal to the compliance of its tender and to its subsequent legal challenge.

In its 2002 decision in *J. Oviatt Contracting Ltd. v. Kitimat General Hospital Society*, the British Columbia Court of Appeal also found that a purchaser is entitled to reject a tender that contains qualifications. The case involved a tender call for site preparation work for the construction of a community health centre. One of the issues was whether the bidder had inserted qualifications in its tender by excluding the construction of a temporary road from its bid price. The bidder argued that its price included that cost. The Court of Appeal disagreed and found that the bidder had intended to exclude the cost of the temporary road from its tendered price:

> The trial judge concluded...that the reference to the temporary road did change the specifications and qualified the Oviatt bid. The bid did not include a price for the temporary road.
>
> Oviatt submits that the temporary road was not part of the work and its cost would have had to be absorbed by Oviatt if it had been awarded the contract. That was not the view taken by Mr. McIntyre from Oviatt's bid submission which included the statement, "We have not allowed for a temporary road".
>
> I think...the Society could reasonably take the statement in the bid submission as implying that the cost of the temporary road was an extra for which Oviatt would expect to be paid in addition to the tendered items, and Oviatt's bid was thus qualified.

By stating that "we have not allowed for a temporary road," the bidder rendered its tender non-compliant.

As these cases illustrate, bid variations can undermine a bidder's compliance and the eligibility of the bid for contract award.

Courts Prohibit Post-Bid Changes to Awarded Contracts

Purchasers are typically restricted from making material post-bid changes to a tendered contract since the contract awarded under a formal binding bidding process should be consistent with the contract that was originally put to tender.

For example, in its 1993 decision in *Protec Installations v. Aberdeen Construction Ltd.*, the British Columbia Supreme Court found that the purchaser was not allowed to make changes to the tender call rules or negotiate material changes to the contract after the close of bidding. The case involved a tender call for the construction of a mall in Richmond, British Columbia. With full knowledge of the low bidder's price, the second-lowest bidder entered into post-bidding negotiations with the purchaser and submitted a revised bid for $5,000 less than the low bid. That bidder was awarded the contract. The low bidder sued. The court found that the purchaser was not allowed to cut the low bidder out of the process while permitting a competitor to re-negotiate the terms of the deal and re-tender its price. The court found that the low bidder was prejudiced by the post-close indulgences granted to the competing bidder and awarded the low bidder damages.

Similarly, in its 1996 decision in *Health Care Developers Inc. v. Newfoundland*, the Newfoundland Court of Appeal recognized that a purchaser's good faith duties include the duty to avoid varying the terms of the awarded contract from the terms contained in the tender call. The case involved a tender call for the construction of health facilities and other buildings. The

Court of Appeal noted that "In respect of the decision to award a contract other than that contemplated by the tender call, the trial judge found this was also a violation of the common law principles of contract." The Court of Appeal agreed, finding that the need to award a contract that is consistent with the contract contained in the tender call is one of the primary implied duties that applies under the duty of fairness and good faith:

> The doctrine of good faith is applicable in this case.... [T]he necessity for its application to Government tendering to "protect the integrity of the bidding system" was expressed in *Kencor* and I need not state the principle more broadly than that it is a part of the law of tendering for Government contracts. As to the standard of conduct demanded by good faith, at a minimum, it would require that a party not act in bad faith.

As this case confirms, any post-bidding changes to the awarded contract can undermine the integrity of the formal bidding process and the equal footing upon which all bidders are entitled to compete.

Furthermore, in *Emery Construction Ltd. v. St. John's Roman Catholic School Board*, the Newfoundland Court of Appeal also found that a privilege clause does not allow a purchaser to award a contract that varies from the Contract B contained in the tender call. The case involved a tender call for the construction of a new school. The low bidder was bypassed in favour of the second-lowest bidder. The low bidder sued. The Court of Appeal stated that the school board was not permitted to use its privilege clause to apply undisclosed award criteria or vary the terms contemplated in the tender call:

> [S]uch clauses do not permit the owner to choose among bidders on the basis of criteria not disclosed to the bidders nor does it permit the owner to award something other than contract B.

As these cases illustrate, post-close improprieties can undermine the fairness and transparency of the bidding process and expose purchasers to potential legal challenges.

Fixing Tender Defects Breaks Bid Repair Rule

During a formal bidding process, purchasers are typically under an implied duty to reject non-compliant tenders. This implied duty prohibits the post-bidding correction of material defects in a tender. While the practice of correcting tender defects is often justified as a "clarification" or "correction" exercise aimed at addressing "minor irregularities," the following examples illustrate how these post-tendering activities can constitute "bid repair" and result in significant legal liabilities to the purchasing institution.

For example, in its 2008 decision in *Jarlian Construction Inc. v. Waterloo (City)*, the Ontario Divisional Court upheld a prior trial judgment which found that the City of Waterloo had improperly accepted a non-compliant low bid. The case dealt with a mistake in the selected bidder's rate bid form. The municipality had corrected an obvious error in the low bidder's tender and awarded the construction contract to that bidder. A competing bidder sued. The trial court concluded that the error made the low bid legally incapable of acceptance and that the municipality had accepted a non-compliant bid:

> Xterra's bid was clearly non-compliant and therefore not capable of being accepted by the City in accordance with the terms and conditions of the tender. By accepting Xterra's bid, the City was in breach of its implied obligation to only accept a compliant bid.

As this case illustrates, purchasing institutions should be careful to avoid engaging in post-tender "bid repair." The correction of bid errors, particularly mistakes relating to price, can constitute a breach of the implied duty to reject non-compliant tenders.

Similarly, in its decision in *Maystar General Contractors Inc. v. Town of Newmarket*, released the same year, the Ontario Superior Court of Justice found that the defendant municipality improperly corrected a mathematical error in a tender and held the municipality liable for awarding a contract to a non-compliant bidder. The case involved a tender call for the construction of a recreational facility. The plaintiff, Maystar General Contractors, was an unsuccessful bidder. It alleged that the contract was awarded to a non-compliant competing bidder. It sued for $3.3 million in lost profits. Newmarket, the defendant municipality, argued that the selected tender was compliant and that its mathematical corrections were permitted within the tendering rules.

The court disagreed, finding that the bid price in the selected tender was uncertain and that the post-bid "clarifications" and "corrections" amounted to improper bid repair:

> [T]he uncertainty of the price that existed in Bonfield's bid could not, in my view, be corrected or rectified by the subsequent communication from Bonfield to the Town and in particular, Bonfield's facsimile letter of September 20, 2005 purporting to clarify its Bid Price. As I have held, the Bid was non-compliant and therefore incapable of acceptance ....

The court concluded that the "clarification" process resulted in the improper post-bidding alteration of the tender. The Ontario Court of Appeal subsequently upheld that decision.

Turning to the federal sphere, in its 2008 decision in *Surespan Construction Ltd. v. Canada*, the Federal Court of Appeal upheld the Canadian International Trade Tribunal's decision to summarily reject the complaint of a non-compliant bidder. In its May 2007 determination, the CITT dismissed the rejected bidder's complaint after noting that the bidder had failed to submit a signed front page with its tender as was required by the Invitation to Tender. While the rejected bidder argued that this was a "minor irregularity," the Tribunal disagreed. It found that signing the front page was a mandatory requirement and that the government had acted appropriately in rejecting the bid for non-compliance.

The Federal Court of Appeal agreed and rejected the bidder's subsequent appeal:

> We are of the view that there is no reason for us to intervene in the decision of the CITT. The applicant asked the CITT to commence an inquiry into the rejection of its bid for the construction of a bridge because the face page of the bid was not signed by an authorized official of the applicant as required by Tender documents. The CITT declined to embark upon an inquiry and dismissed the complaint summarily…. In our view the necessary implication which flows from that conclusion is that the CITT did not consider the absence of a signature to be a minor irregularity.

As this case illustrates, what some may see as "minor irregularity" may actually be a fundamental flaw that calls for the rejection of a tender.

Engaging in the post-bidding rectification of tender defects can be a risky business practice. To avoid being on the receiving end of the next bid repair claim, purchasing professionals should tread with extreme caution when assessing tender compliance.

Budget Constraints Trigger Bid Shopping Battles

While the courts have traditionally deferred to budget-based bidding decisions, a flurry of lawsuits over the past decade reveals that the tides are turning against purchasers who terminate tender awards based on financial constraints. As the following bid battles illustrate, purchasers should think twice before pushing the cancel button on their latest tendering process:

- In its 2003 decision in *Air-Tite Sheet Metal Ltd. v. N.D. Dobbin Ltd.*, the Newfoundland and Labrador Supreme Court found Defence Construction's general contractor N.D. Dobbin Ltd. liable for bid shopping against a subcontractor. While N.D. Dobbin claimed that it terminated the subcontractor for performance issues, the court found that the real reason behind the termination was the subcontractor's refusal to lower its bid price. The court also found the purchaser, Defence Construction, partially liable to the subcontractor for failing to take steps to protect the subcontractor from the budget based-termination decision of the prime contractor.

- In its 2006 decision in *Port Hawkesbury (Town) v. Borchert Concrete Products Ltd.*, the Nova Scotia Court of Appeal found the Town liable for attempting to in-source a project after receiving over-budget bids. The case involved the construction of bleachers for the new $15 million Port Hawkesbury Civic Centre. Since the low bid was well over budget, the Town decided to act as its own prime and in-source the work. Without cancelling the original tendering process, the Town sought new quotes from third-parties. The Nova Scotia Supreme Court found that this conduct was an "egregious attack on the integrity of the bidding process" that amounted to bid shopping. The Nova Scotia Court of Appeal agreed and found the Town liable for $45,000.

- In its 2007 decision in *Hub Excavating Ltd. v. Orca Estates Ltd.*, the British Columbia Supreme Court found the defendants liable for cancelling a tendering process. The case involved a tender call for a road and sidewalk construction project in a residential subdivision. The low bidder alleged that the defendants failed to act in good faith when they informed it that its bid was close to the engineer's estimate although in fact it was substantially higher. The court found that the purchaser's agent made negligent misrepresentations when it told the low bidder that it would get the "go-ahead" to perform the contract prior to the cancellation of the process. The court awarded the low bidder $300,000 in damages. While the purchaser was ultimately able to overturn the decision on appeal, the case illustrates the perils of pulling the plug on a bidding process.

- In its 2008 decision in *Amber Contracting Ltd. v. Halifax (Regional Municipality)*, the Nova Scotia Supreme Court found the Region liable for bid shopping after it cancelled and retendered due to purported budget constraints. The case involved a tender call for the construction and upgrade of a sanitary pumping station in Dartmouth, Nova Scotia. After the initial bids came in over the budget estimate, the Region issued an almost identical new tender call. The Region then awarded a contract to a different bidder, whose tender also exceeded the original budget estimate. The original low bidder sued. The court determined that the Region relied on a flawed and undervalued original budget estimate to cancel its initial tendering process. It also found that the Region's real reason for retendering was to seek price improvements. The court determined that this constituted bid shopping and awarded lost profits to the original low bidder. While the Region managed to get this judgment overturned by split decision at the Nova Scotia Court of Appeal, the case illustrates how even the courts can be divided on whether purchasers can pull the plug on a bidding process due to budgetary constraints.

- In its 2008 decision in *G&S Electric Ltd. v. Devlan Construction Ltd.*, the Ontario Superior Court of Justice found a prime contractor liable to its named electrical subcontractor after a "post-tendering addendum" resulted in the selection of a competing subcontractor. The case involved a tender call for a major renovation project at the Tillsonburg Community Centre. The defendant, Devlan Construction, was the low bidder. However, its bid was 30 percent over the Town's budget. The Town asked for revised bids. Devlan sought revised pricing from its named electrical subcontractor, G&S Electric. It also sought new pricing from another electrical subcontractor and received a bid that was $31,000 lower than G&S's bid. Devlan included the lower bid with its revised tender and awarded the electrical work to the other subcontractor. G&S sued Devlan. The court found Devlan liable for $65,000 in lost profit damages.

As these cases show, purchasers should not assume that budget constraints provide an unfettered and risk free route out of a tendering process. In fact, pushing the cancel button may prove to be a costly exit strategy when potential litigation costs and lost profit claims are factored in.

Escape from the Planet of the 'A's
By Marilyn Brown

Since the seminal decision of the Supreme Court of Canada in the case of *Ontario v. Ron Engineering and Construction Eastern (Ltd)* in 1981, purchasing entities in Canada have struggled to survive in the world of Contract A. It's a world in which a notional contract full of express and implied legal obligations, with the power to override even clearly articulated disclaimers, generates a steady flow of costly litigation. After thirty years of battling claims and allegations of breach of the express and implied duties of Contract A, and struggling unsuccessfully to fight back from within, many institutions are ready to leave the strange and unpredictable world of Contract A behind them. The problem is, getting out is not that simple. In fact, even figuring out whether you're living in the world of Contract A can be a challenge.

How did I end up in the world of Contract A?

The first step to avoiding Contract A is understanding how this mysterious contract is created in the first place. Essentially, it works like this: When a purchaser issues a tender call, it's offering to enter into Contract A, while also inviting bidders to make it an offer for Contract B. If a bidder submits a compliant tender, the bidder is both accepting Contract A and offering to enter into Contract B. The offer to enter into Contract B is binding because of the terms of Contract A. When the purchaser accepts a bidder's tender, it is accepting the Contract B offer.

However, in various decisions since *Ron Engineering*, the Supreme Court of Canada has recognized that not every procurement document constitutes an offer to enter into Contract A. By issuing an appropriately drafted document, purchasers can elect to operate outside of Contract A and govern themselves by the law of traditional negotiations. In the 1999 decision of the Supreme Court of Canada in *M.J.B. Enterprises Ltd. v. Defence Construction (1951) Ltd.*, the court held that the creation of Contract A depends on intention, specifically "whether the parties intended to initiate contractual relations by the submission of a bid in response to the invitation to tender." The following year, in *Martel Building Ltd. v. Canada*, the Supreme Court emphasized that the wording of the tender call is crucial: "whether the tendering process creates a preliminary contract is dependent up on the terms and conditions of the tender call."

It is clear that the courts will look to the substance and not the form of the procurement document to determine the contractual rights of the parties. The clearest indicator of Contract A is irrevocability of bids. The requirement for bid security, or an expressly stated requirement that bids remain binding during an irrevocability period, would almost certainly be considered clear evidence of an intention to create contractual rights and obligations in the procurement process. While purchasers may find the concept of irrevocable bids attractive, requiring bidders to honour their bids comes at a cost. In many cases, the right to enforce irrevocable bids is simply not worth the legal risks and inflexibility inherent in a traditional Contract A process.

How do I escape the world of Contract A?

Having come to the conclusion that the risks outweigh the benefits, how can a purchaser ensure that the process it undertakes keeps it safely outside the world of Contract A? Unfortunately, it may not be enough to leave out the bid bond or delete the statements that speak to binding bids and irrevocability periods. Where the document does not expressly state what is intended, the question will depend on the court's interpretation of the presumed intention of the parties. In some cases, the courts have found that Contract A has been created by procurement documents that are silent or ambiguous with respect to irrevocability of bids.

The bottom line is that if you aren't clear in expressly stating your intentions in your procurement document, you may be surprised by what a court finds was intended. A simple statement that the procurement process is not intended to create a formal legally binding bidding process is a good start, but be careful that express statements in one part of your document are not inconsistent with other parts. Taking your old traditional tender call template and tossing in a statement of intent won't do the trick if you've forgotten to remove the reference to binding bids or irrevocability buried elsewhere in the document. These sorts of ambiguities and inconsistencies will inevitably be held against the purchaser. If you've decided it's time to leave the world of Contract A behind, make a clean break with a new set of carefully developed simplified procurement formats that won't leave the courts guessing at your intentions.

Cape Breton Bid Battle Proves Defensibility of Flexible RFPs

Guysborough v. Resource Recovery Fund Board Inc. Nova Scotia Supreme Court, 2011

The *Guysborough (Municipality) v. Resource Recovery Fund Board Inc.* decision of the Nova Scotia Supreme Court illustrates how the use of flexible RFP formats can protect purchasers from protracted lost-profit claims. In this case the court granted the purchaser's application for summary dismissal of a bidder's lost-profit lawsuit after finding that the RFP in question did not create a binding Contract A bidding process.

The case dealt with an RFP issued by the Resource Recovery Fund Board Inc. ("RRFB") for the processing and recycling of scrap tires. The Municipality of Guysborough ("Guysborough") submitted an unsuccessful proposal and sued for its lost profits due to alleged problems with the evaluation process. RRFB brought an application for summary judgment, maintaining that the RFP in question did not create a Contract A bidding process and was therefore not subject to lost profits claims.

The court summarized the issue in the summary dismissal application as turning on whether the RFP in question had in fact created a Contract A:

> The Municipality's claim is first grounded upon an allegation that the RRFB owed the Municipality a duty of fairness arising out of a contract that resulted from the submission of the Municipality's proposal. RRFB takes the position that there was no such contract, and as a result, there was no such duty. If a contract is found, then this application for Summary Judgment must fail. If no contract is found, then this application will succeed on this ground.

The court held that the issue should be decided by reviewing the terms and conditions of the RFP in question. In its defence, RRFB cited a number of detailed provisions from the RFP that supported its assertion that the procurement process did not create Contract A. After reviewing those provisions, the court agreed and concluded that the RFP did not create a binding Contract A bidding process and instead was a mere invitation to submit proposals for the opportunity to enter into negotiations for a potential contract:

> I have come to the conclusion that these parties did not create a Contract A as defined in *Ontario v. Ron Engineering*, *supra*. I find that the RFP language makes it clear to all proponents that this is anything but a tender call. It is not obliged to accept any of the proposals and it has clearly reserved to itself the right to reject all proposals. I accept the RFL does provide that the Proponents are to provide details in their submission as well as proof of financial stability. I find that the RFP provides only very general guidance. The details are left to the Proponents. I do not find that the provision of some detail by RRFB changes this from a proposal call to a tender. As stated in *Buttcon Limited v. Toronto Electric Commissioners*, [2003] O.J. No. 2796:
>
>> Established timelines and deposit requirements are common to both requests for proposal and formal tender situations. They alone do not establish whether a particular situation is or is not a formal tender situation. Deposits were required in *Mellco*, *supra*, yet the court there held the request for proposal to be a mere invitation to treat and not a formal call for tenders.

I am satisfied that the RFP represented an invitation to propose and nothing more. The benefit at the end of the exercise was the opportunity to negotiate a contract to recycle used tires. There was no intention by the issuance of the RFP to create contractual relations with the Municipality. Consequently the Municipality has no case for a breach of a contract, and as such, this aspect of the application must succeed. The RRFB has satisfied me there is no genuine contractual issue for trial.

After finding no Contract A, the court summarily dismissed the bidder's lawsuit. As this case illustrates, by conducting a competitive RFP process outside of the Contract A framework, purchasers can significantly decrease the risk of lost profit claims and, if legally challenged, can potentially avoid protracted legal entanglements by launching successful summary defences. To help leverage these positive risk mitigation strategies, purchasing institutions should ensure that they develop flexible tendering formats that allow them to engage in open competition while avoiding lengthy litigation.

Chapter 4:
DOCUMENT DRAFTING

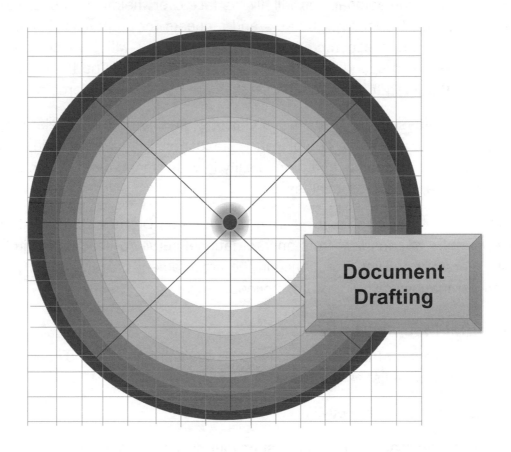

Introduction

Just as many downstream issues can be proactively avoided through proper institutional and project governance, proper document drafting processes can also help mitigate risk and increase the prospect of project success. The following discussion summarizes some of the key concepts that should be integrated into your drafting process to help mitigate your legal risks, accelerate your tendering cycle and meet your project objectives. The subsequent case studies focus on developing clear requirements and defensible evaluations, on establishing properly understood roles and responsibilities within the drafting team and on managing technical content in the tendering document.

Time Pressures Compel Precision Drafting

As they stood in the grip of a global economic crisis, government leaders around the world embarked on unprecedented spending sprees. Their plan was to inject billions of dollars into the marketplace to stimulate an economic recovery. Much of that spending occurred through procurement projects in every conceivable area from construction to technology. This was not the first time that procurement professionals were called on to deliver extraordinary results under pressing conditions. Nor will it be the last.

As a procurement professional, you will always face overwhelming pressure to get to market as quickly as possible with your tenders and requests for proposals. Paradoxically, as your tightening timeframes are compressed even further, you will also be put to the highest standards of probity in spending and transparency in process. The initial rush to market will be replaced with a rush to judgment if mistakes are made or standards are not met.

Procurement professionals face the conflicting pressures of accelerating timeframes, shrinking resources and rising due diligence standards. To help you achieve rapid assembly, solid construction, readability and defensibility in your procurement documents, you have to take a proactive approach to legal issues.

The following seven stages, derived from my Precision Drafting Code, distil concepts from a quarter century of case law, from an international survey of leading institutional practices and from years of front line experience in the procurement process and offer a streamlined framework for managing your drafting process:

1. The Initial Mapping Statement

The first step in your drafting process should be designing a clear and concise initial mapping statement that accomplishes the following:

- Explains what you are buying;

- Provides the road map for the rest of your document; and

- Serves as a framework to organize your team for the drafting process.

2. Detailing Requirements

Once you have summarized your requirements, you need to flesh them out. To build efficiency and precision in your drafting process, you have to balance plain language with technical content by leveraging the principles of legal construction and interpretation. You need to structure your documents so that technical details (e.g. detailed specifications, legal agreement terms, etc.) are left to the subject-matter experts in their discrete subdocuments while the main document uses plain, accessible language.

3. Material Disclosures

To meet transparency standards and fulfill your disclosure duties, you need to address two discrete but related streams of information:

(a)   information relevant to the contract, including all information that could affect the supplier's decision to bid or the supplier's bid price; and

(b)   the evaluation rules that will apply to the competition, including the threshold eligibility requirements for supplier screening and the scoring criteria for supplier ranking.

4. Eligibility Requirements

Assessing supplier compliance can attract legal challenge. You need to draft clear eligibility requirements that lend themselves to transparent and defensible evaluation decisions. Since the duty to reject non-compliant bidders typically applies to a tendering process, you should limit your eligibility requirements to essential minimum standards.

5. Ranking and Selection Criteria

You need to ensure the thorough disclosure of bidder ranking and selection criteria. These transparency principles are a cornerstone of the open procurement process. They prohibit the use of hidden evaluation criteria and call for the disclosure of the following information:

- The pricing structures, volume estimates and scoring formulas that will be relied upon to calculate the total bid price;

- A clear indication of whether supplier ranking will be based on the "lowest bid" rule or on criteria that combine price and non-price factors; and

- All of the scored criteria that will be used to evaluate bids, including the methods of evaluating and weighting those criteria.

6. The Pricing Form

Given the core significance of price to the procurement process, you should integrate pricing into your procurement documents in a coherent and thorough fashion so that the evaluation of price is clearly connected to the required goods and services and to how payments will be made under the contract.

7. The Legal Agreement

The proper final assembly of a procurement document requires the vertical integration of the statement of requirements and the pricing structure with the terms and conditions of the legal agreement. Purchasing institutions should ensure that they properly integrate all of the document components together with a legal agreement that incorporates the business requirements and payment terms of the contract.

Meeting the Challenge

The high-stakes challenges of the modern procurement era require you to meet the twin goals of accelerating deadlines and meeting increased due diligence standards. The seven stages of precision drafting should serve as your reference points and help you keep your projects focused and on track as you face these mounting challenges.

Does your organization have a clearly defined document drafting process that avoids duplication and delay and enables accelerated drafting?

A purchasing institution should implement a clear and consistent drafting process that focuses on the development of clear requirements, proper pricing structures and transparent evaluation criteria.

Seven Stages of Precision Drafting

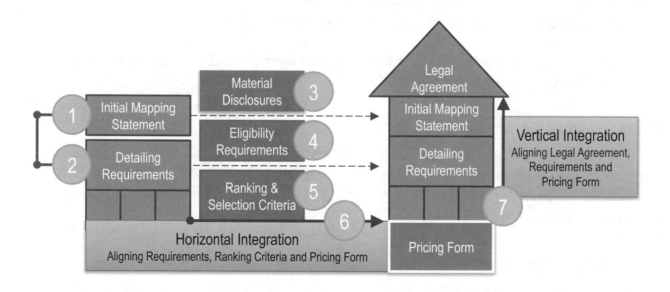

Accelerated Procurement:
The Secrets of Aerodynamic Drafting

While purchasers are often called upon to procure at Autobahn speed, many institutions continue to employ drafting methods drawn from the horse and buggy era. To meet modern purchasing challenges, institutions need to implement techniques that can accelerate tender call drafting while producing clear documents capable of withstanding the turbulence of high-speed bidding. This article surveys five critical steps for injecting aerodynamic drafting into your purchasing cycle.

Platform Documents Build For Speed

Building a good procurement document is a lot like using a high-performance race car: while technicians constantly adapt to specific conditions, they rarely re-invent the wheel. The same goes with tender call drafting. Like the car race pit crew, purchasers need the tools to ensure the rapid responses demanded by today's procurement cycle. Drafters should therefore have a good set of template documents and modularized components that can be quickly adapted to the specific circumstances. To accelerate document preparation, institutions need to deploy a flexible suite of procurement formats that eliminate the inefficiency of unnecessary duplication. This is a necessary precondition to optimizing drafting efficiency.

Drawing a Clear Road Map

Every tender call needs a succinct statement of requirements, which should typically be one page or less in length. This initial mapping statement should provide the clear, thorough and concise roadmap to the rest of the tender call requirements. The more complex the procurement, the greater the need to carefully craft this roadmap. Once this big picture overview is provided, the various components should be detailed in later sections of the documents. The structure of your drafting process should map to the structure of your procurement document: the team should start with the clear general understanding of the requirements and then proceed to fill in the specifics. Rushing head long into the details without first setting out a commonly understood and agreed upon plan can result in a lot of dead ends and delays in the drafting process. It can also result in serious design flaws in the final product. Establishing a clear statement of requirements is therefore a critical checkpoint for aerodynamic drafting.

Highlighting Recurring Hazards

Knowing the legal terrain of the tendering process is crucial to avoiding head on collisions with suppliers. To properly meet disclosure duties, purchasers need to notify prospective suppliers of known risk factors in the contemplated contract. They also need to properly describe their evaluation plan by drafting: (i) clear tender compliance requirements; (ii) transparent supplier ranking criteria; and (iii) simply stated process rules. As the case law clearly illustrates, the procurement roadway is fraught with legal hazards and strewn with the wreckage caused by poor past drafting practices. Avoiding legal potholes through proper disclosure is a crucial risk mitigation measure for maintaining aerodynamic procurement.

Achieving Horizontal and Vertical Integration

To run a streamlined procurement process, all of the components of the tender call document need to work together properly. This requires horizontal integration across the document: the statement of requirements needs to line up with the evaluation criteria which need to line up with the pricing structure in the rate bid form. Aerodynamic drafting also requires vertical integration: the statement of requirements needs to line up with all of the operational and technical details which, in turn, must integrate with a properly tailored legal agreement. To complete the assembly, the pricing structure must also align with the legal agreement. The integrity of the procurement process can be seriously undermined if any of these components are out of alignment. Proper document integration is therefore a critical step in achieving aerodynamically designed tender calls.

Using Clear Drafting

There is no value added to your procurement documents by speaking in riddles, using unnecessarily complicated legalistic drafting conventions or importing extraneous deadweight content cribbed from prior procurements. Document drafters need to get back to basics and reclaim control over their content. The use of clear, direct and jargon free language is the proper starting point. Legalistic drafting techniques – such as defined terms, cross-referencing and shorthand phrases – should be used sparingly and only with a proper understanding of their effect. Inserting unnecessary filler from the institution's past documents should be avoided at all costs. Aerodynamic drafting leaves no room for tricky terminology, cumbersome techniques or deadweight content.

Time to Start Your Engines

To avoid being left behind in the next procurement cycle, purchasers need to be trained to use a flexible suite of procurement tools and a streamlined set of drafting techniques. As timeframes continue to tighten, the use of aerodynamic drafting will likely become an increasingly common industry practice. Purchasers should therefore get a head start and gear up early for the ride ahead.

What Are We Buying?
Drafting Your Initial Mapping Statement

With all the rules, regulations and red tape entangling the tendering process, we often spend more time dealing with secondary issues than we do focusing on the critical purpose of the purchasing process: buying. As procurement professionals, that's what we do, we buy things. As this section explains, to succeed at this task, the first thing you should do in any tender call drafting process is develop an initial mapping statement that answers the basic question: What are we buying?

Clear Thinking

For us procurement professionals, time is always of the essence, so we can't afford to rush things. Our endless cycles of bidding and buying leave little margin for error. We can't squander our time by leaping headlong into the drafting process without a clear game plan. Cutting corners at the front end only compromises the quality of our documents, causing downstream delays and increasing the business and legal risks. The more complicated the procurement project and the larger the drafting team, the more critical the need to slow down and get the initial mapping statement down right. This requires discipline and clear thinking.

Thinking About Your Reader

As purchasing professionals, we need to think clearly about the suppliers who read and respond to our tender calls. They want to know, "Should I keep reading this document or should I turn my attention to the next document on my desk, the next email in my in-tray, the next phone message in my voicemail?" As a procurement professional, you need to get to the point and you need to do it fast. You shouldn't speak in riddles or force your prospective suppliers to decipher impenetrable jargon.

Focus on the Objective First

As William Zinsser observes in *On Writing Well*, to communicate effectively to your distracted reader, you need to first have a clear idea in your own mind of what you are a trying to communicate:

> The answer is to clear our heads of clutter. Clear thinking becomes clear writing; one can't exist without the other. It's impossible for a muddy thinker to write good English. He may get away with it for a paragraph or two, but soon the reader will be lost, and there's no sin so grave, for the reader will not easily be lured back.

To avoid losing your reader, you need to find your focus and then stay on message.

In the field of media communications this is referred to as preparing an "intentional message statement." As former television producer George Merlis explains in his book *How to Make the Most of Every Media Appearance*, formulating intentional message statements is critical to properly preparing for an interview:

> The first step in fulfilling that preparedness commandment is to formulate an agenda. That agenda should be composed of what I call intentional message statements (IMSs). These are the points you feel must be made during the interview.

While media interviews may require the preparation of many message statements, a procurement process only requires you to prepare a single initial mapping statement: the one that frames your requirements and aligns those requirements to a clear pricing structure.

In *Thinking Like a Writer: A Lawyer's Guide to Effective Writing and Editing,* Stephen V. Armstrong and Timothy P. Terell explain that readers absorb information best if they understand its significance as soon as they see it, if the form of the information mirrors the substance and if the information can be absorbed in pieces. To help the reader absorb your information, you need to provide the reader with a structural container for that information:

> When you set out to communicate complex information, therefore, your first task is to create a container in your reader's mind *before* you give

them information. And that task never ends, because you should continue to create containers throughout the document whenever you are about to dump new information on the page. The containers' function is to make readers smart – smart enough to understand the significance of every detail that follows as soon as they see it.

The first container in your tender call document should address the reader's "Why should I care?" question by clearly and concisely providing the "What are we buying?" answer. That statement should serve as the container and road map for the rest of the information that follows in your tender call. It should be the touchstone for everything else you do in your drafting process. If you find yourself getting lost along the way, chances are it's because you forgot to focus on what you're buying. When that happens, don't be afraid to reach for your roadmap and ask for directions.

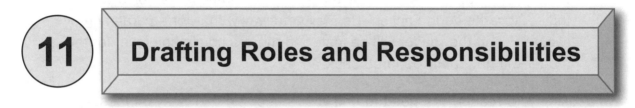

11 Drafting Roles and Responsibilities

Does your organization have clearly identified roles and responsibilities for procurement advisors, legal counsel, technical experts and decision-makers in the drafting and assembly of its tendering documents?

The drafting process should not be improvised. To accelerate the drafting process and properly coordinate document content, roles and responsibilities should be established before the drafting process begins. The following case studies illustrate the importance of properly coordinating roles and responsibilities to better ensure the success of a drafting initiative.

Drafting the Declaration of Independence

Almost everyone's work can be improved with a careful edit. However, that editing process needs to be implemented after the lead author has first had the opportunity to engage in the creative phase of the writing process.

Thomas Jefferson's drafting of the Declaration of Independence is a good example. The Continental Congress met in Philadelphia in June 1776. Thomas Jefferson served as a representative from Virginia. On June 7, another Virginia delegate, Richard Henry Lee, introduced a resolution declaring, "That these United Colonies are, and of right ought to be, free and independent States." (M. Lincoln Schuster, ed., "Thomas Jefferson Prepares to

Write the Declaration of Independence," *A Treasury of the World's Great Letters* (New York: Simon & Schuster, 1940)). That short resolution served as the initial mapping statement for the Declaration of Independence.

Once the objective was confirmed, the Congress delegated the drafting of the document to a five-person committee, which gave the lead to Jefferson. Jefferson sat down for four days to produce the draft he presented to Congress. After much debate and some revision, the Declaration of Independence was proclaimed.

The drafting of the Declaration of Independence is a good example of a controlled editing process. The group as a whole confirmed its main objective through an agreed-upon initial mapping statement that declared that the "United Colonies are, and of right ought to be, free and independent States." It then delegated the actual writing to a smaller committee that, in turn, selected a person to hold the pen and put the ideas into words.

During the drafting process, other members of the committee provided input before the draft was submitted to the main group. As illustrated following, the famous introductory paragraphs received some help from Benjamin Franklin during Jefferson's initial four-day drafting phase. Those same paragraphs then received further edits when the Continental Congress debated the document over a subsequent three-day period.

Introductory Paragraphs of Thomas Jefferson's Working Draft

(Adrienne Koch and William Peden, eds., *The Life and Selected Writings of Jefferson* (New York: Random House, 1944))

> A DECLARATION BY THE REPRESENTATIVES OF THE UNITED STATES OF AMERICA IN *GENERAL* CONGRESS ASSEMBLED
>
> When, in the course of human events, it becomes necessary for a people to dissolve the political bands which have connected them with another, and to assume among the powers of the earth the separate and equal station to which the laws of nature and of nature's God entitle them, a decent respect to the opinions of mankind requires that they should declare the causes which impel them to the separation.
>
> We hold these truths to be sacred and undeniable: that all men are created equal; that they are endowed by their Creator with inherent and inalienable rights; that among these are life, liberty and pursuit of happiness...

Introductory Paragraphs of Thomas Jefferson's Working Draft, with Revisions by Benjamin Franklin

(Schuster, *A Treasury of the World's Great Letters*, supra)

> A DECLARATION BY THE REPRESENTATIVES OF THE UNITED STATES OF AMERICA IN *GENERAL* CONGRESS ASSEMBLED
>
> When, in the course of human events, it becomes necessary for <u>a</u> *[replace with "**one**" – Ben]* people to dissolve the political bands which have connected them with another, and to assume among the powers of the earth the separate and equal station to which the laws of nature and of nature's God entitle them, a decent respect to the opinions of mankind requires that they should declare the causes which impel them to the separation.
>
> We hold these truths to be <u>sacred and undeniable:</u> *[replace with "**self-evident**" – Ben]* that all men are created equal; that they are endowed by their Creator with inherent and inalienable rights; that among these are life, liberty and the pursuit of happiness...

Introductory Paragraphs of Thomas Jefferson's Submitted Draft, with Approved Revisions by the Continental Congress

(Koch and Peden, eds., *The Life and Selected Writings of Jefferson*, supra)

> A DECLARATION BY THE REPRESENTATIVES OF THE UNITED STATES OF AMERICA IN *GENERAL* CONGRESS ASSEMBLED
>
> When, in the course of human events, it becomes necessary for one people to dissolve the political bands which have connected them with another, and to assume among the powers of the earth the separate and equal station to which the laws of nature and of nature's God entitle them, a decent respect to the opinions of mankind requires that they should declare the causes which impel them to the separation.
>
> We hold these truths to be self-evident: that all men are created equal; that they are endowed by their Creator with <u>inherent and</u> *[replace with "**certain**" – Congress]* inalienable rights; that among these are life, liberty and the pursuit of happiness...

Consolidation of Revisions by Benjamin Franklin and the Continental Congress

A DECLARATION BY THE REPRESENTATIVES OF THE UNITED STATES OF AMERICA IN *GENERAL* CONGRESS ASSEMBLED

When, in the course of human events, it becomes necessary for a [replace with "**one**" – Ben] people to dissolve the political bands which have connected them with another, and to assume among the powers of the earth the separate and equal station to which the laws of nature and of nature's God entitle them, a decent respect to the opinions of mankind requires that they should declare the causes which impel them to the separation.

We hold these truths to be sacred and undeniable: [replace with "**self-evident**" – Ben] that all men are created equal; that they are endowed by their Creator with inherent and [replace with "**certain**" – Congress] inalienable rights; that among these are life, liberty and the pursuit of happiness...

Final Draft of the Introductory Paragraphs of the Declaration of Independence

A DECLARATION BY THE REPRESENTATIVES OF THE UNITED STATES OF AMERICA IN *GENERAL* CONGRESS ASSEMBLED

When, in the course of human events, it becomes necessary for one people to dissolve the political bands which have connected them with another, and to assume among the powers of the earth the separate and equal station to which the laws of nature and of nature's God entitle them, a decent respect to the opinions of mankind requires that they should declare the causes which impel them to the separation.

We hold these truths to be self-evident: that all men are created equal; that they are endowed by their Creator with certain inalienable rights; that among these are life, liberty and the pursuit of happiness...

As this case study illustrates, you have to carefully organize your drafting process, agree on your objectives, and give your team members the time and space to engage in a more-detailed writing process. As your documents become more complicated with discrete parts written by different authors, proper planning and coordination at the outset becomes all the more essential to ensuring the overall success of your drafting process.

Contract Rocked by Inconsistent Use of Terms

Fournier Excavating v. Nanaimo-Ladysmith School District No. 68
British Columbia Supreme Court, 2002

The December 2002 decision of the British Columbia Supreme Court in *Fournier Excavating v. Nanaimo-Ladysmith School District No. 68* dealt with an interpretive dispute over the wording of a contract for the construction of the Cedar Secondary School in Nanaimo, British Columbia.

The parties disagreed over how much the contractor was entitled to bill for the excavation and removal of rock from the site. The court highlighted the cause of the interpretive dispute as follows:

> The interpretation of the contract between the parties arises because the contract uses three terms: "bedrock", "trench rock" and "mass rock" and defines none of them. The contentious clauses of the contract read as follows:
>
> Original Tender Document:
>
> 6. Unit Prices
>
> 6.1 Rock Blasting
>
> The estimated volume of bedrock to be blasted or broken and excavated is approximately 400 cu.m. The actual quantity of bedrock that is blasted or broken with a rock breaker will be measured in the field. Overbreak beyond the trench section will not be measured. The unit price quoted will be used to deduct or add to the contract price if measured quantities of rock differ from the estimated quantity. Additions and deductions will be authorized by approved change order.
>
> Addendum #3:
>
> 6. Unit Prices
>
> 6.1 Rock Excavation
>
> The unit rates for this item will apply to <u>trench rock only</u>. Any mass rock excavation of the rock face above the drainage ditch from station 3+100 to station 3+220 shall be included in the tender price. No measurement or payment will be made for mass rock blasting or breaking. Contractors shall determine the volume of mass rock (if

> any) that will be required to install the foreemain [*sic*], and
> shall include this in the stipulated tender price [emphasis
> in original].

> From these two clauses, it is unclear whether "bedrock" and "trench
> rock" are the same thing.

To help clarify the matter, the School Board attempted to introduce a diagram that illustrated its original intention regarding the "bedrock" and "trench rock" terms. However, the court refused to accept this into evidence, since the diagram was not contained in the original tender call documents and was, in fact, created after the contract was formalized:

> Mr. Sabo, an employee of the School Board, prepared a diagram meant to
> show that the two terms ["bedrock" and "trench rock"] are synonymous.
> However, the diagram is not admissible as an aide to interpretation of
> the contract since it was created after the work was completed and
> once litigation was commenced, and certainly did not form part of the
> original tender documents. As counsel for the defendant conceded, the
> intentions of the parties are not admissible for the purpose of construing
> the contract. It is therefore necessary to turn to the general principles of
> contract interpretation.

The court then relied on the plain meaning of the disputed words to determine that the price adjustment would apply only to subsurface rock and not to the rock that was above the ground's surface.

The contractor was therefore entitled to charge extra only for the rock that it removed from below the ground, not for the rock that it removed from above the ground. In coming to this conclusion, the court relied on ordinary dictionary definitions:

> Words of a contract are to be construed in their grammatical and ordinary
> sense, except to the extent that some modification is necessary in order
> to avoid absurdity, inconsistency or repugnance: *Grey v. Pearson* (1957),
> 6 J.L. Cas. 61 at 106. The *Oxford Encyclopaedic English Dictionary* defines
> "bedrock", the term used in Article 6.1 of the original tender document,
> as: "solid rock underlying alluvial deposits...". Applying this definition
> to Article 6.1 of the original tender documents, it seems that the 400
> cubic metre estimate refers to rock beneath the surface, particularly
> when considered in conjunction with the phrase "overbreak beyond the
> trench section will not be measured". On a plain reading of paragraph
> 6.1 of the original tender documents, it appears that rock above the
> surface will not be measured, nor will additions or deductions at the
> unit price apply to it. It is the rock beneath the surface that is to be

measured and it is to that rock which additions or deductions based on the unit price will apply. The last sentence of the paragraph states that the unit price applies to additions or deductions to the contract price, if measured quantities of "rock" differ from the estimated quantity. While it is not clear from the words themselves whether "bedrock" and "rock" are synonymous, they clearly are when the paragraph is read as a whole. According to that paragraph, rock beneath the surface is to be measured and actual quantities excavated will be compared with the estimated excavated quantity, namely, 400 cubic metres. Any difference will be adjusted using the unit price. The terms used by the defendant are not consistent and could have been expressed more clearly; however, the meaning of Article 6.1 of the original tender document seems fairly clear.

While siding with the School Board's interpretation, the court noted that the School Board's Addendum #3 (which was issued after the original tender call was released and formed part of the final contract) had added more confusion to the contract:

> Whatever the defendant's intentions, Addendum #3 actually muddied the waters of interpretation in respect of their original tender documents dated October 19, 1998. Article 6.1 of Addendum #3 makes no reference to "bedrock" (the term used in Article 6.1 of the original tender document) but, rather, uses the terms "trench rock" and "mass rock" which, like "bedrock" are not defined. Addendum #3 states that unit rates apply to "trench rock only" and that any "mass rock excavation of the rock face above the drainage ditch shall be included in the tender price".

As this case study illustrates, when the meaning of a particular term is unclear, the courts may rely on the entire document rule to use other parts of the document to come up with an interpretation. This gives new meaning to the old expression "Anything you say can be used against you in a court of law." Drafters should therefore strive for precision by using terms consistently and defining them accurately.

The Virtues of Version Control

By Jennifer Marston

In procurement, where template use is common and documents are often assembled by multi-disciplinary project teams working concurrently under time pressure, proper version control is essential. Unless revisions are carefully tracked and integrated through an organized process, the final result is likely to include gaps and inconsistencies that will undermine certainty of terms and open the door to legal exposure. Version control systems allow organizations not only to track historical versions of documents, but to keep tabs on what has or hasn't been incorporated into a current version during the development or revision stage.

Why Version Control is Important

The following examples illustrate the kinds of version control issues that can plague procurement operations:

Example 1:

An Invitation to Tender is nearing the final stages of completion and the technical specs need to be finalized and incorporated. The Purchasing Department forwards the draft Invitation to Tender to Engineering. An engineer inserts the specs, but while doing so inadvertently highlights a "boilerplate" paragraph and deletes it. The document is saved and sent back to Purchasing, where a buyer checks to ensure that the technical section has been incorporated, but doesn't notice the deletion. In fact, no-one notices the deletion until the bids all come in over budget. At that point, Purchasing discovers that the tender cancellation provisions were accidentally deleted by Engineering.

Example 2:

A draft information technology RFP is circulated for review and edit. Someone in Purchasing makes changes in the document, then passes it on to the contact person in the IT department, who makes more changes and then returns it to Purchasing. The IT contact then circulates his version to the broader project team. Other project team members proceed to make further changes to that version of the document. Meanwhile, Purchasing has sent the original version over to Legal. Legal reviews the original version, only to have to repeat its review a second time two days later when it learns of the further revisions made by the broader project team.

Most organizations now use document management systems to ensure that files are saved in a secure, centralized location accessible to all staff of the organization. While these systems eliminate some document management concerns, they don't prevent against version control issues and can sometimes exacerbate them, as the following example illustrates.

Example 3:

A new buyer is certain that the template she needs exists somewhere in the system, but she can't find it. She asks her co-worker in Purchasing to email it to her and then saves it in the system, somewhere where she'll be sure to find it next time. Two versions of the document now exist. When it comes time to update or revise the document, only one version is changed. Months later, when another new buyer needs the template, he unwittingly uses the outdated version.

These types of version control problems increase the risk of drafting errors and lead to both duplication of effort and project delays. They could be avoided by putting proper version control systems into play.

Techniques for Version Control

There are simple steps that can be taken within existing systems to ensure that revisions are made in a seamless fashion. While there is no single method of version control that will work for all organizations, the following tips can serve as a baseline for developing a version control policy:

- During the drafting process, one person should be assigned to "hold the pen" on each document. That person will be responsible for assembling the final draft, and should personally input all changes into the master version of the document. The drafting of particular sections can be assigned to various departments, but incorporation of those sections – and all other revisions or additions – should be done by the person holding the pen.

- Only the person holding the pen should assign new version names to the document. Version names need not be complex – "RFP Draft 1" is fine – but a common convention for documents that are subject to multiple drafts, like tendering documents, is to use a numerical system where major revisions are reflected by a new primary digit (e.g. "RFP v. 2.0"), and minor changes are reflected by a new decimal digit (e.g. "RFP v. 2.1").

- When the master version of the document is circulated for review and comment, it should be saved in "read only" format, to ensure that changes can be made only after the document has been saved under a new file name.

- The person circulating a draft for review (usually the person holding the pen) should include instructions in the cover email asking recipients who intend to make electronic changes to save the file under a new file name that includes their name and the date of the changes (e.g. "RFP Draft 1 – changes by AB March 1").

- Where a document is likely to be used over an extended period and to be subject to multiple revisions, consideration should be given to maintaining a version control or "change history" table that reflects the dates of the various versions and the nature of any significant changes. The same kind of table can be used to track multiple concurrent versions of related documents, such as template pricing grids that reflect different pricing structures. Depending on the nature of the document, the table can be included within the document itself or in a separate file. It should include columns for the document name and/or version number, date, variation, and person responsible.

While version control protocols may take some advance planning to implement, they tend to deliver substantial downstream dividends in combatting version drift, unnecessary duplication and the risk of errors and omissions. Purchasing institutions would therefore be wise to take heed of the virtues of version control and integrate version control protocols into their drafting processes.

12 Document Readability

Does your organization ensure better readability by using plain language in the main body of its tendering documents and properly incorporating technical content within appendices and schedules?

Procurement documents can become unnecessarily complicated when the content is not properly organized. To help promote document readability, purchasing institutions should strive to use plain language in the main body of their tendering documents and leave the complex technical content to schedules and appendices. The following case studies focus on the importance of managing technical content, and of ensuring careful editing for details, including punctuation and cross-referencing.

Detailing Requirements

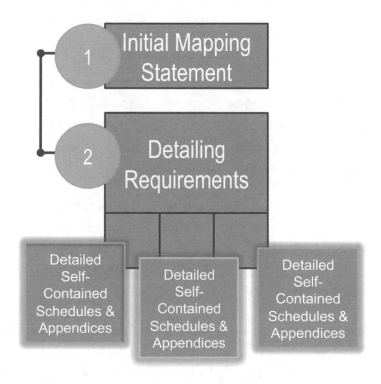

Why Plain Drafting is Tricky Business

Using plain language in your contract documents isn't as easy as it sounds. While plain language advocates argue for using plain words in legal documents and for interpreting those words based on their ordinary meaning, achieving this objective is complicated by two factors. First of all, using technical language is sometimes essential to the accurate and succinct expression of complex ideas. Secondly, there's no consensus on what we mean by the "ordinary meaning" of a word. As this section explains, drafting technical details in plain language may be harder than you think.

The plain language philosophy has significant influence in international legal circles. For example, the European Parliament's *Joint Practical Guide* for legislative drafting recognizes plain drafting as its first principle and calls for legislation that is: (a) clear, easy to understand and unambiguous; (b) simple, concise, containing no unnecessary elements; and (c) precise, leaving no uncertainty in the mind of the reader. While no-one can reasonably disagree with these objectives, achieving them is not nearly as simple as proclaiming them. There are, unfortunately, complicating factors awaiting us on the path to plain language utopia, particularly when we apply plain writing to our contract documents.

The things we buy are often described in the marketplace in technical terms. Our use of plain language needs to be tempered by this commercial reality. For example, try going into a technology store and asking a clerk for an MP3 player without using the term "MP3 player." Try saying that you are looking for "one of those small devices that you attach to your computer to record music that you can then detach and walk around with to listen to music with your headphones." As this example illustrates, technical terms often serve as the succinct shorthand of the marketplace. The trick is to distinguish between helpful technical terms that facilitate accuracy and brevity in communication and gratuitous technical terms that serve no purpose other than showing off knowledge in obscure subject areas. Knowing the difference is critical to precise contract drafting.

Once you cut your content down to the essential technical terms, you still face a challenge in achieving contractual certainty since your technical terms may have no universally understood meaning. Much may depend on your audience. In fact, the common meaning of a term, as generally understood by a non-expert, is often inconsistent with the more precise meaning of that term as understood by an expert.

In *Sullivan and Driedger on the Construction of Statutes*, Ruth Sullivan provides two good examples dealing with "fruits and vegetables" under Canada's *Excise Tax Act*. In the first case the court determined that the statute did not apply to the defendant peanut importer since nuts (which, technically speaking, fall within the category of "fruits and vegetables") did not fall within the common understanding of "fruits and vegetables". In the second case the court found that the statute did apply since mushrooms (which, technically speaking, are a type of fungus) were commonly understood to be vegetables. In both of Sullivan's examples, the outcome would be reversed if the court had applied a technically precise meaning over an "ordinary meaning" interpretation. This illustrates the big risk of plain language interpretations: they may not line up with what you originally intended when you used a technical term in your contract.

Furthermore, there is no consensus on what we even mean by an "ordinary meaning" or on when it should trump the technical meaning. As F.A.R. Bennion notes in *Bennion on Statute Law,* the "ordinary meaning" of a term can be "impacted by education levels, regions and class variations." In other words, whose "ordinary meaning" applies? Furthermore, Bennion notes that: (a) a technical term should be given its technical meaning when used within its specialized area; but (b) a term that has both a technical and ordinary meaning should be interpreted based on the context. This begs the question: what interpretation applies when that context is unclear? Is it my understanding of "MP3 player" or that of some teenage techno-wizard? Does it depend on where we're standing?

It may give you little comfort to know that your next contract interpretation dispute could land you in a courtroom where lawyers may be unable to agree on the meaning of "ordinary meaning," let alone on whether that meaning should prevail over the technical meaning of your disputed term. Contract drafters should therefore define their technical terms as precisely as possible since, as it turns out, keeping things simple is much harder than it appears.

Bad Punctuation Leads to Legal Liability

Re MTS Allstream Inc.
Canadian International Trade Tribunal, 2009

In its February 2009 determination in *Re MTS Allstream Inc.*, the Canadian International Trade Tribunal awarded lost profit damages to a complainant after finding that the government relied on vaguely drafted compliance requirements to improperly reject the complainant's proposal. The case dealt with an RFP for portable and mobile radios for the Royal Canadian Mounted Police. The RFP contained the following technical evaluation criteria:

> 1.1 Technical Evaluation
>
> It is recommended that the Bidders include a compliance checklist in their proposals, cross-referring each mandatory technical criteria with the relevant portion in their proposals.
>
> 1.1.1 In order to establish full and unreserved compliance with all mandatory provisions, the bidder must:
>
> (a)   specify that its Proposal is COMPLIANT or NON-COMPLIANT to those paragraphs/requirements which are associated with the bolded word "must" which are mandatory/essential requirements. The bidder

can describe its compliance to these paragraphs/requirements by using the word "COMPLIANT" or the word "NON-COMPLIANT";

(b)   clearly demonstrate compliance to mandatory/essential requirements by providing a statement which clearly supports/justifies the response provided;

and/or

Clearly demonstrate compliance to mandatory/essential requirements by providing features or characteristics with Original Equipment Manufacturer (OEM) or vendor published specifications, manuals, brochures or test data. This documentation must be included with the proposal;

(c)   include clear directions regarding where the relevant information required for evaluation can be found in its proposal. References to Web pages are forbidden. The bidder's proposal must be complete by itself.

The complainant was rejected for failing to meet the technical requirements. It challenged its rejection, arguing that by "specifying" that it complied with the requirements, as called for in part (a) above, it had satisfied the technical requirements. The government disagreed, arguing that the complainant had failed to meet all three parts of the requirements (i.e., parts (a), (b) and (c)) and that the proposal was therefore non-compliant.

The Tribunal noted that Article 506(6) of the *Agreement on Internal Trade* requires the clear identification of the criteria to be used in the evaluation of bids and the methods of weighting and evaluating the criteria. It found that the government breached this treaty duty by using ambiguous evaluation requirements:

> [T]he Tribunal notes that an ambiguity exists in section 1.1.1 of Part 4 of the RFP. A close review of that provision reveals the absence of a conjunction between paragraphs (b) and (c). The absence of the word "and" or "or" at the end of paragraph (b) leaves this section open to more than one reasonable interpretation. One interpretation would be to read in the word "and" between paragraphs (b) and (c). Doing so would make the requirements of all three paragraphs mandatory. On the other hand, if one read in the word "or" between paragraphs (b) and (c), then it would be reasonable to infer that only one of the three requirements needs to be met. Applying the principle of *contra proferentem* to this matter, any ambiguities should be construed as against the party that drafted the ambiguous provision.

The Tribunal determined that the interpretation and application of the applicable requirements was unreasonable and unfair and that the disqualification of the complainant breached Article

506(6) of the *Agreement on Internal Trade*. It therefore awarded lost profits to the complainant. As this case illustrates, bad punctuation can lead to legal liability so institutions would be wise to carefully proof their solicitation documents, particularly those sections that relate to tender compliance requirements.

Avoiding Cross-Referencing Chaos

Nothing disrupts the flow of a document more than cross-referencing. Repeatedly forcing the reader to pinball from one part of the document to another deadens the aerodynamic flow of your ideas. Additionally, cross-referencing can create gaps in the document or result in circularity as one concept is explained in reference to another, which, in turn, is explained in reference to the first.

Cross-Referencing Crackdown:
European Parliament's Joint Practical Guide Regulates Cross-Referencing

You know there's a serious problem when it becomes necessary to formalize model laws to regulate how cross-referencing is used. In fact, Article 16 of the European Parliament's *Joint Practical Guide* (Luxembourg: Office for Official Publications of the European Communities, 2003) asserts the following rule:

> References to other acts should be kept to a minimum. References shall indicate precisely the act or provisions to which they refer. Circular referencing (references to an act or an article which in itself refers back to the initial provision) and serial referencing (references to a provision which itself refers to another provision) shall also be avoided.

This principle should also apply to contract documents. Cross-referencing can create an incoherent mess that wastes time during the drafting cycle as you review and repair loose threads. Even after it is edited for consistency and accuracy, cross-referencing undermines the flow of the document for the reader.

In his *Legislative Drafting Guide*, Kenneth L. Rosenbaum offers some practical advice and warnings about cross-referencing:

> [C]ross-references complicate revisions. The drafter must verify cross-references after every change in the text. A simple renumbering or minor edit to the content of the target section can ruin a cross-reference hiding in another section.

> Also, if you regularly use cross-references to incorporate substance, you may end up with a section that refers to another section that refers to another section that refers to another section. These chains of references drive readers crazy.

For these reasons, you should use cross-references with forethought. Use them to help the reader understand the text. Avoid references that force the reader to read several places in the law to understand what you could have just as easily put in a single place. And remember that keeping cross-references accurate will add work to later revisions.

Preparing and reading procurement documents is hard enough. You don't need to create additional work for yourself or the reader through the unnecessary use of cross-referencing.

Mitigating the Adverse Impact of Cross-Referencing

There may be some instances where cross-referencing is necessary. Article 16.7 of the European Parliament's *Joint Practical Guide* provides some useful direction for incorporating a cross-reference while maintaining the flow of your ideas:

> 16.7   A reference should be worded in such a way that the central element of the provision to which reference is to be made can be understood without consulting the provision.
>
> Example:
>
> Rather than: "Article 15 applies to exports to countries..."
>
> use: "The control procedures laid down in Article 15 shall apply to exports to the countries..."

As this example illustrates, the use of cross-referencing should be consistent with the proper use of definitions: The reader should be able read and understand an entire passage without having to consult another part of the text. Once the general idea is conveyed, the reader can then decide whether to refer to the cross-reference. Whenever possible, avoid forcing your reader off the page, since the momentum of your ideas will be lost.

Chapter 5:
BIDDING RISKS

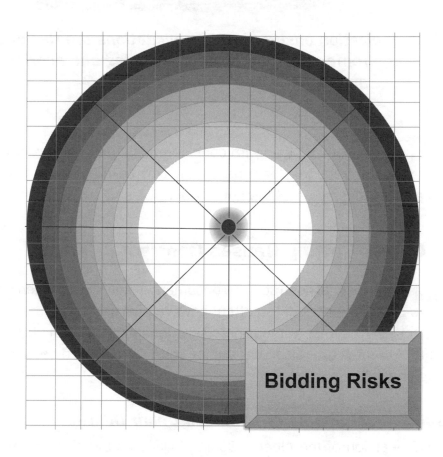

Bidding Risks

Introduction

Many of the inherent risks of the bidding process can be proactively mitigated by proper drafting and planning. With a view to avoiding bidding risks, purchasing institutions should ensure that tendering processes include properly designed and scoped contracts, thorough pre-bid disclosures and defensible evaluation protocols.

Does your organization ensure that its solicitations are designed with clearly drafted requirements, properly aligned pricing and scoring structures and well-tailored legal agreements?

Every procurement process should begin with considerations of proper contract scoping. The following case studies illustrate the legal risks that can be created by improper contract drafting practices and discuss some of the guiding principles of proper contract design.

Corner-Cutting Causes Contracting Chaos

The core purpose of a commercial contract is to document a deal so that each party has a clear understanding of its commitments. All too often, however, parties enter into negotiations and proceed into contract performance without precisely defining their deal. The following cases show how this kind of corner-cutting can undermine the much needed certainty of terms and lead to contracting chaos.

Invisible Oil Sands Deal Sparks Multimillion Dollar Dustup

As the March 2007 decision of the Alberta Court of Queen's Bench in *Klemke Mining Corp. v. Shell Canada Ltd.* illustrates, an enforceable contract may be created even where there's no formal written agreement. In this case, the court awarded $26 million in damages for the breach of an oral contract. The plaintiff, Klemke Mining Corp., claimed it had negotiated an oral agreement for a mining project in the Athabasca oil sands with a group of oil companies operating as Albian Sands Energy Inc. Klemke claimed that Albian had breached the agreement by failing to proceed with the project.

In its defence, Albian claimed that it never entered into an agreement in the first place. The court disagreed, finding that the parties had formed an enforceable contract, even if that contract was never reduced to a formal written agreement. The court determined that the parties had engaged in a series of discussions (which were recorded through a document referred to as a "Memorialization"), and through those discussions had established all of the terms necessary to form a contract at law. The court found Albian in breach of contract for failing to follow through with the oral agreement and awarded $26 million in damages.

Dalhousie Deal Hits Wall of Uncertainty on Pricing

As the January 2006 decision of the Nova Scotia Supreme Court in *Alumitech Architectural Glass & Metal Ltd. v. J.W. Lindsay Enterprise Ltd.* illustrates, failing to firm up your pricing structure can have costly downstream consequences. The case dealt with a dispute over a building project at Dalhousie University. Alumitech agreed to pay $240,000 for Lindsay to install approximately 39,000 square feet of wall. However, the project ultimately required only 31,000 square feet of wall. A dispute arose over payment.

Lindsay maintained that the parties had agreed to a lump sum contract and it claimed the full $240,000. Alumitech disagreed, arguing that the payment structure was based on a unit price of $6.1538 per square foot, which entitled Lindsay to a lesser pro-rated amount of $191,000. The court concluded that the pricing structure was vague and that there had been no meeting of the minds on whether the deal was a lump sum or unit price contract. Since Alumitech failed to provide any useful evidence to support its lower price calculations, the court was left with little choice but to award Lindsay the full $240,000 even though it erected only 31,000 of the originally contemplated 39,000 square feet of wall.

No Clear Cut Answer on Rate Review Clause

In its May 2005 decision in *Stratus Contracting Ltd. v. Abitibi Consolidated Inc.*, the British Columbia Supreme Court dealt with a contract interpretation dispute. The case involved a contract for the transportation of logs. The plaintiff, Stratus Contracting Inc., had entered into a contract with Abitibi to transport logs to sawmill sites. The contract included an annual rate review clause which guaranteed Stratus a minimum 12 percent net profit per annum.

A dispute arose over whether this clause was intended to apply from the second year onwards or whether it was intended to apply retroactively to adjust the first year of payments. Stratus argued that the clause should be applied retroactively to increase its first-year rates. Abitibi disagreed. It argued that there should be no rate adjustment for the first year, since the clause applied only to the second and subsequent years.

Since there was more than one reasonable interpretation available, the court determined that it was free to consider additional evidence to determine the true intentions of the parties when the contract was created. The court considered a lengthy series of discussions that had preceded the formation of the contract. While the court ultimately sided with Abitibi and rejected the retroactive interpretation, this case demonstrates how vaguely drafted provisions can undermine the certainty of pricing under a contract and lead to interpretive disputes and litigation.

Due Diligence in Deal Design

As these cases illustrate, contracting parties should exercise a great degree of diligence when negotiating and drafting their contracts. While purchasing professionals will often face intense pressure to dispense with formalities and paper a deal quickly, they should never forget that the time saved in the initial rush to cut corners will be lost many times over when informal negotiation practices and imprecise deal-drafting causes downstream contract disputes.

Laying the Foundation of Contract Design

To properly leverage their purchasing power and effectively manage their supply chain, purchasing organizations need to proactively integrate contract design concepts into their procurement cycles. This article will introduce the four cornerstones of contract design – (i) contract anatomy; (ii) contract architecture; (iii) contract assembly; and (iv) contract award – and will explain how they serve as the foundation for effective contract management.

Purchasing professionals need to understand the anatomy of their contracts at an organic level. They need to dissect the terms and conditions and understand how the various components should work as part of a living agreement between the contracting parties. The basic organs of any properly designed procurement contract include performance terms and payment provisions. The performance terms should clearly define the requirements, performance standards, warranties and delivery schedules. The payment provisions should establish payment structures and schedules and clearly connect those components to the performance terms. This basic DNA of contractual anatomy serves as the foundation onto which more specialized terms can then be added to adapt the procurement contract to the specific industry and particular transaction. These specialized terms can include, among other things, change control provisions, confidentiality clauses, insurance and indemnity terms, limitation of liability clauses, dispute resolution and termination protocols, and document retention and audit provisions. Understanding basic and advanced contract anatomy helps to avoid complicating contracts with the dead weight of unnecessary provisions.

The components of a contract can be housed in different architectures. Some contract structures are designed for speed, others for long-term endurance. The most evolved architectures synthesize speed and endurance with multi-module formats that allow purchasers to lock down standard terms while permitting the rapid incorporation of more complex components as required. Organizations need to direct their purchasing into appropriate format streams. Proper contract design takes pressure off of the system by allowing purchasers to direct standard "one-time delivery" transactions into rapid use purchase order formats while also identifying situations that call for more complex legal agreement formats. It also enables the implementation of user-friendly multi-module formats that can help to quickly navigate the middle ground between these two extremes.

Contract assembly is the third critical cornerstone of contract design. It takes skill, judgement and experience to properly assess the specific situation and incorporate the necessary elements of contract anatomy into the appropriate contractual architecture. Some situations are more self-evident than others. While a one-time delivery of a standard commodity can often be handled through simplified purchase order terms, a fifteen-year outsourcing deal will typically require a formal legal agreement with a complex set of tailored schedules and appendices. These conceptual extremes may be easy to identify, but it's the unclear middle ground that often leaves purchasers bogged down in a contractual no-man's-land. It's in this legal grey zone that proper contract design can bring the greatest gains to the purchasing institution through the implementation of a contract assembly process that enables the rapid creation of modularized contracts tailored to the nuances of the specific industry and adapted to the requirements of the specific good or service.

Contract award is the fourth and final pillar of contract design. There's no use having a perfectly assembled contract that no one will sign. Since it takes two to contract, purchasing organizations should incorporate commercially reasonable terms into their contract design process. Building a sustainable contractual relationship, particularly with strategically significant suppliers, often requires the precision of a scalpel, rather than the blunt force of a "standard form" hammer. While an adversarial "winner-takes-all" approach may be suited for certain courtroom situations, getting mired in a "battle of the forms" with your suppliers and their lawyers will only lead to purchasing gridlock. To avoid unnecessary legal entanglements, the right starting point is to establish a proper contract design process that allows purchasing professionals to quickly adapt to the circumstances, identify real deal-breakers, and distinguish fundamental terms from the nuisance clauses that tend to unnecessarily bog down the contracting process.

Given the current economic conditions, purchasing professionals are under increasing pressure to find efficiencies and create competitive advantages for their organizations. Those purchasing institutions that properly adapt to today's purchasing challenges by integrating contract design concepts into their procurement cycle will be better positioned to survive and flourish in our increasingly competitive marketplace.

Selecting an Appropriate Pricing Structure
By Rosslyn Young

When public sector entities are putting goods or services to market through a competitive procurement process, they often spend a great deal of time developing detailed specifications and business requirements, without turning their minds to the pricing structure underlying the delivery of those goods and services until the very end of the drafting process, if at all. However, the pricing structure is the foundation of a contract and should be one of the primary issues considered during the planning stages of a procurement process.

The selection of an appropriate pricing structure will depend on what is being purchased, and will often involve ensuring that the pricing structure aligns with industry standards. Examples of various pricing structures and the factors that inform their choice include:

Lump Sum (also referred to as "flat fee," "firm price," "total price," or "stipulated sum")

The bidder submits a total price to provide the deliverables, which is not subject to adjustments after the contract is awarded. This model is only appropriate where all specifications are known in advance, all conditions affecting price are known and the terms of the contract are clear.

Unit Prices

The bidder submits a per-item price for the required goods or services and then that unit price is multiplied by the required amount. Similar to the lump sum pricing structure, this pricing structure requires exact specifications for the goods or service required, along with clear metrics (e.g. hourly rates or price per kilogram). In order to get the most competitive pricing, it is important to ensure that historical or estimated volumes are disclosed in the procurement document. Unit prices may be applied to a one-time purchase or may be attached to a specific term of contract during which the successful bidder will be expected to honour its pricing.

Lump Sum or Unit Prices with Price Adjustments

Where an industry is subject to increases in pricing for products or labour, but a firm estimate on pricing is required, the lump sum or unit price model can be used in conjunction with a pre-determined price adjustment. The price adjustment should be tied to objective criteria in the marketplace or subject to an objective, predetermined formula that is set out clearly in the contract.

Time and Materials

This pricing structure is used to solicit competitive pricing for a project or purchase where it cannot be estimated in advance how much time or materials will be required to complete the project. This pricing structure allows some flexibility in pricing. However, in order to avoid costly budget overruns, this pricing model must include clearly described deliverables and requires careful project management to ensure efficient use of public funds. The time and materials pricing components should each have clear metrics (e.g. hourly or per diem rates, set pricing for required materials).

License Fees

Common in the software industry, this pricing structure involves a set licence fee payable by the purchaser that is tied to specific rights of use (e.g. number of users, number of computers on which software can be installed).

Budget-Based Bidding

This is a less common form of pricing for use when there is a set amount of money budgeted for a project and the public sector purchaser wishes to get the most value for that spend. The total budget is disclosed in the solicitation document and the bidders propose solutions that set out the most products and services they can provide for that set amount.

Additional issues to consider when developing a pricing structure include:

- The need for clear indications as to what is in or out with respect to pricing. For example, is the submitted pricing "all-inclusive" or are certain expenses allowed to be charged in addition, such as delivery charges? The inclusion or exclusion of applicable taxes should also be addressed.

- The payment structure. For example, will the entire amount be paid at the end of the contract or will the supplier be able to bill monthly?

The selection and development of an appropriate pricing structure should be given careful consideration at the beginning of a procurement project. It should be informed by careful industry-specific research, as well as consideration of all possible costs associated with the project and the development of clear contractual parameters for how those costs will be paid for or reimbursed. In order to ensure that public sector entities are insulated from legal risk and that public funds are being spent in a sound and efficient manner, the development of a defensible and clear contract should begin with a solid foundation of a clear pricing structure.

Does your organization have the proper material disclosure protocols built into its document drafting and tendering processes to mitigate against project delays and supplier extra-cost claims?

Purchasing institutions are subject to strict transparency obligations during a tendering process. The following case studies illustrate the significant legal risks that can be created by unclear disclosure practices and underscore how important proper material disclosures are to keeping projects on time and on budget.

Disclosure Dispute Leads to Protracted Court Battle

Welcon (1976) Ltd. v. South River Newfoundland and Labrador Court of Appeal, 2009

The Newfoundland and Labrador Court of Appeal's split decision in *Welcon (1976) Ltd. v. South River (Town)* shows how uncertainties over project conditions can create protracted legal battles with uncertain outcomes.

The case dealt with an extra cost claim for unforeseen work made by a contractor on a municipal water and sewage project. The contractor claimed that the additional work was created by unexpectedly adverse soil conditions. The trial took fifty days, during which twenty-nine witnesses were called to testify in order to determine whether the contractor had encountered "extraordinary conditions" that entitled the extra payment. Ultimately, after considering the detailed evidence, the trial court ruled against the contractor:

> Reviewing the evidence regarding the soil conditions, I am satisfied on balance that the soil conditions encountered at South River should have been expected. I recognize that Mr. White, the principal of Welcon, and those employed with him, state that the conditions were severe, however, their evidence has to be viewed with the reality of the fact that they have an interest in the outcome. I am also satisfied that Welcon did little or nothing to prevent water from contaminating the soil, as well as failing to segregate the wet soil from the dry.
>
> The evidence of the experts, Paul Green, Calvin Miles, Leo Brown, Sean Kavanagh, and Thomas Kendall have satisfied me that the glacial till encountered on this project is typical of the glacial till found on the whole of the Avalon Peninsula. In that regard there should have been no surprise for the contractor when he encountered some poor soil conditions after the soil was exposed to moisture. The risk of adverse soil conditions rests with the contractor. *Bruce Butler (1974) Ltd. v. Bonavista Peninsula Interfaith Senior Citizens' Foundation et al.* (1989), 83 Nfld. & P.E.I.R. 318, 260 APR 318. I am also satisfied that because of the optimum moisture content of the soil it had to be carefully handled in order to be reused. In that regard, I am satisfied the plaintiff did not take adequate precautions to protect the soil from moisture. In relation to Mr. Neville's testimony, I accept the fact that he says contaminated glacial till is difficult to work with, but I reject his evidence that the circumstances here were extraordinary. I find that Mr. Neville's opinion is based on the fact that most of the project was affected by contaminated soil. The reality is that only a portion was affected. Regarding the soil conditions throughout the project, I accept the evidence from Sean Kavanagh and Thomas Kendall that only a small portion of the project was affected by poor soil conditions and that would not be "extraordinary" considering the makeup of the soil not only for South River, but for the whole of the Avalon Peninsula.

However, the fifty-day trial did not put the matter to rest. The contractor appealed to the Newfoundland and Labrador Court of Appeal. The majority of the Court of Appeal agreed with the trial decision. However, the third judge disagreed, finding that the trial court failed to properly interpret the contract terms. In a lengthy dissent, the minority judge maintained that the contractor should have been awarded damages from both the municipality and the municipality's engineer.

As this case study indicates, to reduce project risks, purchasers would be wise to proactively plan for an orderly disclosure process and confirm which party is responsible for inspecting and bearing the cost of unforeseen project conditions. Win or lose, leaving these material issues to be retroactively resolved through litigation can be a costly and time consuming alternative to due diligence in the pre-award stage of the tendering process.

Brockville Disclosure Case Establishes Cardinal Rule

Cardinal Construction Ltd. v. Brockville
Ontario High Court of Justice, 1984

In its decision in *Cardinal Construction Ltd. v. Brockville (City)*, discussed above in Chapter 2, the Ontario High Court of Justice held that the purchaser was under an implied duty to disclose all information that could potentially influence the supplier's decision to submit a tender and the price bid in that tender. The case dealt with a construction contract for the reconstruction of sewers and water mains in the city of Brockville, Ontario. Performance issue arose. The contractor sued, alleging that the city and its advisors had failed to properly disclose relevant information in relation to the project. The court agreed and held the purchaser was under a duty to disclose material information in its tender call. More particularly, the court held that:

1. Information should be provided with the average bidder in mind.

2. Information should be correct and complete.

3. All material information should be disclosed.

4. Unreliable information should be disclaimed.

5. Material facts that arise during the tendering process should also be disclosed.

The plaintiff maintained that "cable" markings on the relevant diagrams failed to properly highlight potential issues regarding the presence of a concrete duct structure and the complications that this could present in performing the work. The city argued that the markings were sufficient to inform a knowledgeable bidder. The court held that this was insufficient disclosure to warn the individuals preparing the bids of the work conditions:

> Thus the defendants' witnesses are of the opinion that the "clues" in the contract documents and on site should have led a knowledgeable bidder to inquire further as to the nature of the Bell structure…. [M]r. Mangione did not accept the warning signs as calling for investigation in face of the plain labelling of the cable as such. Mr. Solomon in fact, as I find, did not deduce anything from the clues and assumed it to be cable as labelled.

The court held that bidders should not be required to search for clues or perform detective work in order to uncover the true state of affairs with respect to a tendered project. Rather, to meet its disclosure duties, a purchaser should prepare its tender call documents with a view to the average bidder's level of knowledge and sophistication:

> [B]idders are not expected to play the detective or read between the lines to identify the nature of the work. On all the evidence the defendants do not satisfy me that an average bidder not having special knowledge of Bell systems would be likely to "read between the lines" and question the clear labelling by the engineers of cable or at most conduit which would make no difference. I am therefore unable to find that Solomon ought to have made further investigation on the basis of the indicia as submitted by the defendants. I add that the evidence as a whole is equivocal and the defendants have not discharged the onus of showing that Cardinal ought to have investigated further by reason of these indicia; I also interpret the contract documents, including the contract documents as whole, *contra proferentem*.

As the court stated, since the purchaser is the party drafting the tender call documents, any ambiguities can be held against it in accordance with the *contra proferentem* rule.

By inducing bidders to submit tenders on the basis of inaccurate information, the city had breached the duty of care it owed to those bidders and was therefore liable for damages. As this case illustrates, the institution issuing the tender call can be found liable for failing to meet its disclosure duties.

New Brunswick Liable in Disclosure Dispute

Goodfellow's Trucking Ltd. v. New Brunswick New Brunswick Court of Queen's Bench, 2003

In its decision in *Goodfellow's Trucking Ltd. v. New Brunswick*, the New Brunswick Court of Queen's Bench found the purchaser liable for failing to properly disclose soil conditions in relation to a highway construction project. When it issued the tender call, the New Brunswick Department of Transport was aware of poor soil conditions that could adversely impact the project and increase the contractor's costs. It failed to disclose those conditions.

The court rejected the Department's reliance on a general policy against disclosing such information, finding that this internal policy did not extinguish its duty of care or trump its duty to act fairly and in good faith:

> In the case before me it is submitted that the Province made a policy decision not to disclose the water or moisture on its tender call — soil profiles. I believe, as do others, that a policy decision does not eliminate the prima facie duty of care .... Nor do I believe a policy decision trumps the duty of acting in fairness and good faith. There is no question that the

clauses in the contract and standard specifications...are specific. But I believe the Court has an obligation both to the process and this particular tender to require the Province to disclose the very important fact of moisture and water. I acknowledge that there may be circumstances when the disclosure will not be required because the moisture is not significant but that is not the situation in this case.

This failure on the part of the Province resulted in the soil profiles being substantially different from the actual soil conditions on the Woodstock side of the project. In my opinion, the information was readily available to the province and in fairness ought to have been disclosed. This duty of care owed by the Province to the company has been breached and the Company has been damaged.

The court awarded the plaintiff contractor over $226,000 in damages for the breach of the disclosure duty. The New Brunswick Court of Appeal subsequently upheld this finding of liability.

This case provides a good example of the disclosure duties and liabilities that can apply to purchasers during the tendering process. Purchasers are typically under a duty to disclose material information about the contemplated contract to all bidders. The failure to do so can create liabilities, give rise to litigation and cause significant problems in contract performance. The cases on point have reflected the following governing principles:

- A purchaser should disclose all material information about the contemplated contract including information that could influence a bidder's decision to bid or influence the price the bidder quotes in its tender.

- A purchaser should disclose any unusual or dangerous conditions that it is aware of and cannot typically avoid these duties by creating internal policies against disclosure.

- Tender call information should be correct and complete and be provided with the average bidder in mind. Tender call specifications should be drafted clearly and coherently.

- A purchaser should clearly disclaim any information that may be unreliable. However, disclaimers may not guard against inaccuracies or misrepresentations.

- A purchaser will be expected to honour the representations it makes during the tendering process, including the representations it makes regarding its roles and responsibilities during contract performance.

- A purchaser's external advisors may also be liable to prejudiced bidders for failing to meet disclosure duties. However, any residual liability not allocated to the external advisors will tend to flow back to the purchaser.

As the cases illustrate, the bidding process is fraught with hidden risks and potentially significant liabilities for purchasers who fail to meet their disclosure duties.

15 Evaluation Defensibility

Are your organization's evaluations based on clear compliance standards, transparent scoring mechanisms and defensible award processes?

The bid evaluation process is a minefield of potential legal liability. To navigate this perilous tendering terrain, purchasing institution should ensure that they use clear tender compliance standards, transparent evaluation criteria and solid contract award processes. The following case studies provide examples of the legal exposures that can arise when these high risk areas are not properly managed.

Supreme Court Delivers Split Decision in Compliance Controversy

Double N Earthmovers Ltd. v. Edmonton
Supreme Court of Canada, 2007

The Supreme Court of Canada's January 2007 five-to-four split decision in *Double N Earthmovers Ltd. v. Edmonton (City)* serves as a perfect case study to illustrate the contentious nature of tender compliance disputes. The case involved a City of Edmonton tender call for refuse removal services that required contractors to use equipment dated 1980 or newer. The Supreme Court was deeply divided on whether the city had a duty to confirm allegations that the winning bidder's equipment did not meet the required standard. The majority decided that the city could take the winning bidder's assertions of compliance at face value without further investigation. The minority disagreed, finding that this undermined the integrity of the tendering process by allowing a deceitful bidder to win a contract based on an inaccurate tender.

Under Canadian law, the parties in a formal tendering process create a preliminary contract, known as Contract A, which governs the competitive phase of the procurement process from the time that tenders are submitted until the award of the tendered contract, which is referred to as Contract B. Under Contract A, the purchaser owes compliant bidders an implied duty to reject non-compliant tenders. Contract A gives competing bidders legal standing to sue purchasers for contract awards made to non-compliant bidders. The plaintiff, Double N Earthmovers, raised the alleged non-compliance of its competitor prior to the award of the contract. The city failed to investigate this allegation and awarded the contract. When it later discovered that the winning bidder had misrepresented the date of its equipment, the city waived the requirement and proceeded with the performance of the awarded contract. Double N Earthmovers sued. Twenty years later the case culminated with a controversial Supreme Court split decision.

The five-judge majority held that the city was not under a duty to investigate the allegations of non-compliance, stating that "contrary to Double N's suggestions, allegations raised by rival bidders do not compel purchasers to investigate the bids made by others. This would encourage unwarranted and unfair attacks by rival bidders and invite unequal treatment of bidders by purchasers. This would frustrate, rather than enhance, the integrity of the bidding process." The majority concluded that the city was not aware of the winning bidder's deceit until after the contract was awarded and found that by this point in the process, the issue was a matter to be dealt with between the purchaser and bidder. Competing bidders no longer had standing to challenge the process under Contract A since Contract A came to an end once Contract B was awarded.

The four-judge minority found that this result seriously undermined the integrity of the tendering process, stating that the case was a "cautionary tale of a tendering process gone badly wrong. Although in some business contexts parties might decide to turn a blind eye to contractual inaccuracies and ambiguities, the tendering process is different. It is a process in which fairness and integrity are of paramount importance." The minority concluded that the city was under a duty to confirm the compliance of a tender, noting that the "obligation to accept only a compliant bid would be meaningless if it did not include the duty to take reasonable steps to ensure that the bid is compliant. In my view, checking the equipment particulars – particulars which the city itself called for – against its own records was one such reasonable step the city was obliged to take in evaluating the bids for compliance. I agree with the trial judge's conclusion that, if there was such a duty, the city was negligent in failing to check its own records."

The minority found that this failure to investigate encouraged dishonesty in the tendering process, stating that a "bidder can submit a bid that is either ambiguous or deliberately misleading but compliant on its face in some respects, secure in the knowledge that if it is awarded Contract B it will be in a strong position to renegotiate essential terms of the contract." To support its point, the dissenting judgment noted that the city failed to enforce the relevant contractual requirement, thereby allowing a deceitful bidder to win a contract award based on an inaccurate bid and then reap the rewards of that deceit.

As this controversial case illustrates, tender compliance is a certified danger zone, fraught with inherent risk and uncertainty. To reduce their risk, purchasers should exercise a high degree of diligence when establishing tender compliance requirements. The fact that the city waived the requirement once the contract was awarded begs the question of why it was included as a tender compliance requirement in the first place. While the contract award was ultimately upheld, fighting a twenty year legal battle to defend a tendering process based on an unnecessary tender compliance requirement is a far cry from victory for either the purchaser or the taxpayer. To help avoid the risk and uncertainty of similar future controversies, tender call drafters would be wise to limit their compliance requirements to those essential minimum requirements that are capable of a clear and objective assessment at the time of tender submission.

Nova Scotia Liable for Arbitrary Evaluation

Zutphen Brothers Construction Ltd. v. Nova Scotia
Nova Scotia Supreme Court, 1993

A fairly run process is key to the integrity of the tendering system. In a formal binding bidding process, purchasers are required to conduct a fair competition and fair evaluation process. This duty includes the requirement to conduct a transparent evaluation process consistent with the rules that were pre-established in the tender call and to avoid arbitrarily changing those pre-established rules when making contract award decisions.

For example, in its decision in *Zutphen Brothers Construction Ltd. v. Nova Scotia (Attorney General)*, the Nova Scotia Supreme Court found that the government unfairly evaluated the plaintiff's tender when it failed to apply the evaluation criteria stated in the tender call. The case involved a project for the construction of a bridge in Cape Breton. Originally Nova Scotia wanted to limit the materials to pre-stressed concrete but, as the court noted:

> [T]he steel industry lobbied the Department to permit them to bid on the final phase of the construction and eventually it was agreed that parties be permitted to tender on a steel alternative. In the tender documents were special provisions: Barra Strait Crossing, Phase III, Contract 91-001, which indicates "Bidders on this contract are hereby advised that they will be permitted to submit an alternate bid based on a structural steel type of superstructure if they so desire". The last portion of that information to bidders states: "To be acceptable a structural steel alternative must show a substantial saving over the precast, prestressed concrete design".

Against staff advice, Nova Scotia eventually awarded the contract to a bidder who submitted a $7.3 million bid for a structural steel alternative. In the opinion of the engineer advising the Deputy Minister, the $151,000 savings of the structural steel bid over the best concrete bid was insufficient to represent a substantial savings in light of the higher future maintenance costs. However, the Deputy Minister ultimately wrote the Minister stating that the steel alternative represented a substantial savings and recommending a contract award to that low bid. The court noted that the Deputy Minister's conclusion in the recommending memo was not supported by any analysis and did not mention the contrary staff recommendations:

> It is to be noted here that the Minister's evidence on discovery was that there was no analysis attached to the memo and the Minister did not know that the staff, from the Senior members down through, were opposed to the awarding of the contract for a structural steel alternative.

The court therefore concluded that the contract was improperly awarded and that the integrity of the bidding process had been violated:

[T]he Province did not realize a substantial savings...the Deputy Minister ignored all recommendations from his Department and, in fact, decided arbitrarily in the face of all advice to award the contract to Maritime Steel and, subsequently, did not apprise his Minister fully of the situation. The integrity of the bidding system was violated.

As this case illustrates, when contract award decisions are challenged, a purchaser may be required to establish that its evaluation was conducted on the basis of an accurate application of the facts to the pre-established criteria. Any internal decisions to overrule the evaluation team's recommendations, particularly expert recommendations, should be made with caution since the failure to support such decisions with a reasonable justification can ultimately compromise the fairness of the process. In this case, the purchaser's arbitrary contract award process resulted in a successful lost-profit claim by the prejudiced plaintiff bidder. The duty to conduct a fair evaluation process will continue to be a risk factor for purchasers who engage in improper evaluation and award decisions.

BC Hydro Authority Liable For Undisclosed Price Calculations
Berwick West Development Inc. v. BC Hydro
British Columbia Supreme Court, 1996

In its decision in *Berwick West Development Inc. v. British Columbia Hydro Authority and Power*, the British Columbia Supreme Court found that the purchaser could rely on its general privilege clause to apply undisclosed evaluation factors when those factors were recognized industry customs. However, the court also found that other undisclosed factors constituted undisclosed preferences that could not be saved by the privilege clause.

The case dealt with a British Columbia Hydro and Power Authority ("Authority") tender call for a debris cleaning contract. The Authority bypassed the low bidder. That bidder sued. The dispute revolved around the Authority's reliance on an industry "blue book" to factor in the "added value" of tenders based on the machinery that the bidder proposed for the work. As the court explained, the Authority had applied its own undisclosed additional calculations in making its assessment:

> The evaluation process employed by B.C. Hydro in 1992 and 1993 involved attempting to determine the "added value" to B.C. Hydro, by using the equipment rental rate guide prepared for B.C. Hydro and B.C. Rail by the Province of British Columbia, commonly referred to as the "blue book". That book lists standard hourly rates for each kind of cat. It recognizes that older and smaller horsepower machines are less productive and efficient than newer and larger horsepower machines, and assigns hourly rates to each category of cats, depending on its horsepower and age.... [B]ids were assessed, not according to the lowest absolute dollar

> amounts, but by calculating the difference between the hourly rate bid
> for a particular machine, and the rate for that machine as set out in the
> blue book. The theory was that such an evaluation would determine the
> bid which gave the greatest value to B.C. Hydro. However, the equipment
> rental guide only referred to cats built in 1976 or later. [BC Hydro] thus
> adopted a practice...[o]f reducing the blue book rate of older machines
> by 5% for each three years before 1976 to the year in which the machine
> was manufactured. Thus, a 1974 machine was assigned the 1976 blue
> book rate, less 5%.

The court found that the Authority's 5 percent deduction fell outside of industry practices. Accordingly, the undisclosed calculation could not be saved as a reasonably implied term of the process. Instead, it constituted an improper hidden preference:

> With respect to the 5% deduction from the blue book rate for machines
> older than 1976, that was a practice which had not been used in previous
> years, nor was it generally known to the contractors submitting bids.
> I accept the evidence that the custom in the industry with respect to
> vehicles older than the years shown in the blue book was to use the rate
> for the oldest year of machine shown in the blue book. Although the 5%
> deduction for older machines may have been applied to all bidders, it
> was, in effect, a secret preference, not set out in the tender documents,
> preferring bidders with newer machines. In the words of Legg J.A. in
> *Chinook Aggregates*,...[i]t was "an undisclosed term that is inconsistent
> with that tendering process". I thus find the use of the 5% deduction to
> be improper. What properly should have been done was to use the rate
> of the oldest equipment shown in the blue book.

The court therefore concluded that the 5 percent deduction did not fall within the legitimate exercise of the Authority's general privilege clause. As this case illustrates, a privilege clause has limited utility in saving undisclosed criteria and is no substitute for proper disclosure.

Manitoba Auditor Raises Transparency Concerns Over "Value Adds" Report of the Auditor General of Manitoba, May 2010

In its May 2010 report entitled *Winnipeg Regional Health Authority – Administration of the Value-Added Policy*, the Manitoba Auditor General noted that the acceptance of "Value-Add" contributions from bidders during a public tendering process creates public perception issues and raises the potential of undermining the transparency and integrity of the competitive procurement process.

As the Auditor General noted, the acceptance of over $20 million annually by the Winnipeg Regional Health Authority ("WRHA") of "money, equipment and other gifts" from its suppliers raised media queries that included an article entitled "What's in the Envelope?" In its review, the Auditor General was careful to note that it found no evidence of impropriety in the administration of the "Value Adds" policy:

> The Value-Adds that WRHA received took the form of cheques as well as product, equipment and education. We found no evidence that anyone benefitted personally from Value-Adds. The cheques were received in the form of unrestricted or restricted funding. Our audit confirmed that all such funding was properly recorded by WRHA. There was no indication that there was ever any "cash" in "brown envelopes". Controls around the Value-Adds for product, equipment and education were weak, but this control weakness was isolated to these items. Tendering for goods and services and construction contracts was well controlled and included a competitive bidding process, except for the project consultants for construction contracts, which were not tendered.

However, the report also noted that a "Value Adds" policy, if not properly handled, could undermine the transparency and integrity of the bid evaluation process. As the report stated, "Value-Adds must be separated from supplier bids during the bid-evaluation process. WRHA followed this policy. The intention of the Value-Added policy is to ensure impartial bid selection. In theory, this is good practice, but in reality, there could be an influence from Value-Adds on vendor selection over time."

The Auditor General explained how WRHA had attempted to establish safeguards in the administration of its "Value Add" policy but noted that the policy had led to practical problems in the implementation of transparent and defensible competitive bidding practices:

> As part of the procurement process, WRHA issues a competitive bid document, which tells bidders to put any Value-Adds they want to offer in a separate envelope from their proposal and clearly mark it as a Value-Add. When a vendor includes a Value-Add with their bid, it consists of a document outlining the Value-Add offering. The analysis of proposals that Logistics Services staff prepare for the decision-making group excludes any Value-Adds. This exclusion is intended to ensure that the award decision is fair and impartial and based on the best product or service at the lowest price — without considering any Value-Add.

> Beginning in 2007, the President and Chief Executive Officer issued a memo indicating that the WRHA would no longer accept restricted Value-Adds. The Value-Add Policy was not changed but the competitive bid documents have been changed to reflect this directive.

> All bids, including Value-Adds, are opened with at least two Logistics Services employees present. The actual Value-Add, should WRHA choose

to accept it, is provided to WRHA after it signs a contract with the winning bidder. In some situations, WRHA declines the offer when there is no benefit to accepting the Value-Add.

An example of an actual Value-Add in a proposal for infant formula was funding of $330,000 a year allocated as follows: the Women and Child Health Program ($100,000), Research ($210,000), and staff education ($20,000). Funding these programs was not a requirement of the competitive bid document that WRHA issued. In some cases, bidders include the Value-Add with their proposal, not in a separate envelope. Logistics Services staff must then remove all Value-Add references from the proposal before the evaluating committee can see it. They know that a Value-Add exists, but not its details.

While, as the report noted, efforts were made to buffer evaluators from the particulars of the "Value Add" offers, evaluators were in some cases aware that offers were being made and this raised questions with respect to their ability to be unbiased and objective in the assessment of those bids. As this case study illustrates, introducing non-scored factors into bid evaluation decisions can create unnecessary complications. "Value-Adds" can also undermine downstream procurements where the "free" products become the de facto standard for scoping future solicitations.

Jamaica Sets Standard for Transparent Price-Evaluation Formulas

When bids are evaluated on the basis of price alone for a single price category, the assessment of the low bid is typically a straightforward exercise. However, this process becomes more complex when there are multiple pricing categories and where anticipated volumes need to be added to the equation to calculate the total cost for each bid.

The evaluation process becomes even more complex when proposals are evaluated on the basis of best overall value and qualitative non-price criteria are factored into the supplier ranking. In these situations, evaluators must combine their price evaluation with their evaluation of other qualitative factors to arrive at a total score for the particular proposal. This requires the conversion of pricing information into a score that can be added to the other scored categories. In order to score proposals in a transparent and defensible fashion, a purchasing institution should establish a formula for converting a proponent's pricing information into a score that can be tallied with the other scored categories.

The Jamaican *Handbook of Public Sector Procurement Procedures* provides a clear method for this scoring process. The Handbook recommends a three-step process where qualitative factors are evaluated first. Only those proposals that meet a minimum threshold on quality proceed to the price evaluation. The other proposals are returned with the pricing envelope sealed. Pricing information for the remaining proponents is scored in accordance with a predetermined mathematical formula. In the third step, the scores for the qualitative and cost categories are added together to arrive at a final score for the proposal. Highlights from the Handbook's recommendations, which include the prescribed price-scoring formula and an illustrative example, are set out following.

Government of Jamaica

Handbook of Public Sector Procurement Procedures

5.1.2.10 Evaluation of Financial Proposals: Cost Considerations

After the evaluation of quality is completed, the procuring entity shall notify those consultants whose proposals did not meet the minimum qualifying mark or were considered to be non-responsive to the RFP and TOR, indicating that their unopened financial proposals should be collected.

…

The total score shall be obtained by weighting the quality and cost scores and adding them. The weight for the "cost" shall be chosen, taking into account the complexity of the assignment and the relative importance of quality. The weighting shall also depend on the degree of innovation sought by the procuring entity. Where, however, unusual approaches are sought, for instance to provide designs for a building of a type that is seldom required or where a wide variety of design solutions may exist, then the technical quality of the proposals should be accorded more importance. The greater the intellectual input required the more the evaluation should be weighted towards technical excellence. As a general rule, the weighting for cost should normally not exceed 30 points out of a total score of 100. The proposed weightings for quality and cost shall be specified in the RFP. The consultant obtaining the highest total score shall be invited for negotiations.

…

For those firms that have passed the technical evaluation, the National Contracts Commission recommends the use of the following methodology to determine the proposal with the highest total score:

Legend:

- ◆ TS – Total marks (out of 100) for technical (quality) criteria
- ◆ q – Quality Weighting (%)
- ◆ c – Cost Weighting (%)
- ◆ LT – Lowest Tender
- ◆ XT – Other Tenders

Step 1 — Technical (quality) Weighting

$$\text{Quality Score (Q)} = \frac{TS}{100} \times q$$

Step 2 — Cost Score Weighting

$$\text{Cost Score (C)} = \frac{LT}{XT} \times c$$

Step 3 — Total Score

$$\text{Total Score} = Q + C$$

A Typical Example Is:

The Weighting for Quality is : 75%

The Weighting for Cost is : 25%

Step 1 – Technical (quality) Weighting

Proposal	Score	Weighted Quality Score		
A	96	$\frac{96}{100}$	x 75	= 72
B	93	$\frac{93.5}{100}$	x 75	= 70
C	100	$\frac{100}{100}$	x 75	= 75

Step 2 – Cost Score Weighting

Proposal	Adjusted Financial Offer	Weighted Financial Score		
A	$ 8,288,108.00	$\frac{7,956,584.00}{8,288,108.00}$	x 25	= 24
B	$ 7,956,584.00	$\frac{7,956,584.00}{7,956,584.00}$	x 25	= 25
C	$ 8,999,562.00	$\frac{7,956,584.00}{8,999,562.00}$	x 25	= 22

Step 3 – Total Score

Proposal	Total Score
A	72 + 24 = 96
B	70 + 25 = 95
C	75 + 22 = 97

Chapter 6:
CONTRACT MANAGEMENT

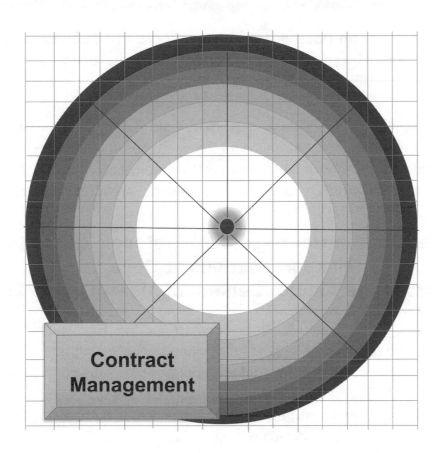

Introduction

While the bidding process may be fraught with legal risks, purchasing institutions should also be mindful of the perils of the post-award stage of the procurement process. To meet their due diligence duties during the contract management phase of the purchasing cycle, organizations should establish clear contract administration accountabilities to properly manage vendor payment. They should also develop proper monitoring protocols to keep their projects within scope and keep their vendors to their commitments.

Contract Administration Accountability

Does your organization have a proactive and clearly defined accountability structure for the contract administration stage of the procurement process?

Purchasing institutions should establish clear roles and responsibilities for dealing with the administration of their contracts. The following case studies focus on the need to establish effective checks and balances within the organization to protect against internal irregularities in contract administration and to proactively manage vendor-related performance issues.

Lack of Contract Approval Protocols Leads to Misappropriations at College
Report of the Auditor General of Alberta, April 2009

In its April 2009 report, the Alberta Auditor General found that Bow Valley College lacked the appropriate checks and balances to guard against inappropriate contract approvals. According to the Auditor General, this lack of clear contract approval protocols contributed to the alleged misappropriation of $189,000 by a college director. The report called for the creation of stronger internal controls, along with ethical guidelines that include clear reporting protocols in instances where staff suspect spending irregularities.

The Auditor General found that this lack of proper contract approval protocols allowed a director within the Bow Valley College International Educational and Workplace Training Department ("IED") to approve the award of contracts and the payment of invoices for expenditures under $50,000 without seeking any further internal approvals. The director allegedly used this gap in internal governance to direct funds to his own businesses for work that was never completed:

> Weaknesses in the College's system of internal controls enabled the Director to allegedly prepare and submit invoices for payment of commissions to businesses controlled directly or indirectly by him pursuant to contracts for which no services were provided. The Director could initiate and approve personal services contracts without any secondary review, initiate and approve new vendors in the computer systems, initiate and approve invoices, and arrange to have the payment hand-delivered to his department. We identified opportunities for management to improve internal controls over contracts, vendor maintenance and payment processing, and improve processes for dealing with unethical conduct in the workplace.

To protect against similar future fraud, the Auditor General advised the college to establish proper processes to review contracts before they are signed in order to ensure that they are valid. It also recommended the creation of an appropriate selection method for the award of contracts, along with clear invoice payment protocols.

The Auditor General found that existing policies allowed college deans and directors to approve their own contract awards. It also found that this practice ran contrary to the guidelines established in other college departments, which called for a separation of roles between the individuals who initiate a contract, approve its award and approve invoices under the contract:

> IED did not follow the typical guidelines other College departments follow when entering into personal services contracts with vendors. The Director initiated contracts with agents of international students that included terms and conditions different from those of the standard contract template. The deviations in certain contracts the Director signed were never reviewed or approved to ensure the College was aware of and had approved, the terms for paying commissions to these agents. We were advised by the College that the Director kept all signed personal services contracts with these agents in an IED file and did not share the final contracts with other departments. The Finance Department processed the vendor invoices without having copies of these contracts, so it could not match the payments to the contract. An effective control process would define separate roles for initiating and approving contracts.

Given this gap in the system, the Auditor General called for the creation and implementation of appropriate internal controls across all departments of the college.

The Auditor General also called for more transparency in the college's vendor selection process. It noted that many personal services vendors were hired through "word of mouth" and that the college policy was silent with respect to an appropriate selection process. The Auditor General recommended the creation of clear rules to provide guidance on how to run a proper vendor selection process:

> College policies did not provide guidance to departments on the proper process for contractor selection. As a result, IED did not use an appropriate method to evaluate agent vendors. Our interviews with staff revealed that the desired method for evaluating agents is to require them to complete a proposal for contract. But nearly all personal services contracts in IED were prepared without a proper proposal process. Only 1 of 13 personal services contract files related to these agents we tested had a completed proposal form. Staff said that an informal process was generally used for these contracts.

The report noted that the failure to implement these recommendations could compromise the college's value-for-money objectives and increase the risk of future fraudulent activity. The Auditor General also recommended that the college's ethics policy be enhanced to: (a) provide clear direction to staff on how to report suspicions of irregular spending activities; and (b) provide protection to employees who report any suspected problems.

Ontario Auditor Finds Tax Authority in Breach of Spending Rules
Annual Report of the Auditor General of Ontario, 2010

In its 2010 annual report, the Ontario Auditor General found that the Municipal Property Assessment Corporation, the government body established to prepare the annual tax assessment roll for the collection of $20 billion in taxes for municipalities and school boards, was not following proper procurement protocols. In particular, the Auditor General found significant weaknesses in the corporation's contract administration practices.

The Auditor General found many instances where the corporation failed to follow its mandatory purchasing policies and procedures when awarding contracts and where the corporation failed to follow appropriate protocols when managing those contracts:

> We also found that the Corporation had established reasonable requirements for determining the need for goods and services, and for acquiring them competitively. However, when the Corporation acquired goods and services, it often did not comply with good business practices, including its own mandatory purchasing policies and procedures. For example:
>
> - Almost half of the goods and services that should have been acquired competitively were not. In addition, we found many instances where contractual agreements for relatively small amounts were amended numerous times, thereby increasing the value of some original agreements by more than $1 million, or by as much as 1,500%, in some instances.
>
> - In many cases, written agreements between the Corporation and its suppliers either were not in place or were prepared and signed after the goods and services had already been delivered and the underlying invoices had been received and paid.
>
> - Paid invoices we examined from consultants and contractors often lacked sufficient detail to assess if the amounts billed were in compliance with the contractual agreement or to determine if the goods and services paid for had actually been received.

The report also found that the corporation's major computer system overhaul, which was originally budgeted for $18.3 million, eventually exceeded $50 million and failed to deliver the system components required for the valuation of business properties.

The Auditor General also found that the corporation failed to properly document its payment processes to show that suppliers were actually entitled to the payments made under awarded contracts:

> [T]he Corporation was unable to demonstrate — and we were unable to determine — whether, for example, amounts were paid only for goods and services actually received and, ultimately, that they represented value for money spent. In addition, we noted many instances where reimbursements for travel, meal, hospitality, and other expenses appeared excessive or otherwise inappropriate in our view.

The report found that in some instances the corporation inadequately documented its contractual commitments and that it was often playing catch-up and papering transactions after payment had already been made:

> Our review of a sample of documentation supporting contractual arrangements between the Corporation and its suppliers found that:
>
> - For some purchases of up to $300,000, a purchase order was the only document covering the transaction. However, the purchase order is a poor substitute for a contractual agreement because it contains no evidence that its terms were agreed to by the supplier and it lacks many of the usual terms and conditions that would normally be included in a proper written agreement.
>
> - Although written agreements were in place for many of the acquisitions we reviewed, their usefulness was extremely limited for a variety of reasons, including the following:
>
>   - 40% of the agreements were prepared and signed after the goods or services had been delivered and the underlying invoices had been received and paid; and
>
>   - about half the agreements lacked normal prudent business terms and conditions, such as a ceiling price, project deliverables, and associated time frames. Without mutual agreements to cover such issues, it becomes more difficult to monitor the work of the supplier or consultant, and to resolve any subsequent disagreements.

In addition, many of the agreements had been approved by individuals who did not have the authority to do so.

The Auditor General noted that as an arm's-length body, the corporation had historically operated outside of the government's standard procurement practices and had been given the discretion to establish its own practices. However, as the report observed, after the procurement practices at eHealth Ontario received significant public attention, the Ministry of Finance began to prescribe more specific controls on the manner in which the corporation governed its procurement. This case study serves as a useful reminder to those public institutions operating at an arm's-length basis from senior levels of government of the need to establish and maintain proper contract management practices.

Mastering Contract Management
By Maud Murray

Effective contract management can help an organization meet its performance goals, minimize its legal and financial risks, and achieve value-for-money in its procurement process. This article explains why contract management should be an integral part of an organization's procurement strategy and introduces the five pillars of contract management.

What is Contract Management?

Contract management is more than an administrative function. It requires a thorough understanding of the terms of the contract, detailed documentation of key developments during the contract performance stage, management of all post-award changes, and timely resolution of any issues that arise during the performance of the contract.

The contract management process begins with the proper design of a contract and encompasses all dealings between the procuring entity and the supplier from the formation of the contract to the complete performance or early termination of the contract. The specific complexity of the contract management process will depend on the requirements of the contract, and the nature of the goods or services to be provided. For example, the process required for a contract involving a one-time purchase of a simple commodity would be different from that required for a multi-phased design-build project.

An effective contract management process ensures that the procuring organization properly designs its contract, carries out its obligations according to the terms set out in the contract, monitors and resolves any issues that develop during contract performance, and obtains the requisite quality of goods or services that it paid for on time and within budget.

Why Is Contract Management Integral to the Procurement Process?

Purchasing organizations can gain great benefits by proactively integrating a proper contract management process into their procurement strategy. An all too common practice is for organizations to treat contract management as separate from and less important than the competitive stage of the procurement process. This practice is based on a narrow understanding of the procurement process as linear in nature. However, at its best and most efficient, the procurement process is cyclical rather than linear. If the contract performance stage is properly integrated into the planning stages of a procurement process and is properly managed it will inform and improve the proposal or bid solicitation stage of the procurement process, minimize the inherent legal risks that exist in all contractual relationships, and yield great efficiencies in subsequent procurement processes.

Relying on your contract only after the contractual relationship has deteriorated and the legal risks have materialized reduces the contract's utility. Rather than serving as a shield (to protect interests) or a sword (to attack the other party), a properly designed contract should serve as the vehicle by which a purchasing entity improves its bottom line and manages its core business functions effectively and efficiently.

The Five Components of Mastering Contract Management

There are five pillars of any effective contract management process:

1. **Contract Design:** Leveraging the four cornerstones of contract design: anatomy, architecture, assembly and award; and building a contract that is suited to a particular purpose;

2. **Performance and Payment:** Monitoring supplier performance and linking payment to the completion of objective benchmarks;

3. **Change Management:** Effectively dealing with unforeseen circumstances to successfully reduce delays and cost overruns;

4. **Issue Management:** Implementing a coordinated approach to issue resolution and managing the escalation of issues up the organizational hierarchy; and

5. **Performance Tracking and Bidder Barring:** Designing and implementing a systemic approach to track supplier performance and screen out problematic suppliers.

In these times of fiscal constraint, it is imperative that purchasing organizations reject the outdated practice of filing away contracts and looking at them only when the relationship between the parties has deteriorated beyond repair and legal risks have materialized. Even in the best-case scenario, where the parties do not end up in litigation over a contract, there is no disputing the fact that a proper contract management process can prevent lost time, lost money, and lost opportunities. To enhance the efficiency of their procurement processes, organizations should go back to the drawing board and make contract management an integral part of the purchasing cycle.

Does your organization have proper scope-management practices to protect against improper scope increases?

Purchasing institutions should establish proper protocols for protecting against the risks of project "scope creep." The following case studies focus on the importance of contract design and project planning to keeping projects on time and on budget. These case studies also illustrate how contract administration decisions are subject to supplier legal challenges and how post-award contract scope increases can constitute breaches of the relevant trade treaties.

Proper Contract Management Critical to Avoiding Contractor Claims

Proper contract management is critical to avoiding contractor claims. The following cases provide some examples of performance-based claims launched by contractors against purchasing institutions. The first example shows how the failure to properly design contract pricing structures can prove fatal to the prompt resolution of a performance dispute, the second illustrates the risks of not honouring the project scope commitments contained in a contract and the third underscores the inherent risks of contract termination decisions.

The 2007 decision of the Nova Scotia Supreme Court in *Millwood Band Council v. Wilmot (c.o.b. Wilmot Drywall)* illustrates the contract management problems that can be created by unclear project specifications. In this case, the court found a council liable to a local drywall contractor in a dispute over a project for the construction of an administration building. Poor specifications, coupled with a lack of proper contract management, led to a legal dispute as the parties disagreed over their respective obligations. As the court stated, "This case is fundamentally a fact finding exercise. The parties rushed into a commercial arrangement with little thought or documentation. Once the conflict emerged, there was no foundation for a summary resolution. The players' recollections differ greatly and, as such, they all have a different view on the terms of their commercial arrangement." The court ultimately found that the council had failed to pay the drywall contractor for all of the work that had been performed. Much of the controversy revolved around the initial failure to properly design the pricing structure in the contract, since the parties never clarified if the initial quote was for a set price or cost-plus pricing structure.

The 2007 British Columbia Court of Appeal decision in *VSA Highway Maintenance Ltd. v. British Columbia* provides an example of the liabilities that can be created when an institution fails to properly manage its project scope commitments. The road repair contract in question included provisions for extra emergency work. According to those terms, if emergency work was directed to the contractor, the contractor would be entitled to the entire scope of the particular project. Government officials triggered those contractual clauses when they instructed the contractor to commence emergency work to address flooding on a provincial highway. However, instead of assigning the entire scope of the emergency work to the contractor as required under the contract, the government only deployed the contractor for the initial emergency set up work and then performed the rest of the work internally. The contractor sued and the British Columbia Court of Appeal ultimately found the government liable for $680,000 in damages for breach of contract.

The 2008 British Columbia Supreme Court decision in *Wise v. Legal Services Society* shows how contract termination decisions can also lead to litigation. The dispute involved a lawyer whose vendor number for legal aid services was deactivated for administrative reasons by the Legal Services Society. The court reviewed the Legal Services Society's contract termination decision. While it found that "the decision to terminate the Petitioner's vendor's number after 25 years of service may have been harsh, there is nothing in the analysis that provides a basis for quashing the decision as patently unreasonable." The Legal Services Society maintained that it considered "the amount of administrative effort put into the LSS's dealings with the Petitioner relative to other private bar lawyers" and found that the terminated contractor "created a higher administrative burden that was not warranted by any exceptional value" and therefore concluded that the contract should be terminated. Even though the decision to terminate the contract was not overturned, this case illustrates how contract termination decisions remain subject to lawsuits and therefore call for proper contract management practices that include the detailed documenting of the reasons behind a termination decision.

As these examples illustrate, purchasers should ensure that all of their procurement decisions are reasonably made in order to ensure their defensibility in the face of legal challenge.

$385 Million Cost Overrun in BC Olympic Convention Centre Project
Report of the Auditor General of British Columbia, October 2007

In October 2007, the Office of the Auditor General of British Columbia released a report entitled *A Review of the Vancouver Convention Centre Expansion Project: Governance and Risk Management*. The report reviewed the convention centre expansion project that was initiated in preparation for the 2010 Winter Olympics in Vancouver. The report found significant cost overruns, which were attributable to poor project scoping and which resulted in significant scope management issues during the construction phase of the project:

192 - Contract Management

Accelerating the Tendering Cycle

Thoughts of expansion started in earnest in the late 1990's. The initial capital cost estimate for the project announced in 2000 was $495 million. Little happened for several years, then, in early 2003, the provincial government announced that it would undertake the expansion project, using a Crown agency (VCCEP), to have it designed, constructed, commissioned, and owned. The announced capital cost of the expansion was still $495 million.

VCCEP's first approved project budget of $565 million was announced in June 2004. This amount was subsequently revised to $615 million in July 2005. Since then, government has approved three interim budget increases to ensure construction would not be interrupted while it considered a final project budget and schedule. By early 2007, the project was drawing significant public attention because of the changes in the announced schedule and repeated increases in the budget. The current budget, approved by government in July 2007, is $883.2 million.

Among other things, the report noted that the original estimates were not based on detailed project budgets and concluded that there were no guarantees to guard against even more cost escalations or project delays. As the report highlighted, additional risks were created by the need to complete the project within tight timeframes:

As far back as 2000, a convention centre task force recommended an expansion of the existing facility. The government agreed to a July 2008 completion date and considered using an expanded convention centre as part of the 2010 Olympic and Paralympic Winter Games (the Games) if Vancouver was selected to host the Games. After Vancouver was selected to host the Games in mid-2003, the intention was to complete the new expanded centre before the Games, to take advantage of the international exposure it would receive. In late 2004, the expanded centre was chosen to house all Games-related press and broadcast activities. This meant that the facility needed to be ready well before the Games to allow for some preliminary use and time to prepare it for those using it during the Games.

This showcasing opportunity, however, had several drawbacks. First, the hard deadline, combined with a year of elapsed time during an unsuccessful attempt at a public-private partnership agreement prior to the formation of VCCEP, meant that VCCEP's choices regarding a procurement approach were somewhat limited. Instead of proceeding with a traditional staged procurement approach such as design-bid-build, VCCEP felt obliged to proceed concurrently with construction of the marine and platform works while design of the building was being completed and retain a private sector construction management company to provide pre-construction services. Second, the procurement approach assumed that VCCEP would be able subsequently to negotiate a stipulated lump-sum contract with the construction management company. None of the early cost estimates reflected any risk premium that would be needed to compensate the construction manager for accepting the transfer of risk that would be the result of a stipulated lump-sum contact. The stipulated lump-sum contract was not completed until the first part of 2007, by which time most of the large contracts had already been let by VCCEP. This has left VCCEP to bear the originally unanticipated cost escalations.

In addition, the risk transfer premium has proven to be significant, resulting in increased fees in excess of $35 million.

As this case study illustrates, the failure to properly plan a project prior to the commencement of performance can cause significant contract management issues. This provides another reminder of the increased procurement risks created when major public procurement projects blend urgency with political intervention and transform contract management into crisis management.

Alberta Auditor General Calls for Better Coordination of IT Projects
Report of the Auditor General of Alberta, October 2010

In its October 2010 report entitled *Athabasca University – IT Governance, Strategic Planning and Project Management*, the Alberta Auditor General noted that the university's multiple IT projects, which over a ten-year period were budgeted at $90 million, lacked overall coordination or a clear definition of objectives. The Auditor General made a series of recommendations relating to governance of these technology projects.

The Auditor General noted that the university's major technological overhaul is "critical for the University to deliver online courses to students and provide the financial and administrative systems that support the academic environment and student services." However, to avoid becoming overwhelmed by the thirty concurrent IT projects, the Auditor General recommended that the university implement a solid project governance framework aimed at avoiding delays, cost overruns and project failures:

> These diverse, costly and often complex IT projects require that the University's governance and project management processes provide clear oversight and accountability. Without clear governance and project management processes, these IT projects can overwhelm the University's resources and may not meet the University's needs or be delivered cost-effectively and on time.

The Auditor General's report noted that the university had failed to establish these project governance frameworks and that the "University still does not have well-designed and effective IT policies, processes, standards and project management systems."

The Auditor General also found that university management had failed to ensure cost-effectiveness, coordinate its multiple projects or consistently define technical standards for its specific procurements:

> Management was unable to demonstrate that it is implementing its IT strategic plans cost-effectively, and that it achieved the expected results and benefits. The University had not:
>
> 1. developed an integrated IT delivery plan to link the University's individual IT projects to its IT Strategic Plan, in order to highlight project priorities, critical sequence, inter-dependencies, and high-level risks
>
> 2. consistently prepared business cases to provide key project planning information to the steering committees and executive committee, including details on project objectives, development costs and projected maintenance costs, benefits and risks
>
> 3. consistently measured and reported sufficient and relevant project status information to the steering committees and executive committee to allow them to effectively govern projects and provide oversight to the IT strategic planning process
>
> 4. formalized project management standards to provide clear and consistent procedures on how to manage IT projects
>
> 5. defined a clear mandate and authority for its project management office to establish and enforce standards and processes for successful portfolio management, project governance, reporting and effective risk management for all IT projects
>
> 6. defined a formal systems development methodology and architectural standards to ensure that systems are developed and implemented using an efficient, consistent and cost-effective approach.

The university's failure to establish proper governance frameworks to coordinate between the different projects undermined its ability to set the consistent technical standards required to ensure compatibility and interoperability between the acquired products and systems.

As noted above, the failure to establish a proper governance framework in a multi-project initiative undermines an institution's ability to define project specifications or ensure that discrete project deliverables result in a properly integrated overall system. As the Auditor General noted, the lack of interoperability remained an ongoing problem since the university "has not progressed with its 2005 plan to improve the integration and efficiencies in its financial, human resources and payroll systems. IT strategic planning documents do not clearly reflect this system integration initiative as a priority project. The University's business processes remain inefficient, as significant manual processes are required."

When working as part of a broader initiative, project teams require clear and consistent technical standards so that they can clearly define the requirements of their particular procurements. As the Auditor General's report indicates, the failure to coordinate multi-project initiatives can undermine the ability to set consistent standards and achieve properly integrated end results. The review of Athabasca University's IT initiative provides a useful project governance case study for all institutions and underscores the importance of proper project planning to the future development of project specifications.

Post-Award Scope Increases Contravene Treaty Duties

While directly awarded contracts have long been a source of controversy in government procurement, another lesser known form of improper sole-sourcing involves the post-award expansion of previously tendered contracts. As the following Canadian International Trade Tribunal cases illustrate, the expansion of contract scope during the contract administration phase of the procurement cycle can put a public entity in breach of its trade treaty obligations.

By way of example, in its 2008 determination in *Bell Mobility v. Canada (Department of Public Works and Government Services)*, the Tribunal determined that the government's contract amendments constituted an improper sole-source that breached the applicable trade treaty procurement rules. The dispute revolved around the federal government's amendment of two mobile products and services contracts. The complainant alleged that the amendments improperly expanded the scope of the originally competed contracts and precluded competition. The Tribunal agreed. It found that adding a 1GB service for heavy users to the 30MB service plan that was scoped out in the original RFP constituted a substantial change which was not permitted under the "service enhancement" clause in the contract. The Tribunal determined that the amendment constituted a new non-competed procurement that breached the *Agreement on Internal Trade*. While the Tribunal declined to award lost profits to the complainant due to the small number of additional users that would be using the enhanced 1 GB service, the case serves as a useful reminder that post-award out-of-scope acquisitions can constitute improper sole-sourcing in contravention of the trade treaties.

Similarly, in its 2008 determination in *Colley Motorships Ltd. v. Canada (Department of Public Works and Government Services)*, the Canadian International Trade Tribunal awarded the complainant lost profits and ordered the government to compete future work after finding that a post-award contract amendment constituted an improper sole-source. The case involved a contract amendment which expanded the scope of an existing personal household goods relocation services contract to include the provision of private motor vehicle relocation services. The complainant, an existing provider of private motor vehicle relocation services, challenged the contract amendment. The government acknowledged that the complaint had merit and asked the Tribunal to recommend reasonable compensation. The Tribunal awarded the complainant one-third of its lost profits.

Conversely, in its 2010 determination in *Microsoft Canada Co. v. Canada (Department of Public Works and Government Services)*, the Canadian International Trade Tribunal rejected a sole-source challenge launched by Microsoft Canada. The case dealt with the acquisition of a new unified portal software solution by Health Canada under an existing contract with Sierra Systems Group. Microsoft claimed that the acquisition fell outside of the scope of the previously tendered contract and was therefore an improper direct award. After engaging in a detailed analysis of the newly procured software and of the software licensing and maintenance terms in the original contract, the Tribunal determined that the acquisition properly fell within the scope of the contract. While in this instance the sole-source challenge proved unsuccessful, this case illustrates how the failure to properly scope contracts to take post-award changes into account can result in a sole-source challenge and can potentially fetter the proper downstream acquisition of services and technologies from incumbent suppliers. As this case illustrates, institutions should carefully craft their tendered contracts to ensure that they are able to properly procure successor technologies and services.

Finally, in its 2011 determination in *AdVenture Marketing Solutions Inc. v. Canada (Department of Public Works and Government Services),* the Canadian International Trade Tribunal found that the government's post-award contract amendment constituted an improper sole-source and contravened the applicable trade treaties. It also found that the treaty duties regarding post-award scope changes are more strict than the equivalent common law duties. The case dealt with the acquisition of USB drives for the Department of National Defence. The complainant alleged that the DND made significant improper changes to the mandatory specifications after the contract was awarded to a competing supplier. The Tribunal agreed, finding that this post-award amendment constituted a new procurement and that suppliers had the right to challenge these post-award changes under the trade treaties. In coming to its conclusion, the Tribunal rejected the government's argument that post-award contract administration decisions are generally not challengeable by losing bidders. The Tribunal distinguished the court-based common law duties under the law of tenders that tend to regulate the bidding process from tender submission to contact award from the broader treaty-based duties that compel the public entity to use open tendering for its acquisitions. The Tribunal awarded the complainant lost profits due to the treaty breach.

With a view to complying with their treaty obligations, all public institutions should establish internal governance rules for the use of direct contract awards. To that end, Canadian International Trade Tribunal determinations dealing with post-award scope changes provide useful guidance for adhering to treaty duties during the contract management phase of the procurement cycle.

Does your organization have the performance tracking measures in place to deal with problematic contractors and properly bar them from future work?

Clear and objective performance criteria, coupled with the establishment of performance tracking protocols, are critical elements for ensuring that contractors keep to their commitments or are dealt with effectively when they fail to do so. The following discussion focuses on the importance of establishing clear performance standards. The subsequent case studies illustrate the importance of properly monitoring and documenting vendor performance.

Managing Supplier Performance

By Maud Murray

For many purchasing organizations, supplier performance management is a key aspect of a comprehensive strategy for maximizing contract value. The deliverables and performance criteria set out in a contract can be a useful set of tools. Effective performance management requires the deliverables and performance criteria in the contract to describe the outcomes expected by the purchaser, to set out measurable performance standards and to explain the applicable performance evaluation process, including payment incentives and disincentives.

Describing Expected Outcomes In the Contract

Purchasers often make the mistake of prescribing the manner in which their suppliers must provide the deliverables, as well as the quantity and type of material the supplier must use in its provision of the deliverables. This practice diminishes the supplier's ability to provide the deliverables efficiently and innovatively. For example, a purchaser's prescribed performance process may not always be the most cost-effective way for a supplier to provide the required goods or services. In developing performance requirements under a contract, purchasers should shift the focus from process to desired outcomes, and consider the problem the contract is meant to resolve in the first place as well as the timelines for achieving that outcome.

Setting out Measurable Performance Standards

A purchaser needs to establish clear and measurable performance standards. The level and complexity of the performance standards will depend upon the value of the contract and the nature of the services or goods being provided. The measurable performance standards should flow from the desirable outcomes of the contract and should focus on the key performance indicators required for the achievement of such outcomes. Some key performance indicators to consider include, where appropriate, compliance with regulatory requirements such as health and safety, the completion of well delineated milestones or phases applicable to the deliverables, the performance of the deliverables by the specific timelines, the expected quality of the deliverables, and the attainment of end-user satisfaction requirements.

In developing and setting out their performance standards in the contract, purchasers should ensure that each performance standard is necessary, measurable, and not unduly burdensome. Purchasers should also ensure that the performance standards in their contracts are not set so high that they drive up the overall cost of deliverables or so low that they act as a disincentive to good contract performance.

Establishing A Performance Evaluation Process

Suppliers should be aware from the outset that their performance will be monitored and evaluated throughout the term of the contract. Suppliers should also be advised of the criteria that will be assessed, what effective performance is and what will be done to correct underperformance. For example, at early stages of underperformance the purchaser could use informal remedial measures such as requesting the addition or replacement of personnel, or increasing the report-back requirements. For more egregious underperformance, purchasers may need to take more formal action such as involving senior management.

To add even more rigour to the performance evaluation process, the purchaser should align payment of the supplier with the performance standards and evaluation process set out in the contract. Payment incentives (positive, negative or a combination of both) can also be used when necessary to induce better quality performance. Purchasers should use caution when utilizing and calling on such incentives and ensure that the incentives apply to the most important aspects of the work, rather than to every individual task required in the provision of the deliverables.

To leverage an effective performance evaluation process, a purchasing organization should establish the proper infrastructure to support the management of the supplier's performance. For example, the purchaser should ensure that it has the appropriate contract managers in place since managers are crucial in the performance evaluation process. Training is also critical since managers must have the right skills and authority to monitor and evaluate the supplier's performance while ensuring that the purchaser meets its own obligations under the contract.

Establishing a strategy for supplier performance management can require a significant investment of an organization's time and resources. However, if the strategy is executed effectively, an organization can quickly realize its return on investment.

Procurement Ombudsman Calls for Vendor Management Strategy

In its 2009–2010 report entitled *A Management Approach to Vendor Performance,* the Office of the Procurement Ombudsman of Canada recommended that public institutions establish clear vendor management strategies to better ensure value-for-money for the taxpayer. As the report states, proper vendor management strategies are "of interest to our stakeholders due to the significant amount of money that is spent by the federal government on procuring goods, services and construction to deliver programs to taxpayers." The report also notes that holding "vendors accountable for their performance is an important tool for making sure the government receives good value from its contracts. This also fosters better communication and results in improved relationships between the government and its vendors." In fact, the report notes that leading institutions have implemented clear vendor performance strategies within their organizations:

> Eight Canadian government organizations responsible for the procurement of goods, services and construction at the federal, provincial, and municipal levels participated in the Study. It is important to note that five of these organizations, which are not covered by our mandate, contributed on a voluntary basis.

> We carried out research that included a review of academic and government literature related to vendor performance. We also interviewed officials responsible for procurement, contract management and project management at participating organizations.

> We found that vendor performance management is best supported by a vendor performance program with an established framework and policy. The elements of the framework need to be aligned with corporate strategic goals and objectives, as well as risk mitigation strategies.

> All organizations we interviewed have best practices that address elements of a framework for a vendor performance program. For example, they have established processes; use performance clauses in contracts; use tools and automated systems to monitor, evaluate and report performance results; follow contract file close out procedures; and can apply corrective measures on vendors for poor performance.

> A good vendor performance program helps to protect Crown interests and provides transparency on what the government's expectations are.

Vendors are also entitled to know the rules of engagement. If government organizations apply corrective measures by clearly communicating, in advance, evaluation criteria coupled with due process, it is more likely to be defensible in a legal action.

As the report states, the federal government's Supply Manual also recognizes the importance of establishing and maintaining a vendor performance monitoring system:

Public Works and Government Services Canada, as the government's common service provider for procurement, states the following in its Supply Manual:

- Contract management is the process of systematically and efficiently managing contract development, implementation, and administration for maximizing financial and operational performance and managing inherent risk. Contract management encompasses the life cycle of a contract and involves many stakeholders including, but not limited to the contracting officer, the client department and the supplier.

  Contract administration is an important part of contract management, which includes those activities performed after a contract award, to ensure files are properly maintained and that the contractor meets the requirements of the contract.

  Contract management is an essential element of the procurement process that protects the interests of Canada while ensuring that suppliers are being treated fairly.

- Whenever the satisfactory fulfillment of a contract is jeopardized, contracting officers should take the necessary steps to serve and protect the interests of Canada. Contract disputes should be dealt with fairly, and as promptly as possible. Contracting officers should keep procurement files complete and up to date, to provide a record of actions taken.

- Contracting officers should also keep themselves informed about such things as the proposed contractor's performance history, financial situation and practices, before recommending a contract award. It also means keeping up to date with a contractor during the performance of a contract.

These policies highlight the importance of good contract management and the need to ensure the monitoring and evaluation of the performance of the vendor during and at the conclusion of the contract. It also provides the basis for establishing the rules for due process and the authority to apply corrective measures.

The Procurement Ombudsman makes the following recommendations with respect to the creation and content of an institution's vendor management policy:

A vendor performance policy formalizes the framework for managing vendor performance. It increases fairness by ensuring that all vendors are treated in an equal and consistent manner. It also enhances transparency of the procurement process by providing information to vendors on what an organization's expectations are, and on what basis decisions will be made and actions undertaken.

Based on our literature research, a good vendor performance policy should:

- be linked to corporate objectives and risk management strategies;

- have full support from senior management;

- support fairness, openness and transparency;

- identify roles and responsibilities;

- establish performance measures and evaluation criteria;

- provide vendors with an opportunity to review and comment on evaluations;

- provide for an independent dispute resolution mechanism;

- establish corrective measures;

- use evaluation results for the validation of procurement strategies, evaluation criteria and contractor selection methodology to support continuous improvement of the procurement process;

- identify reporting requirements;

- provide for a system to capture vendor performance information; and

- indicate the requirement to share vendor performance information with procurement review committees to assist them in future contract award decisions.

As the report maintains, taking a coordinated and strategic approach to vendor performance "holds vendors accountable for their contribution to satisfying operational requirements of the Government and helps achieve best value for the Canadian taxpayer." To better serve the public interest, institutions would be well served to use the recommendations contained in the Procurement Ombudsman's report as a roadmap to bolstering their contract management practices and achieving value-for-money for the taxpayer.

Poor Past Performance Can Justify Low Bid Rejection

Carosi Construction Ltd. v. Niagara
Ontario Court of Appeal, 2005

Sound Contracting Ltd. v. Nanaimo
British Columbia Court of Appeal, 2000

The courts have recognized the right to reject a low bidder for past performance issues. However, this right must be carefully exercised since it remains subject to legal challenge.

For example, the *Carosi Construction Ltd. v. Niagara (Regional Municipality)* case involved two separate tenders, one for the construction of storage tanks and the other for a project involving a water pollution plant. The plaintiff submitted the low bid for both projects but both of its bids were rejected. The low bidder sued but the trial court found that the bidder failed to provide evidence that the region had acted improperly.

The Ontario Court of Appeal upheld the trial court decision and found that the defendant municipality was entitled to reject the low bidder based on a bad reference. The low bidder maintained that it had been "blackballed" by a negative reference from another municipality for which it had previously worked. The Court of Appeal disagreed, noting that the owner was entitled to use a negative reference as a reason to bypass the low bidder and that this did not constitute "blackballing". As this case illustrates, low bids can be bypassed for valid reasons. Proper evidence of poor past performance can be relied upon in the right circumstances to avoid awarding a contract to a low bidder.

Similarly, in its decision in *Sound Contracting Ltd. v. Nanaimo (City)*, the British Columbia Court of Appeal held that the owner was entitled to rely on a privilege clause to reject the low bidder due to past performance problems. The case involved a construction tender call which contained the traditional "lowest tender not necessarily accepted" privilege clause as well as a clause stating that the contract would go to "the greatest value based on quality, service and price." The city awarded the contract to the second-lowest bidder. The low bidder sued and won at trial.

The Court of Appeal reversed the trial decision and recognized that the privilege clauses permitted the city to avoid awarding to the lowest bidder "if there are valid, objective reasons for concluding that better value may be obtained by accepting a higher bid." However, the Court of Appeal stressed that the purchaser's discretion must be exercised fairly, objectively and in good faith.

The Court of Appeal found that the city was justified in considering the low bidder's past performance on similar city projects and in deciding that due to past performance problems, the low bid would not result in "the greatest value based on quality, service and price." The Court of Appeal also found that considering the bidder's past performance was not an improper undisclosed criterion since "past dealings are probably the best indicator of how a proposed relationship will come to work out in practice." However, the Court of Appeal was careful to caution purchasers against using their discretion "in such a way as to punish or to get even for past differences," stressing that "[w]henever the low bidder is not the successful tenderer, any additional factors in the analysis will have to be shown to be reasonable and relevant."

The Court of Appeal also cautioned against the arbitrary use of a privilege clause and found that its exercise remains subject to challenge by bidders and subject to the duty of fairness and good faith.

As these decisions illustrate, a privilege clause does not give an owner an unfettered right to reject the low bidder without valid reasons. The exercise of such rights remains subject to legal challenge by bidders and review by the courts. Owners should therefore exercise their privileges in a legally sound and defensible manner based on clearly documented reasons.

Banning Bad Suppliers

If you owned a company and one of your suppliers sued you, would you invite that supplier to bid on your next tendered contract? This is highly unlikely. However, in many purchasing institutions, there is a widespread reluctance to bar litigious bidders or apply other systemic solutions to deal with problematic suppliers. Purchasing institutions should implement a bidder barring protocol to deal with suppliers who launch frivolous lawsuits, who undermine the integrity of the bidding process or who perform poorly after contract award. This section discusses the benefits of implementing a bidder barring protocol.

Litigious Bidders

As noted above, there is a widespread reluctance to bar litigious bidders. Part of that reluctance is well placed since a barring process should not be used to add insult to injury after a supplier launches a legitimate claim. In such instances, the courts have criticized heavy-handed bureaucracies who attempt to "get even" for past disputes. However, a proper balance needs to be struck. Frivolous claims drain resources from the purchasing operation.

Institutional policies and procedures should be established to help differentiate between meritorious claims, which should be settled in an expeditious and reasonable fashion, and frivolous ones, which should be streamed towards a barring sanction. Such guidelines can help reduce the resources squandered on protracted legal battles and at the same time help increase supplier confidence in the integrity of the institution's procurement practices.

Bidding Abuses

Many purchasing institutions rely on bid security as their primary deterrent against bidder improprieties. However, this remedy has serious flaws. Firstly, using bid security draws the institution into the high-risk Contract A tendering process. This gives the bidders a number of common law rights which have translated into an avalanche of lawsuits. By requiring bid security, the institution increases its litigation risk and diminishes its ability to utilize more flexible, low-risk tendering formats.

Secondly, bid security is an overly broad remedy since it punishes all bidders by tying up their liquidity during the bidding process in order to sanction the few bad players who do not honour their bids. In its procurement review of Samoa, the World Bank recognized this problem and recommended bidder barring as a substitute remedy:

> Although securities can be provided by local banks...this restricts the liquidity of firms in their cash transactions. In place of bid security... the Tenders Board may wish to consider allowing bidders to sign a declaration accepting that if they withdraw or modify their bids during the period of validity...the bidder will be suspended by the Tenders Board for a period of time from being eligible for any bidding involving Government funds.... [T]his would help the liquidity of the firms, while at the same time ensuring that frivolous bids are not submitted.

Canadian institutions can implement similar approaches, which would free them up to use lower-risk non-Contract A formats while still maintaining a credible deterrent against frivolous bids.

Finally, bid security fails to provide a practical remedy against corrupt tendering practices such as bid rigging and bribery. Lawmakers in a number of international jurisdictions have passed bidder barring legislation to deal with these types of bidding abuses. For example, Kenya's *Public Procurement and Disposal Act 2005* established a maximum five-year ban for bidders who engage in corrupt tendering practices. Purchasing institutions in Canada should leverage these international legal developments to create their own policies and procedures for implementing bidder barring protocols as deterrents against tendering abuses.

Poor Performers

When an institution receives a low bid from a poorly performing contractor, its natural instinct may be to rely on its reserved right to "reject any and all tenders" and select a different bidder. However, since the decision to bypass a low bidder is typically subject to legal challenge, purchasers should proceed with caution in these situations. The ability to safely sidestep a poorly performing low bidder is directly related to the evidence available to prove poor past performance and to the relevance of that poor past performance to the evaluation of the current tender. While good record keeping can help in these situations, the low-bid bypass remains subject to costly and lengthy litigation and to lost profit awards if the court decides that the bypass was improper. To avoid risky and resource-draining legal entanglements, institutions should bolster their contract management recordkeeping and conduct post-performance assessments of their contractors. Like litigious bidders and unethical bidders, poor performers should be barred before they are given the opportunity to submit another low bid, mess up another project and launch another lawsuit. We owe it to our institutions to create effective firewalls to protect us from these problematic suppliers.

Bidder Barring Fair Game if Properly Applied

While the courts have in some instances upheld a purchaser's right to bar problematic suppliers, purchasers should ensure that these practices are developed and implemented in a reasonable and measured fashion.

In its 2007 judgment in *Advanced Ergonomics Inc. v. British Columbia (Workers' Compensation Board)*, the British Columbia Supreme Court dismissed an unsuccessful proponent's claim of bias and conspiracy and upheld the purchaser's right to refuse subsequent proposals from the litigious supplier.

The case dealt with an RFP for ergonomics consulting services. The plaintiff responded to the RFP but was unsuccessful. It brought an action alleging bias and conspiracy, claiming that although it had been invited to bid, the purchaser had decided in advance that it would not win. The plaintiff claimed that it had incurred $100,000 in bidding costs.

The court found no basis for the plaintiff's claims and dismissed the action. Furthermore, the court recognized a purchaser's right to deny a supplier the opportunity to bid on contracts due to ongoing lawsuits.

As this case illustrates, barring litigious bidders can be a useful remedy for purchasers in appropriate circumstances.

The 2001 decision of the Alberta Court of Queen's Bench in *Green Country Maintenance Ltd. v. Calgary (City)* illustrates the importance of sound contract management in obtaining value-for-money under current and future contracts. After receiving a complaint that one of its contractors was leaving work early, the city investigated the operations of the particular contractor for one-and-a-half months and discovered that during that period the contractor had submitted inaccurate time sheets which had resulted in an over-billing of $541. The contract was terminated and the contractor's tenders for subsequent contracts were rejected.

The contractor challenged the city's actions but the court upheld both the contract termination and the subsequent tender rejections, stating that "I am of the view, after reading all the evidence and hearing the submissions from counsel, that the City of Calgary acted in a fair manner that was within its authority when it suspended the services of Green Country, and when it subsequently refused the tenders." The contract in question contained a clause that allowed the city to terminate when a contractor failed to provide "quality service." That clause also contained the right, depending on the severity of the circumstances, to declare a terminated contractor ineligible for future tendered work. The reservation of those rights, coupled with a well documented monitoring of performance, allowed the city to address the performance issue on an immediate and ongoing basis. In so doing, the city provided purchasers with a useful illustration of how contract management is an essential part of the procurement cycle.

Conversely, in its April 2005 decision in *Soo Logging Co. v. British Columbia (Minister of Forests)*, the British Columbia Supreme Court found that the government improperly blacklisted a contractor due to alleged past-performance problems. The Ministry had previously terminated the contractor due to the alleged performance problems. When the contractor sued, the Ministry unofficially blacklisted the contractor from subsequent tendering opportunities. The contractor challenged those actions. The court was critical of the Ministry's conduct, noting its unreasonable and intransigent approach in the course of the litigation.

The court found "conduct deserving of rebuke on the part of the Ministry representatives who were instructing counsel." As this case illustrates, purchasers should be careful not to use subsequent tendering processes as an opportunity to "get even" with past performance disputes, particularly in instances where there may have been shared responsibility for prior performance problems.

Chapter 7:
TRAINING

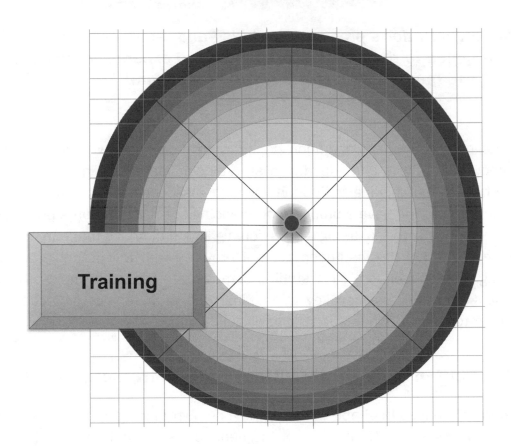

Training

Introduction

Purchasing institutions should ensure that all new personnel who will be intersecting with the procurement function have a proper understanding of the procurement rules. Organizations should also ensure that their core procurement staff are receiving ongoing training to better assist the organization in meeting its due diligence duties. In addition, institutional training programs should be established to create a broader organizational awareness of proper procurement practices.

The following case studies illustrate the risks created by failing to properly train new staff on procurement ethics and by failing to ensure that the right skill sets are brought to bear on procurement projects. These case studies also focus on the need to keep core procurement staff up-to-date on the latest legal developments so that governance frameworks are properly established and a broader organizational awareness of procurement duties is properly maintained.

Hiring Standards

Are your organization's procurement hiring and retention practices properly targeted to the knowledge, skill set and experience required to meet prevailing due diligence standards?

A properly functioning procurement operation depends on the people who work within the system. While knowledge, skills and experience are key considerations in the retention of core procurement staff, purchasing institutions should also consider whether new hires within the broader organization have a proper understanding of the institution's procurement-related due diligence duties. The following discussion highlights the risks that can arise when new staff at all levels within the institution are not provided with the proper procurement awareness training. The subsequent case studies demonstrate the importance of ensuring that the individuals who are assigned key roles within the procurement project have the appropriate skill set to meet the institution's due diligence duties.

Proper Training of New Staff Critical to Procurement Integrity

The *Gomery Report*, discussed in Chapter 1, contains a number of insightful research studies that provide detailed assessments of some of the serious issues that can result from the blurring of the political and administrative spheres of government and the risks that this can pose to integrity of the procurement process. In one such study entitled "The Life and Times of Parliament's Statutory Orphans," Liane E. Benoit highlights some of the significant issues raised by the presence of newly hired political staff working in a Minister's office:

> Of the many footfalls heard echoing through Ottawa's corridors of power, those that often hit hardest but bear the least scrutiny belong to an elite group of young, ambitious and politically loyal operatives hired to support and advise the Ministers of the Crown. Collectively known as "exempt staff," recent investigations by the Public Accounts Committee and the Commission of Inquiry into the Sponsorship Program and Advertising Activities, hereafter referred to as the "Sponsorship Inquiry", suggest that this group of ministerial advisors can, and often do, exert a substantial degree of influence on the development, and in some cases, administration, of public policy in Canada. Further, it is evident from the current and historic record that these powers can be and are, on occasion, open to abuse. Though unelected, often uneducated in the

theory and operation of the machinery of government and regularly devoid of professional qualifications relevant to the ministries with which they are involved, these individuals, by virtue of their political relationship with the party in power and/or the minister they serve, are well placed to influence both the bounce and bobble of bureaucratic political interface and the pace and progress of public policy in Canada.

As this study notes, by acting as an extension of the elected official, political staff can assert inappropriate influence over the government's administrative decision-making process. Benoit cites a 1967 study entitled "The Minister's Office Staff: An Unreformed Part of the Public Services," which was published by Professor J. R. Mallory in *Canadian Public Administration* in the wake of the federal government scandal known as the "Rivard Affair." While Mallory's observations may have been made over 45 years ago, they read as fresh as the day they were first written:

> In the wake of the revelations of the Rivard Affair, Professor J. R. Mallory observed that among the Dorion Report's many contributions, it served to "illuminate certain facets of government which have hitherto escaped the attention of scholars." In redressing this oversight, it was his assessment that, contrary to what some scholars had lauded as the Canadian constitutional system's success in developing a "clear-cut dividing line drawn between the politician and the administrator," there was, in fact, embedded within the machinery of government in Canada, "an intermediate class of persons in the Minister's Office, who are political rather than bureaucratic in their functions, appointed rather than elected, and who operate in an area which strict constitutional theory does not recognize as existing." The presence of this emerging group of operatives in the Minister's lair was, in Mallory's estimation, inappropriate to the Westminster model of democracy.

> > It is clearly undesirable that a considerable number of persons not a part of the civil service should be interposed between a Minister and his department. They lack the training and professional standards of the public service: it may even be the peculiar nature of the appointment means they escape the security screening which is an unpleasant accompaniment of most candidatures for responsible posts in the public service. Not only do these functionaries wield great power because they control access to the Minister and can speak in his name, but they may wield this power with ludicrous ineptitude and in ways that are clearly tainted with political motives.

> There was, he feared, "a danger inherent in having such untrained people, lacking the career motives and professional standards of the civil service, in positions of both influence and power." In his opinion, the duties to be performed by those in a Minister's office should be strictly limited to the writing of the Minister's speeches, the preparation and distribution of press releases and "such mundane matters as supporting the Minister's public image by cultivating the goodwill of the press gallery ... He also conceded the need for a gatekeeper "to act as a buffer between a busy Minister and his constituents and political followers." Beyond that, any role played by the Minister's staff, particularly with respect to policy or program development, was an inappropriate incursion into the realm rightly held by the public service.

As the *Gomery Report* observes, the long-standing failure to properly define the respective roles of political staff and public servants has resulted in ongoing administrative challenges and a less-than-stellar track record of appropriate conduct:

> Perhaps the most honest conclusion that can be drawn following a somewhat exhaustive review of the role of exempt staff in contemporary Canadian government is that there are no absolute truths to be found in the analysis of any aspect of the role and practice of this function, only shades of truth. If my sources are correct, roughly half the time these supporting political roles are carried out in a competent and capable fashion; the incumbents act appropriately with respect to long-standing, if somewhat ill-defined, conventions, and exercise sound and constructive political judgment in the execution of their duties and their relationships with the department. The other half of the time, they don't. Likewise, there remains no absolute consensus, in theory or in practice, either within or outside of government, as to what constitutes the appropriate role of exempt staff in the policy development process. After decades of various attempts by the political centre to wrest control of policy from the bureaucracy, there are still those who maintain that the active involvement of exempt staff in this capacity is illegitimate, inappropriate and sometimes dangerous. Proponents, on the other hand, persist in their belief that an independent policy capacity in the Minister's office is the politician's best defence against the power of an obstinate and self-interested bureaucracy — that democracy demands this direction from its elected representatives; that the political tail should indeed wag the departmental dog.

While the appropriate role of elected officials and political staff within the government's general administrative decision-making process will remain a subject of ongoing debate, one thing is certain: as a general rule there should be no political involvement in government contract award decisions. Political staff, as well as all new staff hired at all levels within an institution, should be provided with proper training on the paramount importance of protecting the integrity of the public procurement process from inappropriate political interference.

Bad Specs Cause Payment Disputes in Atlantic Canada

Coady Construction and Excavating Ltd. v. St. John's Newfoundland and Labrador Supreme Court, 2004

Greenslade's Construction Co. v. Conception Bay South Newfoundland Supreme Court – Trial Division, 2000

As the following examples illustrate, the failure to set sound specifications prior to contract award raises the risk of project failures and legal claims. Institutions should therefore establish clear accountabilities for the drafting of specifications within their project teams.

For example, in its decision in *Coady Construction and Excavating Ltd. v. St. John's (City)*, the Newfoundland and Labrador Supreme Court found the municipality liable for $68,000 in extra contractor costs due to faulty project specifications. Notwithstanding the inclusion of a typical tender call disclaimer warning bidders to inform themselves of existing conditions, the municipality was found liable since its design specifications failed to accurately reflect the complex nature of the required work.

As the court stated, it is "one thing to install an extra catch basin as part of a contract where the drawings are reliable and the work simply involves the acquisition and installation of the unit. It is entirely another thing when the existing underground installation is a double catch basin joined together which has to be busted apart and two new ones installed requiring new holes to be busted into the unit to accommodate the piping which was not shown on the drawings." The court found that "the unpredictable and difficult circumstances found in the field by Coady on this job" entitled the contractor to its extra cost claim.

By way of another example, in its decision in *Greenslade's Construction Co. v. Conception Bay South (Town),* the Newfoundland Supreme Court – Trial Division found a municipality liable for inadequately designed specifications. The case dealt with the construction of a baseball field for the Newfoundland Summer Games. The mayor took a direct interest in the project and overrode engineering advice with respect to both site selection and design specifications. As the court noted, in directions to staff the mayor "specifically instructed them to keep the details of the project to the minimum amount possible. The Mayor was keenly interested in obtaining the lowest possible tender which the town could obtain, and he felt that by keeping the details to the minimum, this could be achieved." The town ultimately issued a tender call with designs based on a rudimentary hand-drawn sketch. As the court noted, this led to significant problems during the construction phase of the project:

On three separate occasions during November the Town changed the orientation of the field. During this period of time a considerable amount of fill was relocated. Because the reorientation twisted the Pad to the west, the side of the field closest to the tennis courts would move up to the west by 7. The result was that the right outfield corner was moved further into the area where there were problems with rock. These sets of changes constituted a fundamental change in the Contract. Greenslade says he told the Town that these changes were not the contract he agreed to. He has been consistent in his position on this ever since. At no time during this process did the Town request an estimate for this work from Greenslade. As a result of the Town's instructions, a considerable amount of fill was removed from the left infield line and replaced behind the pitcher's mound. This fill ultimately became the catcher's sections and was the deepest fill of the whole project. Extra fill was also placed towards the swimming pool area. As a result of the reorientation, Greenslade's were pushed to work in an area which Greenslade's had assumed it would not have to cut or excavate when the project was originally bid. When it became necessary to blast the rock where the right outfield line had been moved to the west, concerns were raised again about the proximity of the houses on Rideout's Road and the nature of the rock. Because of these two problems it was necessary to use very small blasts with a lot of matting in order to avoid fly-rock and also not to cause damage to the concrete bottom of the adjacent swimming pool. This was slower, labour and equipment intensive, and expensive.

The contractor eventually walked off the field in frustration and sued. It was awarded damages by the court. As this case illustrates, to establish clear performance standards and avoid post-award project disputes, institutions should ensure that project specifications are prepared by competent subject-matter experts.

As these cases demonstrate, to mitigate against specification-based project risks, institutions should ensure that their specifications accurately capture performance conditions and are properly aligned with the pricing structures in the tendering documents.

Cut-and-Paste Criteria Lead to Lost-Profit Award in Scottish Tender

Aquatron Marine v. Stratchyde Fire Board
Scottish Court of Session, 2007

In its November 2007 judgment in *Aquatron Marine (t/a Quatron Breathing Air Systems) v. Stratchyde Fire Board*, the Scottish Court of Session awarded lost profit damages to an unsuccessful bidder after the purchasing institution used undisclosed criteria in the evaluation of the bidder's tender. The case involved a tender call issued by the Stratchyde Fire Board for the supply and repair of firefighting equipment.

The plaintiff, Aquatron Marine, submitted a bid but was rejected. It sued, alleging improprieties in the tender evaluation process. The court agreed, finding that the vaguely stated "quality standards" criteria failed to sufficiently disclose the specific factors relied on by the evaluators in rejecting the plaintiff's tender:

> The reasons given for the exclusion of the pursuers were twofold. First it was that the pursuers "did not supply evidence of quality standards achieved by its workforce and on enquiry it appeared that personnel would be employed if [the pursuers'] tender was successful". There are several difficulties with this reason. They stem from the phrase used in the Specification. In the context of a paragraph dealing with the competence of the staff undertaking the work, Clause 11 calls for "copies of any evidence of quality standards achieved by their workforce". The clause does not set down any minimum requirement which a tenderer requires to meet in order to proceed to the evaluation stage. It simply asks for evidence of quality standards to be forwarded with the tender...
>
> [T]he next difficulty is the construction of the phrase "quality standards achieved by their workforce". The impression gained from Mr McKnight was that he had not fully thought out just what he was asking for and had taken this phrase from another, perhaps previous, contract and simply pasted it into this clause. The phrase has to be construed according to what the well informed tenderer would think it to mean, rather than what the drafter intended it to mean. The evidence of what Mr McKnight thought he was doing, the manner in which the defenders sought to implement the clause and the views of an expert in the processing of public procurement contracts may not be entirely irrelevant to the Court's assessment, even if any relevance may be peripheral. I will accordingly repel the objection to that evidence. However, I do not consider that the well informed tenderer could have thought that this phrase was intended to require him to include the *curriculum vitae* of individual staff or any similar documents. As is often said in these situations, if that is what had been intended then it would have been simple to say so in plain unambiguous terms.

After determining that the stated criteria were too vague and imprecise to permit the application of the specific factors relied on by the evaluators, the court found the Board in breach of the tendering rules and awarded the plaintiff lost profit damages. As this case illustrates, purchasing institutions should ensure that their staff draft evaluation criteria with sufficient precision to capture the specific factors that will be relied on to accept, reject and rank competing bidders.

Faulty Evaluation Criteria Cause Recall
of $4.6 Billion Military Tender

L-3 Communications Titan Corporation
United States Government Accountability Office, 2007

In its March 2007 decision in *L-3 Communications Titan Corporation*, the U.S. Federal Government Accountability Office (the "GAO") issued a retender and re-evaluation order against the Unites States Department of the Army after finding that the Department relied on undisclosed evaluation criteria in making its initial contract award. The case dealt with a request for proposals for a $4.6 billion interpretation and translation services contract for the U.S. armed forces in Iraq.

The complainant challenged the Department's evaluation process, arguing that its past experience requirements were not assessed in the manner set out in the RFP. The GAO agreed, finding that the Department was under a duty to follow the evaluation criteria set out in its RFP and finding that the Department breached that duty when it replaced its stated evaluation scheme with an undisclosed pass/fail methodology:

> [A]n agency may not announce in the RFP that one evaluation scheme will be used, and then follow another; once offerors are informed of the criteria against which their proposals will be evaluated, the agency must adhere to those criteria in evaluating proposals and making its award decision. ...

> Here, contrary to the solicitation's express provisions that proposals would be comparatively evaluated against the task order 1 requirements, and would be evaluated as "more advantageous" the greater the extent to which an offeror's recent experience reflected those requirements, the agency applied materially different evaluation criteria, replacing the solicitation's comparative assessments with what was essentially the SSA's pass/fail assessment as to whether an offeror's experience was more than "trivial" or was greater than a previously unidentified "threshold of sufficiency."

> Accordingly, the agency failed to apply the solicitation's stated evaluation criteria with regard to experience.

The GAO ordered the Department to amend its evaluation criteria to ensure consistency between the evaluation criteria in the RFP and the actual evaluation criteria. It also ordered the Department to obtain revised proposals and to evaluate them against those revised criteria.

Misalignments between stated and applied evaluation criteria can undermine the integrity of a tendering process. To prevent unnecessary legal disputes, institutions should ensure that staff assigned to conduct evaluations have the appropriate training to follow proper evaluation protocols and adhere to the pre-established evaluation criteria.

20 Procurement and Legal Training

Are the core procurement staff within your purchasing and legal departments receiving the up-to-date training necessary to ensure that your organization is keeping pace with industry developments and meeting its due diligence duties?

In order to properly meet their due diligence duties, purchasing institutions should ensure that core procurement staff within their purchasing and legal departments are keeping up with the latest industry developments. The following case studies underscore how the proper tracking of case law developments can serve as part of the institution's early warning system and help proactively avoid legal entanglements and other procurement risks.

Bid Shopping Battles Hit Nova Scotia and Newfoundland

Port Hawkesbury v. Borchert Concrete Products Ltd.
Nova Scotia Court of Appeal, 2008

R. v. Crown Paving
Newfoundland and Labrador Supreme Court, 2007

In its unanimous February 2008 decision in *Port Hawkesbury (Town) v. Borchert Concrete Products Ltd.*, the Nova Scotia Court of Appeal upheld a Nova Scotia Supreme Court trial decision that found the town liable in connection with a tangled tendering process. The case, which involved the construction of bleachers for the new $15 million Port Hawkesbury Civic Centre, serves as a cautionary tale illustrating the inherent risks of over-budget bids and post-bid bargaining.

The town had initially issued a tender call for the construction of the concrete bleachers. Since the low bid was well over budget, the town took steps to reduce costs. It decided to in-source a portion of the work by acting as its own general contractor and sought third-party quotes to assist it in building the bleachers. In its October 2006 trial decision, the Nova

Scotia Supreme Court found that this conduct amounted to "bid shopping." The court found the town's conduct to be an "egregious attack on the integrity of the bidding process" that went well beyond the rights afforded under the tender call privilege clause:

> I am satisfied the process as adopted by the defendant is a sufficiently egregious attack on the integrity of the bidding system that it cannot be condoned. If the actions of the defendant are condoned in a case such as this then it would invite various abuses. A general contractor might obtain bid information and then use it to negotiate a better contract either for itself or with third parties at the expense of the bid system. The integrity of the bid system could be undermined to the extent that it would no longer be effective. The issues in this case go well beyond the rights accorded to the defendant by the privilege clause.

The court found the town liable for the low bidder's lost profits in the amount of $69,000.

The Nova Scotia Court of Appeal reduced the lost profits damages award to $45,000. However, it upheld the trial court's finding that the town had contravened the tendering rules by engaging in bid shopping. In so finding, the Court of Appeal adopted an expansive definition of "bid shopping" that included:

> conduct where a tendering authority uses the bids submitted to it as a negotiating tool, whether expressly or in a more clandestine way, before the construction contract has been awarded, with a view to obtain a better price or other contractual advantage from that particular tenderer or any of the others. What I am speaking of here is bid manipulation which can potentially encompass as vast a spectrum of objectional practices as particular circumstances may make available to a motivated and inventive owner, intent on advancing its own financial or contractual betterment outside the boundaries of the established tendering protocol.

As this definition illustrates, the courts tend to frown upon a purchaser's attempt to use the formal tendering process as a springboard to subsequent negotiations. However, not all post-bid bargains constitute bid shopping.

When it comes to considering bid shopping allegations, careful attention is often placed on the timing of events. By way of example, in its July 2007 decision in *R. v. Crown Paving*, the Newfoundland and Labrador Supreme Court found the provincial government not liable for bid shopping. In this case the government cancelled a highway maintenance tender call after the bids came in over budget. It then negotiated an extension with its existing contractor, who also happened to be the higher of the two bidders on the cancelled tender call. The court concluded that this was not bid shopping because the government had cancelled the tendering process prior to initiating the subsequent contract extension negotiations. The fact that the government was able to show that the bids were significantly over budget also helped in the defence against the bid shopping claim by showing that the cancellation was legitimate.

Like the Newfoundland case, the Port Hawkesbury case dealt with an over budget low bid. However, unlike the Newfoundland case, the town failed to cancel its tendering process prior to initiating fresh negotiations for a lower cost approach. Embarking on new negotiations while the low bidder remained bound to its bid proved to be the tipping point that resulted in a finding of bid shopping against the town. As these cases illustrate, navigating the straits between permissible post-bid negotiations and improper bid shopping can be a perilous voyage for purchasing institutions. The best strategy is to avoid over-scoping to prevent over-budget bids in the first place, or to deploy negotiated formats that permit post-bid price adjustments.

A New Frontier of Legal Intervention

Metercor Inc. v. City of Kamloops
British Columbia Supreme Court, 2011

By Rosslyn Young

In keeping with British Columbia's long history at the forefront of high-profile tendering disputes, the B.C. Supreme Court's recent decision in *Metercor Inc. v. City of Kamloops* represents a new frontier of legal risk for public institutions. Rather than applying the traditional law of tendering with its corresponding "duty of fairness" and lost profit awards, the court applied the administrative law principle of "reasonableness," struck down the city's bid process, and ordered that the city conduct a new evaluation. While the immediate impact of the decision may have only been felt in the B.C. interior, its long term impact is likely to echo coast-to-coast across the public procurement landscape for years to come.

By way of background, the city entered into a small scale pilot project with Neptune Technology Group Canada ("Neptune") to install and test new water meter technology. Following the successful pilot project, the city decided to tender the installation of water meters for all its residents. The city divided its evaluation process into two stages: the first stage consisted of a review of proponents' technical requirements and the second stage consisted of a review of proposed pricing. In order to reach the second stage of the process, proponents had to obtain a minimum threshold score on the technical criteria. This methodology, which is often referred to as the "two-envelope system," is widely used by public sector entities for complex tendering processes. Following the evaluation of proposals, the city awarded the contract to Neptune, which was the only proponent to meet the technical threshold and have its pricing evaluated.

One of the unsuccessful proponents, Metercor Inc. ("Metercor"), took issue with the city's decision to award the contract to Neptune, alleging that some of the specifications employed in the RFP gave unfair advantage to Neptune since they were the only supplier able to satisfy those criteria. Because the RFP operated outside of Contract A and no tendering contract was created, Metercor was unable to bring a claim for breach of contract. Instead it chose to bring a petition for judicial review, an administrative law remedy under which the courts can review government decisions. Based on the Supreme Court of Canada's 2008 decision in *Dunsmuir v. New Brunswick*, there are two standards of review available to the courts when reviewing government decisions: reasonableness and correctness. Further, in contrast to the lost-profit damages available under contract-based tendering law claims, the remedies available on judicial review focus on whether the government's decision is legally valid or should be reconsidered or struck down.

The judge in the City of Kamloops decision reviewed the RFP process and found that Metercor's claims of preferential treatment for Neptune were unfounded. The judge concluded that the city was free to conduct its own evaluation and that the process had been transparent for all proponents. The judge also held that the city's purchasing decisions should be given deference and should be assessed on the "reasonableness" standard, as opposed to a more intrusive "correctness" standard. However, notwithstanding the more deferential standard of review, the judge took issue with the city's use of the "two-envelope system," finding that the use of a technical threshold analysis prior to the consideration of price could produce absurd results. Accordingly, the judge ordered the matter be sent back to the city's water meter committee for reconsideration.

This decision represents a new frontier for judicial scrutiny of public sector purchasing decisions. While the court concluded that the city's decision should be afforded significant deference and that the "reasonableness inquiry is not simply the substitution of the opinion of the judge for that of the decision-maker," it nevertheless found the city's use of the two-stage procurement process unreasonable since it resulted in the city not considering the pricing of several proponents. Notwithstanding that the "two-envelope system" is widely employed by public sector entities across Canada, the court seized on the fact that it had not previously been employed by the city as part of its rationale for ordering a re-evaluation.

When compared to contract-based tendering law claims, judicial reviews are widely unexplored territory, unique to the public procurement arena. It is difficult to predict the level of deference other courts will afford procurement decisions in the future. Accordingly, to better withstand legal challenge, public sector entities should, regardless of the procurement format they employ, ensure their procurement processes are transparent and fair and that their evaluation methodologies are reasonable and defensible.

World Bank Recommends Less Centralization and More Training Procurement Assessment Report for Armenia, 2009

In its 2009 review of Armenia's procurement practices, the World Bank noted that an overly centralized procurement system can create undue dependence on senior governing bodies and undermine accountability across the public sector. The report warned that multiple overlapping audit and control functions, coupled with a lack of broader awareness and training, actually increases the risk of procurement-related corruption. To help address these issues, the World Bank called for less centralization and more procurement training across the public sector.

The World Bank's report noted that the centralization of procurement processes under Armenia's Public Procurement Law ("PPL") removed incentives on the part of health care organizations to create their own procurement capacity and undermined the sense of accountability among health care officials:

> Since the procurement process…is centralized in the SPA both for periodic (framework) and targeted tenders, the MOH and other procuring entities in the health sector has little or no incentive to develop their own procurement capacity…. [T]here is a lack of awareness of the requirements of the PPL, which has led to uneconomic and inefficient procurement. Use of poor quality technical specifications for the procurement of pharmaceuticals combined with the lowest price as the major award criterion, is resulting in procurement and distribution of poor quality and ineffective medicines. Finally, internal and external controls…are weak which adversely affects accountability of public officials involved in procurement.

> The case study recommends that procurement authority should be decentralized to the MOH and other health sector procuring entities which should develop their own capacity to conduct procurement.

As the report noted, in order to avoid the erosion of accountability and maintain incentives to improve the procurement system, public institutions need to enhance their internal capacity and implement expanded procurement training programs.

The World Bank report also warned that an overly centralized and non-transparent procurement system, particularly when coupled with multiple overlapping audit and control functions, can actually foster the conditions that lead to corruption. As the report explained, to better protect against corruption, a procurement system requires independent arm's-length oversight and an increase in the education and awareness among the public servants engaged in procurement activities:

> It is recommended that an appeals system be set up which is totally independent of the MOF, AB, SPA and government entities, operates in an environment free from a perception of conflict of interest, builds confidence from participants, and would be efficient [and] effective in providing timely and meaningful remedies. Portals are needed where allegations of fraud and corruption can be reported and followed up. Code of Ethics, asset reporting and disclosure and conflict rules should be implemented in the procurement sector. Appropriate information

systems and freedom of information regimes are needed to be vigorously implemented to promote transparency.... Tender, contract and other model documents should be developed and should include provisions which address corruption, fraud, conflict of interest and unethical behavior. The relevant provisions should also set out the consequences and sanctions for such behavior. Debarment and blacklisting system under the PPL needs to be clarified with articulation of applicable procedures and principles to ensure fairness and prevent abuse.

Capacity building and awareness-raising on fraud and corruption in procurement is also essential. This will ensure that employees engaged in procurement have practical understanding of fraud and corruption schemes. The effectiveness of audit mechanisms is questionable in most cases, undermining the intent of the PPL provisions. Furthermore, having undifferentiated, and multiple entities performing "audits", with no clear demarcation of responsibilities, might provide possibilities for multiple facilitation payments. Similarly, there is generally confusion or overlap of what is considered "audit" and what is "control", which further undermines the quality and effectiveness of audit. It is recommended that functions of various bodies be reviewed and redefined to exclude unwarranted interference in the procurement process and that pertinent laws or regulation be amended accordingly.

The government must devise a systematic and targeted policy and enforcement mechanism for detection and prevention of certain practices (e.g., collusion, pre-determined winner, anti-competitive behavior, bogus disqualifications). Among others, procurement officials should be trained to focus on red flags indicating unusual bid patterns such as: distinct bids by a systematic or uniform percentage; bids inexplicably too close or too far apart; losing bid prices are rounded or of unnatural numbers; unexplained inflated bid prices; losing bidders become subcontractors; apparent rotation of losing bidders; unusual repeated extension of bid security; delay in completing BER or contract award signing indicating efforts to negotiate corrupt terms; cartel like behavior in the market; and a general scheme of coordination of preparation of bids by designated winner.

As the Work Bank's report observes, overly centralized systems can undermine efficiency and accountability in public procurement. To better serve the public interest, public institutions need to enhance their self-governance capacities by promoting broader awareness and accountability through broader training initiatives.

A Three-Pillar Strategy for Bolstering Your Bid Evaluation Process

Bolstering the legal defensibility of a bidding process calls for a three-pillar strategy aimed at addressing the following due diligence requirements: (i) managing mandatories through the use of clear threshold eligibility requirements; (ii) integrating rated requirements so the ranking criteria are clearly disclosed before bids are submitted; and (iii) ensuring procedural integrity through transparent and fairly administered evaluation processes.

Bidders who are prejudiced by non-transparent or otherwise unfair award decisions can be entitled to lost-profit damages. Legal exposure increases with the value of the prospective contracts, and courts have found institutions liable for even minor evaluation irregularities. The greater the ambiguity in the selection process, the greater the risk of disagreement over award decisions. To meet the broadly recognized due diligence standards of transparency and defensibility required in a competitive bidding process, purchasing institutions should ensure that their solicitation documents contain full disclosure of their selection and award criteria and a clear description of their evaluation procedures.

The first pillar of legal defensibility calls for the proper management of mandatory tender compliance requirements. Under the law of tenders, a submission that does not meet a threshold eligibility requirement is legally incapable of acceptance and must be disqualified as non-compliant. Institutions that award contracts to non-compliant proponents face potential lost profit claims by competing proponents. To reduce legal exposure and promote a transparent and clear evaluation process, threshold requirements should be objective, clear and defensible. They should be structured in adherence to the following general principles:

- **Clear Identification:** Threshold eligibility requirements should be clearly identified as mandatory evaluation requirements and should be consolidated in one part of the solicitation document;

- **Essentials Only:** Threshold eligibility requirements should be used sparingly for compulsory requirements that are significant enough to actually disqualify a proponent, rather than for desirable but non-essential requirements;

- **Clear Litmus Test:** Those factors that are not genuinely capable of a pass/fail assessment (e.g. grey areas requiring judgment calls) cannot safely operate as threshold eligibility requirements, and should be either removed from the solicitation document or re-categorized as scored rated requirements;

- **Timing of Adherence:** Those requirements that relate to the post-award contract performance phase should not be included in the evaluation section. Rather, they should be organized in a separate schedule and should be incorporated by reference into the legal agreement.

- **Self-Declarations:** Proponent self-assessment and compliance declarations (i.e. where bidders "swear an oath" of compliance) are inadvisable. The purchasing entity is under a duty to disqualify non-compliant bidders and should therefore take positive steps to screen proponents for each threshold eligibility requirement. Those requirements that cannot be screened and independently verified should be removed from the evaluation. To give legal effect to the proponent's agreement to abide by those standards, a separate schedule can be incorporated by reference into the representations contained in the proposal offer form and legal agreement.

The second pillar of legal defensibility deals with rated requirements and calls for the disclosure of clear ranking and selection criteria. To meet the required standards of transparency and enhance the defensibility of a contract award decision, the purchasing institution should disclose the weightings, formulas and sub-criteria it intends to rely on to arrive at the final score and ranking for each proponent. One of the most critical aspects of the second pillar is the proper evaluation of pricing. The pricing structure needs to be properly aligned with the description of contract requirements in order to: (a) achieve a clear, transparent and defensible evaluation process; and (b) inform how billing and payment will be managed under the awarded contract. To meet these due diligence standards, the purchasing institution should ensure that its pricing structures are clear, thorough and clearly connected to the described requirements and scoring methodology. For example, a solicitation document should include:

- A clearly prescribed pricing structure that lends itself to the consistent evaluation of competing bids without requiring post-bidding clarifications or price adjustments;

- The volume estimates and scoring formulas that will be relied upon to calculate the total price;

- A clear indication of whether supplier ranking will be based on the "lowest bid" rule or on a combination of price and non-price factors; and

- In cases where ranking is based on a combination of price and non-price factors, the process by which price and non-price criteria will be individually scored and then tallied together.

The third pillar of defensible evaluations calls for a "lineal integrity" of the process. Each link in the process chain needs to be solid and based on pre-determined and pre-disclosed procedures. Transparency is paramount across the entire process. There should be no hidden evaluation stages since bidders that lose out based on hidden evaluation stages have been known to launch and win unfair process claims and be awarded lost profits.

To protect against bid litigation, purchasing institutions would be wise to employ a proactive three-pillar strategy based on pre-determined and transparent bid evaluation criteria and procedures. Due diligence training in bid-solicitation drafting will pay big dividends in avoiding unnecessary legal entanglements.

21 Organizational Awareness

Is your organization proactively avoiding procurement crises by promoting a broader organizational awareness of proper procurement practices?

While core procurement staff are the critical hub of due diligence in the procurement process, to proactively mitigate legal risks and better ensure compliance, institutions need to promote a broader organizational awareness of their procurement-related due diligence duties. The following case studies underscore the complexities inherent in the public procurement process and illustrate the risks that arise when institutions fail to maintain an effective internal governance framework and to communicate proper practices across the organization.

Government Procurement Sets Purchasing Standards

There's no question that the public sector does things differently. While some say that government should be run more like a business, there are significant factors that inform the distinctiveness of public sector purchasing. To help ensure compliance with prevailing due diligence standards, there should be a broader organizational awareness of the distinct challenges faced by the public sector in its purchasing activities. This article explains why doing deals in government can be so different from deal-making in the private sector.

Impact of Purchasing Policies

Public administration is about more than the bottom line. While value-for-money is of prime importance, money considerations must be balanced with the policy objectives of transparency and non-discriminatory purchasing.

Public institutions typically seek to achieve both value-for-money and transparency through the use of open public tendering. By harnessing free market forces in a controlled competitive environment, public tendering can provide greater control over deal details and can potentially lower costs.

Non-discriminatory purchasing requires the removal of unnecessary barriers to competition. This tends to open the field of competition to the broadest possible range of potential suppliers.

The public sector's open approach to contracting stands in marked contrast to the traditional behind-closed-doors private-sector approach. While the private-sector approach is more about maintaining existing business relationships, the public sector approach is about repeatedly wiping the slate clean and opening opportunities to new suppliers. In an era of increased shareholder scrutiny over the spending practices of publicly traded companies, large private-sector purchasers may want to consider appropriate situations for introducing similar arm's-length dealings for awarding contracts to their suppliers.

Institutional Rules

Like all large institutions, public institutions are subject to a broad body of institutional rules. These rules can have a significant impact on the legal relationship created between the purchaser and supplier and can vary considerably between and even within different levels of government. Public sector institutional rules are largely drawn from statutory sources (such as treaties, statutes, regulations, and bylaws) and from internal governance frameworks (such as directives, guidelines, policies and practices).

While they may not always be referred to in the purchasing documentation, these institutional rules can significantly impact the legal relationship between the parties during both bidding competitions and contract performance. Knowing the lay of the land is therefore critical to suppliers competing for government work. Many of these institutional rules, such as ethics policies and conflict of interest codes, can also serve as guides to prudent purchasing in the private sector.

Unwritten Rules

In addition to the broad body of institutional rules described above, public purchasers are also subject to a vast and highly developed body of case law that applies unwritten implied rules to purchasing activities. With literally hundreds of reported cases over the last quarter century covering almost every conceivable aspect of the spending cycle, Canadian case law places public institutions and their private-sector suppliers within a complex web of reciprocal legal obligations. While most of these cases deal with public purchasers, the little known fact is that many of these case law rules also apply to private-sector purchasers, thereby presenting hidden dangers to the uninitiated.

Scrutiny and Legal Risks

The law can impose serious risks and remedies when purchasers fail to follow their procurement rules and when suppliers fail to honour their legal commitments. The threat of legal sanction inevitably informs the manner in which both public purchasers and their suppliers govern themselves. Stated simply, the public purchasing terrain is fraught with legal risks. The double-barrel deterrent of high public scrutiny and high legal risk tends to foster a risk-averse culture in public purchasing circles. This can compromise innovation and flexibility. Since increased scrutiny and legal risk is also a fact of life in the private sector, private-sector purchasers may want to revisit their own purchasing practices to assess whether they could use a due diligence overhaul.

Impact on Purchasing Practices

Public institutions are facing increasing pressure to empower their procurement practices. They can build winning conditions for their purchasing professionals by implementing the following measures:

- adopting values-based ethical procurement practices;

- defining clear roles and responsibilities within their procurement cycle;

- entrenching internal checks and balances;

- establishing independent external oversight; and

- empowering innovation by creating a range of flexible procurement tools.

These measures can also assist private-sector purchasers in meeting the challenges of an increasingly complex marketplace.

Final Considerations

Just as no two suppliers are the same, no two purchasers are ever identical. There is a great deal of diversity in the thousands of public institutions that are running purchasing operations across Canada. The public sector can therefore serve as a useful case study for informing the practices of private-sector purchasers.

Calgary Auditor Calls for Update of City's Procurement Practices
Reports of the Auditor of the City of Calgary, 2009 & 2010

After conducting a procurement audit of the City of Calgary's procurement operations, the City Auditor released two reports, the first in November 2009 and the second in May 2010, which made a series of recommendations for updating the city's procurement practices and establishing clearly understood roles and responsibilities across the organization.

As the City Auditor's report noted, there was a lack of common understanding within the Calgary procurement department of procurement processes and procedures:

> We interviewed a number of purchasing agents and buyers within Supply Management to clarify processes, determine the required approvals and assess the consistency of understanding and application given the lack of documented processes and current delegated signing authorities.

> We concluded, based on these interviews, that there was a lack of a common understanding within Supply Management of processes and signing authorities. This has led to inconsistent application of the

requirement to use competitive processes, use of RFPs when a tender may have been adequate and a high level of non-competitive procurement.

The City Auditor found a lack of broader organizational awareness of the role of the procurement department. It also found that the procurement policies and procedures were outdated and incomplete:

> We found the necessary procurement framework had not been established to ensure The city's procurement activities are effectively managed, monitored and controlled.
>
> Our review found that, while some elements of effective program governance existed, it was piecemeal, dated and informal. There was no comprehensive, complete, accurate and authoritative repository available to employees with responsibilities for procurement. More specifically:
>
> - Supply Management is not currently discharging all of the responsibilities of a central purchasing authority.
>
> - Systems had not been established to effectively manage and control delegated signing authorities.
>
> - Existing procurement policies and procedures have not been updated since 1993, even though new systems were implemented in 2001 and The City underwent organizational restructuring in 2006.
>
> - Current administrative practices, which changed over time with implementation of new systems and organizational restructuring, are not aligned with existing policies and procedures.
>
> As a result, there is an increased risk of error and malfeasance from spending that circumvents established business rules and processes (i.e. dissident spending), and litigation from unfair and non-transparent processes.
>
> Without the necessary procurement framework in place, there is no real assurance that The City's procurement activities are always being conducted in a fair, open, and transparent manner, and whether procurement activities are cost effective. Furthermore, employees cannot be expected to follow established business rules and related procedures when they are out of date and not effectively communicated to all stakeholders.

In summary, the City Auditor found that while "some elements of effective program governance existed, it was piecemeal, dated and informal. There was no comprehensive, complete, accurate and authoritative repository available to employees with responsibilities for procurement." The City Auditor noted that many procedures were followed through long-standing undocumented practices:

> We reviewed The City's procurement framework and, while we found some elements of effective program governance, we noted this guidance is provided through a number of documents and sources. In some instances, several versions of the same document were in use; in other instances, reference was made to long-standing practice for which no authority could be located and which was not consistently cited. The procurement framework is not available to staff through a single, integrated, authoritative source.

The City Auditor found that, rather than acting as central stewards of the procurement system, the procurement department had drifted into a reactive approach that focused on transactional issues:

> Supply Management has acknowledged that in recent years it has mainly reacted to business unit requests and issues rather than acting proactively as a central purchasing authority. As a result, its role has primarily been limited to administering individual procurement processes. Supply Management considers business units as having the responsibility for ensuring the integrity of that procurement. This represents a significant weakening of internal controls as it concentrates incompatible functions in the hands of the business unit.

> Although the existing model may have served The City well in the past, recent literature suggests this is no longer enough to ensure value-for-money in the use of public resources.

The report recommended that the role of the procurement department be clearly defined and updated in order to increase broader organizational awareness and increase the procurement department's traction as a strategic corporate undertaking:

> In essence, The City should be managing its procurement activities as a strategic corporate activity. The procurement framework should be reviewed and updated to address procurement from a corporate perspective. Specifically, the framework should:
>
> - Define the role and responsibilities of Supply Management as the central purchasing authority. The model should articulate not only

the service level and performance standards to be provided but also identify what the central authority will not do;

- Clearly assign the decision rights and responsibilities not assigned to the central authority to other stakeholders within The City;

- Establish service levels to substantiate resource requirements and performance indicators to demonstrate that value-for-money is being achieved through strategic procurement; and

- Ensure that the procurement framework is readily available to all employees through the Administration Policy Library.

To achieve this end, the City Auditor recommended that the city's Chief Financial Officer implement "a comprehensive procurement framework." The Calgary case study serves as a useful reminder of the need to approach procurement as a strategic corporate activity that requires proper coordination and integration across the entire institution.

Chapter 8:
INNOVATION

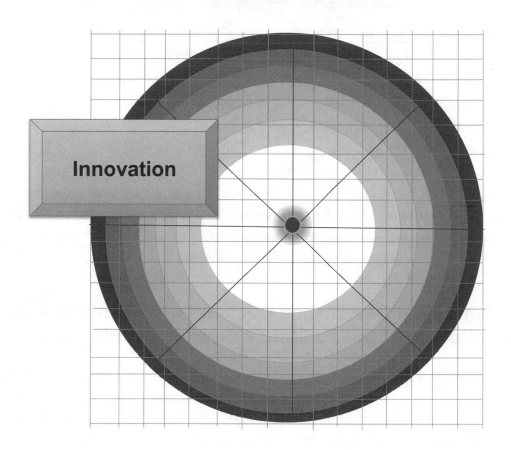

Introduction

Purchasing institutions need to develop innovative strategies to effectively meet their due diligence duties. The challenges of modern procurement call for a migration from a transaction-related focus to the implementation of a bigger-picture perspective that integrates the procurement function into broader institutional governance. It also calls for the development of strategies to proactively interface with the market and effectively leverage technological innovation.

The following case studies highlight the perils of dysfunctional governance and the escalating risks created when the procurement function lacks traction at senior levels within the institution. The case studies also focus on the need to maintain external marketplace traction by properly dealing with vendor interaction before and after the bidding process and by protecting the institution from anti-competitive practices. Finally, this chapter provides a glimpse into the technological innovations that are set to transform and accelerate the tendering cycle in the years to come.

22) Organizational Traction

Does your organization's procurement function have traction on senior management's agenda?

Procurement does not function in isolation from the broader institutional governance of the organization. To be effective, the procurement operation needs to be supported at the senior levels. Procurement must be seen as more than a cost-cutting exercise or sourcing stream. It must be integrated into the institution's overall strategic objectives through a proper internal governance roadmap. The following case studies illustrate the risks that arise when senior officials fail to be part of the solution and instead contribute to the institution's procurement problems.

How Dysfunctional Governance Caused the eHealth Scandal
Special Report of the Auditor General of Ontario, 2009

The Ontario government's $1 billion eHealth scandal serves as a useful case study into the root causes of systemic mismanagement in government procurement. While much of the media attention focused on specific transactional irregularities, including the notable amount of inappropriate sole-sourcing of consulting contracts, the 2009 Special Report of the Auditor General of Ontario noted a number of flaws in institutional governance that contributed to the mismanagement of public resources. These flaws should serve as early warning signs for other institutions that want to avoid similar spending scandals.

As the Auditor General aptly observed, "it has been said that shared accountability means no accountability." It was within this context of "shared accountability" that the originating seeds of the eHealth scandal were sown. As the Auditor General noted, responsibility for the Ontario government's overall electronic health records initiative was divided between the Ministry of Health's eHealth's Program Branch and the Smart Systems for Health Agency ("SSHA"). While SSHA was responsible for acquiring the technological infrastructure for the government's health records information highway, the Ministry's eHealth Branch retained responsibility for the overall stewardship and planning of the government initiative. As the Auditor General's report found, the shared accountability structure resulted in dysfunction and in-fighting between the different government bodies:

> By all accounts, it was not a true partnership and was marred by a
> lack of collegiality and confusion over each party's respective roles and

responsibilities. The Ministry and SSHA blamed each other for many of the failures and delays in system implementation. A telling example of how the Ministry was not working hand in hand with SSHA involves key SSHA employees leaving SSHA to work for the Ministry. Former SSHA executives advised us that they often faced operational problems as a result of employees moving to the Ministry to take consulting contract positions at significantly higher compensation levels.

The Auditor General also found that the creation of this inherently flawed governance structure, together with delays in recognizing the ongoing dysfunction within the program, significantly contributed to the eHealth problems:

> The decision to have two entities at arm's length from each other deliver the EHR solution — SSHA responsible for the underlying infrastructure and the Ministry's eHealth Program Branch responsible for the overall EHR strategy and the related applications — was, in our opinion, inherently problematic. The success of this plan depended on both parties having a cohesive and co-operative working relationship. This was never the case. There was little co-ordination or co-operation between SSHA and the Ministry's eHealth Program Branch. We were informed by numerous parties on both sides that the relationship was marred by mutual mistrust and confusion over roles and responsibilities. The dysfunctional relationship between the two entities and the evident discontent of the medical community should have "raised the red flag" sooner that something needed to be done.

The government eventually responded by spinning off the Ministry's eHealth Branch and merging it with SSHA to form the new eHealth Ontario agency. However, as the Auditor General observed, the new eHealth Ontario agency failed to follow proper procurement practices as urgency became the justification for parting company with due process:

> To sum up, too many procurements at the eHealth Ontario agency and, to a lesser extent, at the Ministry's eHealth Program Branch and at SSHA were the product of rushed decision-making; the acceptance of expediency over thoroughness; the routine defence that the work was of an emergency nature and therefore justified the bypassing of normal procurement controls; procedural shortcuts; poor, absent, or contradictory documentation; and, of particular concern, the concentration of decision-making power in the hands of a few individuals with no compensating controls to ensure their decisions were appropriate. Sound and reasonable policies were in place to ensure that all suppliers could fairly compete for government business and that tax dollars would be prudently spent, but all too often the rules were not followed.

The Auditor General found that these governance problems were compounded by the failure of the eHealth board to rein in a new CEO who "wielded considerable power to make unilateral decisions and essentially ignored procurement policies." According to the report:

- The board did not adequately oversee the CEO's actions and decisions in this area. It appears to have accepted the CEO's assertion that government and agency procurement policies were being followed, without getting sufficient details as to what that meant. For example, it never asked whether any contracts were sole-sourced and, if so, why, and what the value of such contracts was.

- At the same time that a great deal of power was concentrated in the CEO's hands, the agency was faced with the challenge of accelerating progress on the EHR initiative, considered by many to have suffered when it was managed by SSHA and the Ministry's eHealth Program Branch. It was during this period, from October 2008 to June 2009, that millions were paid to consultants who had not been competitively procured. In other words, it was during this time of transition that the CEO and her executive management overrode the normal procurement and contract management controls that SSHA's procurement department had in place. Our discussions with the CEO indicated that urgency and the implied authority she thought she had been given justified and warranted this.

- The Chair told us that the Premier had personally asked him to chair the eHealth Ontario agency. He further informed us that he had told the Premier that his acceptance of the position was largely conditional on his being able to choose the CEO and the agency having the autonomy to act without significant government interference. We were advised that the Premier met with the Chair's choice for the new CEO to impress upon her the importance of her upcoming work. Given that it had no input into the appointment of the CEO, and understanding that the Chair had personally chosen the CEO with the support of the Premier, the board may have had a perception that its oversight role with respect to the CEO was more limited than it would be in normal circumstances.

The Auditor General also cited the board's handling of the new CEO's mid-year bonus payment as further evidence of the board's failure to adequately perform its oversight function due to the spectre of senior government involvement in the decision-making process:

The board's approval of a performance bonus for the CEO midway through her first year on the job is an example of the extent to which the board may have felt it had little power to oversee matters relating to the CEO or question how she should be treated. There are two issues with respect to this bonus — the amount paid and the fact that it was awarded after only four months on the job.

The amount of the bonus paid to the CEO was $114,000, which was 30% of her salary. The maximum bonus rate under eHealth Ontario policy was 15%. However, the CEO had negotiated her 30% maximum bonus as one of the conditions of accepting the job, and it was included as part of her employment contract, approved by the Minister and authorized by an Order-in-Council. Although the bonus was significantly higher than what government Deputy Ministers can receive, we recognize that the government has to have some latitude with respect to executive compensation. The board therefore had no say with respect to the bonus available. It did have a responsibility, however, to assess whether the CEO's performance justified the full 30% and whether the full bonus was warranted only four months into the job.

Under the shadow of government, the board failed to engage in its oversight role. The bonus was approved and the procurement transgressions continued until the public scandal resulted in the dismissal of the several senior officials including the CEO and the Minister of Health.

As the Auditor General's report illustrates, systemic mismanagement created the perfect storm for the eHealth spending scandal. An inherently flawed governance structure based on blurred notions of "shared accountability," coupled with the government's delay in responding to the clear warning signs of bureaucratic dysfunction, caused the high-profile government initiative to run badly behind schedule. The dire situation was compounded by the midstream amalgamation of two dysfunctional government entities into a single agency. That new agency was born in the shadow of a looming crisis caused by ongoing delays in the highly-complex, high-cost initiative. This lethal mix of urgency, complexity and confusion was exacerbated by a board that failed to provide proper oversight as a newly appointed CEO made up for lost time by taking liberties with existing procurement protocols. Having exposed a profound lack of proper institutional governance, the eHealth scandal serves as a cautionary tale for all senior decision-makers who want to avoid similar outcomes within their own institutions.

Post-eHealth Audit Uncovers More Health Sector Spending Abuses
Special Report of the Auditor General of Ontario, 2010

With Ontario tax payers still reeling over the Ontario government's $1 billion eHealth spending scandal, the provincial Auditor General released another report that revealed further procurement improprieties in the health sector. Rather than being contained within a single government agency, the October 2010 *Special Report on Consulting Use in Selected Health Organizations* confirmed widespread spending irregularities within hospitals. The report also found procurement infractions within the Local Health Integration Networks that, ironically, were created to provide oversight and control over health care system spending. As with the prior eHealth report, the Auditor General's 2010 report cited failures in institutional governance as the key contributors to the unhealthy procurement practices.

While they may have initially been created to solve some of the administrative problems faced by Ontario's complex and increasingly expensive health sector, the Auditor General report uncovered significant gaps in the accountability protocols of the Local Health Integration Networks. As the Auditor General stated:

> Local Health Integration Networks (LHINs) are required by their Memorandum of Understanding with the Ministry to comply with certain government directives, policies, and guidelines, including the Management Board of Cabinet's Procurement Directive. For the 2007/08 to 2009/10 fiscal years, the three LHINs we visited had annual expenditures on consultants ranging from $224,000 to $1.4 million per year.

> We concluded that all three LHINs we selected had inadequate processes and practices for most of the period we examined for ensuring that consulting services were planned for, acquired, and managed in accordance with the requirements of the Directive. We recognize that LHINs were established only four years ago and have since been required to quickly implement their key systems and procedures. However, the extent of non-compliance with the mandatory requirements in the Directive that we found was significant. We did note some improvement with recent contracts we sampled following the introduction of the updated Procurement Directive in July 2009....

> In addition, in April 2010, the Ontario Internal Audit Division reported the results of its audit of three other LHINs' compliance with the Directive between April 2008 and August 2009. The internal auditors identified weak control over consulting-services contracts, noted the absence of business cases, found contracts that were single-sourced with insufficient documentation or justification, noted a lack of signed contracts and proper approvals, found consecutive and follow-on engagements that were awarded without competition, and identified consultants that had not been selected from the Ministry's mandatory vendor-of-record listing. The internal auditors informed us that they were planning to review the remaining 11 LHINs by the end of the 2013/14 fiscal year.

As the report indicates, the LHINs appeared to have been rushed into operation without first having the appropriate governance structures put in place to guard against improper procurement practices. The Auditor General determined that "the LHINs did not meet the Directive's requirements most of the time. For example, at least 75% of the single-sourced contracts did not meet the specific exemptions allowed for in the Directive, and they lacked formal documentation and/or prior approval." This represents a far cry from the original purpose of the LHINS, which was to solve existing problems in the health sector, rather than to add to them.

The Auditor General noted that Ontario's hospitals were also not immune from the dependency on sole-sourced consulting contracts. In fact, the report found a prevalence of un-competed and poorly documented consulting contracts across the reviewed hospitals:

> Each hospital we visited had policies requiring competitive procurement practices that met the requirements of interprovincial and national trade agreements. However, most policies lacked specific requirements designed to promote the cost-effective use of consultants. For instance, policies did not require assignments to be well defined or properly justified before consultants were engaged; nor did they require adequate contractual arrangements with fixed ceiling prices, payments tied to specified deliverables, or proper management of consultant performance. Most of the policies we reviewed also lacked the requirement to document and retain the records of procurement decisions.

> Most hospitals had a policy in place to avoid any real or perceived conflict of interest when acquiring consultants, although further guidance was typically not provided to managers on how to administer a conflict-of-interest declaration. Generally, the hospitals we visited did not ensure that conflict-of-interest declarations were obtained from the consultants they engaged. Only a few of the hospitals we visited had established standardized document templates for such declarations from consultants and they were not consistently used.

The report also documented a weak oversight function, noting that "the hospitals had no policies or processes that required senior management to report to the board of directors on their use of consultants, and most boards were not aware of hospitals' procurement practices, since their approvals were required only for total operating and capital budgets on a departmental basis." This lack of transparency allowed the sole-sourcing to persist without effective checks and balances.

As with the eHealth report, the Auditor General's review of health sector consulting revealed systemic deficiencies caused by a lack of proper institutional governance. This report serves as another useful case study for institutions interested in taking a preventative approach to avoiding spending improprieties through the proactive implementation of sound governance structures.

Legislative Hearings on the
Broader Public Sector Accountability Act

Submission to the Standing Committee on Social Policy regarding Ontario Bill 122 (An Act to increase the financial accountability of organizations in the broader public sector)

Queen's Park
November 22, 2010

The following deputation was presented by Paul Emanuelli in the Ontario Legislature on November 22, 2010 to the Standing Committee on Social Policy as part of the legislative consultation process prior to the third and final reading of the proposed law.

I would like to thank the committee for the opportunity to speak today. I have had the benefit of reviewing the Office of the Auditor General of Ontario's October 2010 *Special Report on Consultant Use in Selected Health Organizations* and its findings and recommendations relating to health sector procurement in Ontario. I have also had the benefit of reviewing the text of Bill 122. I am here to speak in support of the Honourable Minister's attempt to enhance the probity and transparency of government procurement in Ontario and to offer some suggestions regarding the implementation of good governance measures for public procurement. My comments will focus on two main points:

1. First of all, we need to be more proactive in dealing with compliance with our public procurement rules. There are far too many examples where tendering infractions and the systemic mismanagement of public funds are only discovered through costly litigation or through after-the-fact audits. We need a clearer operating system that provides proactive guidance to public institutions through the creation of uniform rules.

2. Secondly, there are many international examples we can draw from to help inform our good governance standards to help ensure that we keep pace with other jurisdictions.

1. The Need to Be Proactive With Clear Uniform Rules

We are falling behind in Canada when it comes to establishing clear and uniform public procurement rules. I have circulated copies of *The Laws of Precision Drafting*: *A Handbook for Tenders and RFPs*. In this handbook I attempt to give guidance to procurement professionals on how to properly draft their procurement documents, taking into account case law, policy and statutory developments across a broad range of Commonwealth countries. This project evolved from my main text, *Government Procurement*, which consolidates over a quarter century of Canadian case law. After having completed these two projects I can draw two interrelated conclusions:

1. First of all, when it comes to public procurement, Canada appears to be the most litigious jurisdiction in the English speaking world. Our courts have occupied the field faster and with greater penetration than any other Commonwealth country. That evolving jurisprudence has created a risky and often unpredictable operating system for public procurement. I offer the February 24, 2010, Journal of Commerce article entitled "Supreme Court's Tercon ruling may force new approach to contracts" as just one recent example of the legal uncertainty inherent in our current tendering system.

2. Secondly, relative to other Commonwealth countries, we do not appear to be responding to our past mistakes by implementing effective and consistent remediation measures. We are falling behind the UK, Australia and Africa. For the most part, our procurement operating system lacks a statutory spine. Public institutions are left to their own devices, forced to interpret complex and often contradictory case law rulings and navigate a murky patchwork of treaties, directives and guidelines to develop and implement their own operating rules.

The absence of a clear and uniform operating system is one of the primary reasons why we have so much litigation and why we have so many after-the-fact audit findings. We need to be better at learning from past mistakes and taking a proactive approach to the creation of good governance measures.

2. Drawing from International Examples to Address the Auditor General's Findings

Rather than re-inventing the wheel, if we want to address the issues raised in the Auditor General's Special Report, I suggest that we consider the wealth of examples available from other jurisdictions that have experienced similar challenges. Drawing from the *Precision Drafting* handbook, I will offer you four examples of how other jurisdictions are dealing with the issues raised by our Auditor General:

1. The Auditor General's Special Report speaks to instances in which: (a) there was a lack of advanced planning and approvals with respect to certain contracts; (b) there was a lack of transparency with respect to both contractual objectives and evaluation criteria; (c) higher-priced consultants were given preferred treatment in the procurement process; and (d) contracts exceeded the original cost estimate or were extended without competition. To address similar issues, Ghana's *Public Procurement Act 2003* compels advanced planning by making it a statutory requirement to disclose contact requirements and contract evaluation criteria, including weightings, in public tenders. To draw on another example, the European Parliament's Procurement Directives, along with the UK Regulations which are based on those Directives, create clear statutory rules requiring the disclosure of contract award criteria, including the disclosure of any non-price factors that will inform contract awards. These examples can help inform the creation of clear standardized rules for public procurement in Ontario to help guard

against unclear award criteria, unclear contract requirements and the cost overruns that often result from that lack of initial clarity.

2.   The Auditor General's Special Report speaks to some procurement processes where suppliers were provided with insufficient time to respond to the tender call. Australia's *Commonwealth Procurement Guidelines 2008* and the European Parliament's Procurement Directives both allow for tighter posting timeframes where institutions have provided pre-notice of intended procurements as part of their annual procurement plans. These rules create a clear protocol to help take pressure off the day-to-day tendering cycle by entrenching proactive planning into the procurement process.

3.   Bill 122 speaks to lobbying *by* public institutions. However, as the Gomery and Bellamy reports have detailed, when it comes to government procurement, we have significant issues arising from the lobbying *of* public institutions. The Auditor General's Special Report notes a number of instances where Local Health Integration Networks failed to obtain conflict of interest declarations from their consultants. This deficiency requires clear remediation to help guard against procurement improprieties. Kenya's *Public Procurement and Disposal Act 2005* establishes clear rules against inappropriate conduct within the supplier community, including a ban from government contracts for up to five years for those suppliers who have breached the statute. We should consider implementing similar measures so that our conflict of interest protocols are supported with meaningful sanctions against suppliers who contravene our ethics rules.

4.   The Auditor General's Special Report speaks to the number of consulting contracts that are awarded without competition, particularly in the hospital sector. The United Nations *Model Law on Procurement of Goods, Construction and Services* provides a broad range of recommendations regarding the use of various procurement formats, including prequalification protocols, that can help alleviate the urgency that leads to many non-competed contracts. Malawi's *Public Procurement Act 2003* also provides clear rules regarding the assessment of a contractor's qualifications and serves as an example of the types of factors that can be standardized to help provide guidance to public institutions in the prequalifying of suppliers.

In Summary

In summary, I would like to conclude by reiterating our need to proactively establish clear and uniform good governance rules. We have many international best practices to draw from in the creation of a clear operating system for our government procurement operations.

Drummond Says Cut Red Tape and Pool Purchasing To Save Costs

In February 2012, Don Drummond, the Chair of the Commission on the Reform of Ontario's Public Services, released a cost-cutting report entitled *Public Service for Ontarians: A Path to*

Sustainability and Excellence (the "Drummond Report"). The report makes recommendations on how to balance the provincial budget, maintain a sustainable fiscal environment for government operations and achieve value-for-money. To address Ontario's escalating fiscal crisis, the Drummond Report recommends cutting procurement-related bureaucratic red tape and achieving better value-for-money by removing duplication and consolidating public sector purchasing.

With respect to red tape in procurement, the Drummond Report officially recognizes what procurement professionals have known for years: red tape is paralyzing the purchasing process. The system needs to be recalibrated to achieve better efficiency and properly serve the public interest. As the report states, accountability needs to be balanced against efficiency in order to achieve the parallel objectives of transparency and value-for-money:

Balance the Requirements of Accountability and Efficiency for Government Operations

Accountability is an essential aspect of government operations, but we often treat that goal as an absolute good. Taxpayers expect excellent public-sector management as well as open and transparent procurement practices. However, an exclusive focus on rigorous financial reporting and compliance as the measure of successful management requires significant investments of time, energy and resources. At some point, this investment is subject to diminishing returns.

While acknowledging the importance of transparency and prudent use of taxpayers' money, the implicit costs of accountability measures should be reviewed as well. The Commission has found that little consideration has been given to the appropriate balance between containing risk and the effort and expense diverted to compliance with rules and regulations. The impact of inefficient rules in this regard go well beyond the OPS, and extend throughout the BPS to include hospitals, post-secondary education, elementary and secondary schools, and municipalities. The added cost to the government — and thus by extension to the public, private and non-profit sectors in ensuring compliance — should be considered in gauging the appropriate response to the risk of waste or fraud in operations.

The government should shift to measuring outcomes rather than inputs and process, and should take a risk-based approach to accountability. In trying to balance the goals of accountability and efficiency, the government may well find that there are opportunities both to streamline administration and ensure accountability in the OPS, BPS, private sector and non-profit sector.

Recommendation 16-11: The government should ask the Ontario Auditor General to help find an appropriate balance between ensuring accountability and continuing oversight of compliance with rules and regulations.

These recommendations serve as useful reminders to all public institutions of the need to properly tailor their oversight functions so that they do not place a disproportionate burden on the public purchasing process and undermine the government operations that rely on timely and efficient procurement.

With respect to unnecessary duplication, the Drummond Report recommends an expansion of procurement shared services, stating that the consolidations at the Ontario provincial level within the Ontario Public Sector ("OPS") should be expanded to the Broader Public sector ("BPS") with the consolidation of purchasing within school boards and the health sector:

Back Office Consolidation into Broader Public Sector

In a number of areas, efficiencies already introduced in the OPS should be extended to the BPS. Among these:

- Shared services for back-office functions (e.g., payroll, financial transactions, procurement, collections and insurance) and common administrative services (e.g., printing, mail, translations and asset management) can save money;

- The consolidation of I&IT services in the OPS saved $100 million per year; savings would be greater if this were pushed out to the BPS;

- A standardized framework would enable the BPS to leverage its immense purchasing power through collaborative purchasing, standardization of products and processes, and back-office consolidation; and

- Centralized maintenance practices already established in the OPS should be extended to the BPS.

The Drummond report details how considerable efficiencies could be obtained by increasing procurement consolidation efforts within the health sector:

Recommendation 5-95: Centralize all back-office functions such as information technology, human resources, finance and procurement across the health system. There is redundancy and duplication in the current system design, with hundreds of independent organizations having some level of administrative/corporate structure and backoffice models that result in higher-than-necessary administrative costs. These structures could build on some of the procurement mechanisms in place now (e.g., Plexxus, 3SO, Shared Services West) but need to go further and move forward faster to create stronger single enterprise solutions for all central back-office functions. They should be integrated at a LHIN level (and possibly across all LHINs) to reduce the percentage of overall spending on these services to benchmark levels that have been achieved in other provinces. Assuming a savings benchmark of six to eight per cent of total spending on administration costs, the potential savings in Ontario could be up to $1 billion. In addition, leveraging purchasing power, standardizing procurement practices and managing inventory more effectively would generate savings through lower costs for goods and services purchased.

In addition to recommending health sector consolidation, the report notes that school boards "should also continue to seek out opportunities to foster procurement efficiencies through their expanded buying power." According to the report, this could lead to further cost savings and procurement efficiencies:

School boards should continue to seek opportunities to collaborate with each other and with other parts of the BPS to foster procurement efficiencies. As significant purchasers of similar supplies, equipment and services, school boards can work together to make smart purchasing decisions through their expanded buying power. Important steps have already been taken in this respect through the establishment of the Ontario Education Collaborative Marketplace (OECM), a not-for-profit procurement organization. In consultation with the education and postsecondary sectors, OECM competitively procures common contracts on behalf of school boards, colleges and universities. Additionally, regional buying groups and transportation consortia have encouraged prudent joint procurements.

School boards and other BPS bodies, such as post-secondary institutions, should continue to find ways to create savings and efficiencies through collaborative procurement. Future measures could include a co-ordinated procurement policy framework, strategic sourcing, contract management and product/process standardization. Boards should be required to take advantage of existing organizations such as the OECM and regional buying groups.

Given the increasing fiscal pressures faced within the Ontario public sector, the Drummond Report recommendations are likely to have a significant impact on future provincial procurement practices. The recommendations also serve as useful considerations for other jurisdictions that are seeking to strike the right balance between accountability and efficiency in their own procurement systems. However, as the following case study illustrates, such consolidation efforts must be carefully managed.

Ontario Buys More Bureaucracy in BPS "Cost Saving" Initiative
Annual Report of the Auditor General of Ontario, 2009

In its 2009 annual report, the Ontario Auditor General determined that OntarioBuys, a Ministry of Finance initiative launched to help the broader public sector ("BPS") save money through the consolidation of procurement functions, was unable to substantiate its claimed savings. As the report noted, OntarioBuys failed to properly administer the $148 million in funding it provided to the BPS as part of the "cost saving" exercise. The Auditor General found "three operational areas at OntarioBuys where improvements are required — the review of business cases submitted for funding approval, the monitoring of funded projects for achievement of contract deliverables, and competitive procurement processes."

The Auditor General found that OntarioBuys failed to establish proper business cases to realistically identify potential savings prior to approving funding for the creation of shared services organizations ("SSOs") and that it could not substantiate the cost savings that its programs had allegedly generated. By way of example, the report noted that:

> The underlying business case for the education-sector SSO — the largest SSO funded — projected that its collaborative purchasing and e-Marketplace initiatives would yield benefits/savings of $669 million over five years. This included total savings to group members of $294 million through their use of the e-Marketplace and $375 million from group purchasing. However, our review of the business case, file documentation, and external consultants' reports found that the estimated savings were often based on unreasonable assumptions....

> Similarly, with respect to the $61 million spent on projects for improving supply-chain and back-office processes, evidence was lacking that projected costs and savings were appropriately assessed. For example, one project's projected savings were based on a hospital's extrapolating the results from its emergency unit to the entire hospital without any evidence to support the reasonableness of such a projection. For another project, the estimated costs submitted for funding were revised three times over a four-month period, from $455,000 to over $1 million. The amount of OntarioBuys funding was based on a percentage of estimated costs. However, we found no documentation on file to show that either the cost revisions or the projected savings had been properly assessed.

Of the $45 million in OntarioBuys savings announced in the Ontario Budget, the Auditor General noted that "other than for one project with savings of $20 million, the reported savings provided to us were questionable."

With respect to the $20 million in health-sector savings that could be substantiated, the Auditor General's report noted how those funds, which were originally slated for redistribution into front-line health services, were actually redirected to finance a back-office information technology project for a health-sector shared services operation:

> The government announced in its March 2009 Budget that OntarioBuys had helped BPS entities redirect $45 million in savings toward front-line services. We found, however, that almost $20 million of this reported amount was not redistributed to hospitals to provide front-line services but rather was retained by the SSO that generated the savings to develop information technology for its back-office processes. The balance of the reported savings came from a number of projects; however, OntarioBuys did not verify these savings nor was it able to demonstrate that they had actually been invested in front-line services.

The Auditor General's report also detailed deficiencies in the monitoring of funded projects, finding that OntarioBuys never established proper monitoring protocols prior to launching its "cost-saving" initiatives:

> Once projects were approved and funds provided, OntarioBuys did not have program-specific guidelines for consistent and effective monitoring of their progress. There were no program-specific guidelines for conducting site visits, documenting work performed, verifying deliverables prior to the release of final payments, and closing files for completed projects. We noted that some files contained detailed review notes with good supporting documentation to verify the reported project status. However, many others did not. OntarioBuys indicated that it had hired more staff in 2008/09 to strengthen the monitoring processes. As a result of the insufficient number of staff devoted to monitoring in the earlier years and the lack of program-specific guidelines, projects — especially those approved before 2008 — were not consistently and effectively monitored.

Finally, the Auditor General's report documented how OntarioBuys had spent $45 million on consulting contracts and how, when audited, 40 percent of those consulting contracts failed to comply with competitive procurement requirements. As this case study illustrates, allocating millions of dollars in senior level government funding to the retention of external consultants and the creation of new government bureaucracies offers little assurance of downstream savings in procurement consolidation exercises. Realizing a return on such investments requires that proper project governance frameworks be put in place before the high-cost initiatives are launched. Those institutions that buy into the fallacy that such undertakings can be deployed in the absence of proper planning do so at their peril.

Does your organization have effective market interface and monitoring policies and processes in place to deal with public access requests, debriefings and bid disputes, and is it protecting itself against bid rigging and improper lobbying?

To obtain proper marketplace traction, a purchasing operation needs to think beyond the specific transaction and build protocols that effectively deal with the pre- and post-bidding stages of the procurement process. The following case studies focus on the need to properly manage confidential bidder information and balance that against the disclosure duties that can be created through debriefings, bid protests and supplier lawsuits. They also underscore the importance of establishing early warning systems to protect against anti-competitive supplier practices.

Alberta Liable for Using Proprietary Bidder Information

Pharand Ski Corp. v. Alberta
Alberta Court of Queen's Bench, 1991

When conducting an open tendering process, institutions must balance the need to protect a bidder's confidential information with the need to ensure transparency of the tendering process. Common law confidentiality duties can apply during a tendering process and create obligations with respect to the proper protection of a supplier's information.

For example, in its decision in *Pharand Ski Corp. v. Alberta*, the Alberta Court of Queen's Bench found the government liable for breaching the common law confidentiality duties it owed the plaintiff supplier who had provided confidential business information during a tendering process. This case dealt with a Government of Alberta initiative to build an alpine ski event site for the 1988 Calgary Winter Olympics. Alberta used information contained in the plaintiff's submissions but did not award a contract to the plaintiff. The court awarded the plaintiff $1.3 million in damages due to Alberta's breach of the confidentiality duties it owed to the plaintiff.

The complex background facts in this decision involved a process with multiple proposal calls and mid-stream changes in direction. As the court noted, when it became apparent to the plaintiff that it would not be awarded a government contract, it sought compensation for the use of its confidential information:

Following the rejection of the Plaintiff's proposal, negotiations took place between the Plaintiff and the Defendant with respect to participating in the Government project. The Plaintiff demanded compensation for its confidential information by letter dated May 30th, 1983. The Defendant refused to consider any compensation for the information. This law suit naturally followed.

The court concluded that Alberta had breached the common law duty of confidence it owed to the plaintiff. The court was critical of the manner in which Alberta had conducted its tender call process:

A careful examination of the whole proposals call system shows it was badly flawed and obviously prepared without sound legal advice. It was designed to select a developer with whom the Province would negotiate and conclude a mutually acceptable plan of development of a specific site or sites and the implementation of that plan. But it was unrealistic and failed to provide a proper business base to which a proponent could respond.

This excerpt reflects the importance of conducting a well-organized procurement process, where the governing rules, including the rules pertaining to the protection of confidential bidder information, are expressly and clearly set out in the tender call documents and are honoured during that process.

The court set out the following relevant principles for quantifying damages for breach of confidence:

It now appears that the appropriate measure of damages is the sum which puts the confider in the same position "as he would have been if he had not sustained the wrong." Depending on the position of the particular plaintiff, that loss may be calculated in a number of different ways. The appropriate measure may be: the confider's lost profits; the value of a consultant's fee; the market value of information, as between a willing buyer and willing seller; the development costs incurred in acquiring the information; the capitalization of an appropriate royalty; the depreciation in the value of the information in consequence of the breach of confidence.

The court applied these principles to the particular situation and, given the amount of effort and information provided to Alberta by the plaintiff during the course of the tendering process, awarded $1.3 million, a figure that represented the value of the information and the direct expenses incurred by the plaintiff over the course of the process. As this case illustrates, purchasers should be careful with how they treat the information contained in a supplier's bid.

Debriefing Duties Trigger a Legal Tidal Wave

Ecosfera Inc. v. Canada
Canadian International Trade Tribunal, 2007

In its determination in *Ecosfera Inc. v. Canada (Department of the Environment)*, the Canadian International Trade Tribunal found that the federal government's debriefing duties are far broader than had previously been assumed. By expanding the scope of debriefing duties, the Tribunal launched a legal tidal wave at the federal government. Those institutions outside the federal government that also conduct debriefings may want to brace themselves against the potential ripple effect.

It has long been understood that the focus of bidder debriefings should be forward-looking to help unsuccessful bidders understand how they can improve their future submissions. However, the Tribunal found in *Ecosfera* that these debriefings should also be backward-looking and should provide losing bidders with information that explains why they lost the recent bidding process. While on the surface this may appear to be a minor nuance, in practice this could turn the tide heavily against the government.

Debriefings have always had the inherent risk of becoming fishing expeditions used by losing bidders to contest the outcome of a bidding process or to obtain valuable information about their competitors. Given these inherent risks, an uneasy balance has been struck. While purchasers often discuss the strengths and weaknesses of the supplier's unsuccessful submission, they tend to steer clear of making any comparisons to the winning bidder for fear of disclosing the winning bidder's confidential business information. Given the litigious climate in public tendering, purchasers also try to avoid providing any information that could be used to legally challenge their evaluation process. However, the Tribunal's determination makes it much harder to maintain these litigation barriers.

In *Ecosfera Inc.* the complainant argued that the government failed to provide a sufficient explanation of the evaluation process or sufficient information about the winning tender. The Tribunal agreed, finding that the government had interpreted its debriefing duties too narrowly and that those duties extended beyond merely assisting a bidder in preparing for future bids:

> Contrary to EC's suggestion, the requirement set out in Article 1015(6) (b) of *NAFTA* is intended to do much more than simply allow unsuccessful bidders to understand how they can better respond to future procurement opportunities.... While the Tribunal has stated in the past that the purpose of Article 1015(6)(b) of *NAFTA* is to allow unsuccessful bidders to understand how they can better respond to future procurement opportunities, it is unlikely that the latter meant for the provision to be applied so narrowly.

The Tribunal acknowledged the balancing act that must be struck between promoting the transparency of the process and protecting the confidential business information of competing bidders. However, it found that the legal duty to protect confidential information could not be used as a reason to completely deny a losing bidder an explanation of why it lost the opportunity. The Tribunal then made the following general statements about the government's debriefing duties:

> [T]he information should focus on the considerations of those who were involved in making the decision that resulted in the proposal of the unsuccessful bidder not being selected. This includes, obviously, the communication of the reasons why the proposal was not selected, the communication of the justification for taking those reasons into account and the approach used to examine them. In fact, the entity concerned ought to provide any information that could reasonably be expected to reveal the reasons for which the proposal was not selected.

Since it is often impossible to explain why one tender was not selected without discussing the relative merits of the winning tender, this determination brings the government far closer to the danger zone of having to disclose information that could arguably be the confidential and proprietary information of competing bidders. The clear dividing wall that restricted debriefing disclosures to information about the supplier's own proposal is eroding. In its place is an ambiguous new reality that could place purchasers in a legal whirlpool of conflicting disclosure and confidentiality duties.

This broadly stated obligation to provide "any information" that could "reveal the reasons for which the proposal was not selected" can only serve to strengthen the hands of disgruntled bidders who are fishing for information about their competitors or are looking for information that could help fuel their next legal challenge against the government. While in principle transparency is a good thing, when taken to extremes it only serves to put inordinate administrative burdens on our already strained public purchasing processes. While this decision technically only applies to the federal government, it serves as a wake up call to all public institutions to revisit their debriefing practices and test the strength of their litigation breakwaters.

Access Laws Compel Disclosure of Bid Prices

Ontario v. Ontario
Ontario Superior Court of Justice, 2004

In public sector procurement, common law confidentiality duties are typically supplemented by a number of statutory duties that govern both the protection of bidder information and public access to that information.

For example, in its decision in *Ontario (Ministry of Transportation) v. Ontario (Information and Privacy Commissioner)*, the Ontario Superior Court of Justice considered a public access request for information collected by a government institution in the course of a tendering process. The case involved information collected by the Ministry of Transportation pursuant to a tender call for engineering consulting services for the design and management of highway construction projects. The Ministry received a public access request pursuant to Ontario's *Freedom of Information and Protection of Privacy Act* for the RFP summary charts and construction scores for six highway projects. Six of the nine bidders objected to the disclosure. The Consulting Engineers of Ontario, a professional association, also objected, asserting that "the information had been supplied to the Ministry in confidence; the technical scores are proprietary and trade secrets; and disclosure would prejudice their competitive position in the industry and would result in undue loss." The Ministry decided to deny access to the requested information. The requester appealed to Ontario's Information and Privacy Commissioner. The Commissioner determined that the information should be released. The Ministry filed an application for judicial review of the Commissioner's order.

As the court noted, the Ministry had made the following arguments against disclosure to the Commissioner:

- disclosure would damage the integrity of the consulting bidding system;

- if the scores of the other consultants were to be known, a consultant would be in a position to adjust its bid price to maximize its price while still being awarded the contract;

- consultants might choose not to compete for Ministry contracts if they knew that the scores would be released;

- consultants who believe that their reputation has been damaged through disclosure of the information in the records might take legal action against the Ministry, which would impact negatively on its financial interests.

However, as the court noted, the Commissioner rejected these arguments:

> The Commissioner found that the Ministry's arguments concerning engineering consultants declining to bid on its jobs or suing the Ministry were entirely speculative and did not constitute detailed and convincing evidence to establish a reasonable expectation of probable harm. In addition, given the interest and involvement of the consulting engineering community in the development of an evaluation process generally, it was unlikely that disclosure of the scores could reasonably be expected to result in a disinterest in competing for government contracts.

After providing a detailed analysis of the appropriate standard of review for decisions of the Commissioner, the court ultimately upheld the Commissioner's finding. In so doing, the court articulated the following principles in favour of the transparency and accountability of government in its procurement practices:

> The ability of the public to scrutinize the bases upon which government contracts are awarded is an important aspect of public accountability. Subject to the proprietary interests of third parties, the approaches taken by government, the criteria against which tender documents are assessed, and the degree to which proponents satisfy those criteria, are all integral to the ability of the public to assess the operations of government and to hold it accountable for the use of public funds.

This decision reflects the importance placed on the transparency of government activities and the delicate balance that public institutions must strike between maintaining an open tendering process and protecting the sensitive confidential information of bidders who participate in that process.

Arctic Tender Navigates Confidentiality Crossfire

Savik Enterprises v. Nunavut
Nunavut Court of Justice, 2004

The *Savik Enterprises v. Nunavut (Commissioner)* decision of the Nunavut Court of Justice serves as an illustrative case study on how the government's duty to maintain the confidentiality of sensitive supplier information must be balanced against the need to maintain open and transparent procurement practices. The dispute arose out of a tender call for a ten-year contract for the provision of bulk fuel to Nunavut communities. The incumbent fuel provider, Savik Enterprises, lost the competition to a number of locally owned co-operatives operating as Arctic Cooperatives Ltd. (the "Cooperatives"). Savik sued the government, claiming that there were improprieties in the procurement process.

During pre-trial discoveries, Savik demanded access to the bid documents submitted by the winning Cooperatives. The government claimed privilege over those documents and the Cooperatives also intervened to contest the disclosure. The court granted the Cooperatives standing to contest the disclosure in court:

> There is a growing body of jurisprudence in Canada that has recognized the existence of common law "privacy interests". Given the growing pervasiveness and sophistication of contemporary information technology, particularly that possessed by government, the protection of these privacy interests today is fundamental to the well being of a free and democratic society. Statute has now intervened in four provinces to

create a statutory tort of invasion of privacy. In provinces not having this statutory cause of action, lower Courts have determined that common law remedies do exist to protect a growing variety of privacy interests.

In addition to these common law duties, the court also noted that the Nunavut government was owed a statutory duty to protect bidder information and balance these duties against transparency obligations:

> The privacy interest is also recognized in statutory form by Nunavut's *Access to Information and Protection of Privacy Act 1994* C.20. This legislation maintains a precarious balance; a balance between the need to protect and preserve privacy interests on the one hand, with the need to promote accountability of public bodies through enhanced access to certain types of information, on the other.

The court recognized Nunavut's interest in protecting business information in order to encourage supplier participation in the bidding process, stating that the government "is concerned that release of the requested proposals may impair the future willingness of others to share the detailed information necessary to make informed and effective decisions in a larger government procurement process." However, the court ultimately recognized the need to balance these important confidentiality considerations against the need to promote the transparent and defensible expenditure of public funds, stating that while "the public policy argument advanced by the Defendant in favor of protecting the integrity of the RFP process remains an important consideration, there is an equally compelling, if not greater public policy argument favoring disclosure where the expenditure of public funds is concerned." In so finding, the court stressed the importance of transparency in the public procurement process as a means of ensuring public confidence in government spending:

> Openness and transparency in public administration promotes accountability and fairness in public government. Secrecy breeds suspicion and mistrust. Claims of partiality or discrimination tend to germinate and flourish in a secretive environment. Given the importance of government contracts to the private sector in Nunavut, it is particularly important that those bidding on contracts have confidence in the fairness of the process adopted by government in making its contract awards.

The court also stated that accountability "for public funds and fairness in public administration are values essential to the preservation of a democratically elected government" and that "transparency of process is as integral to the building and maintaining of trust in matters of public administration as it is to the justice system itself."

In striking that balance, the court distinguished between the need for absolute confidentiality during the tendering process to protect the process from external interference and the less absolute need for confidentiality after the contract has been awarded:

> Absolute confidentiality must be maintained during the submission phase of the government procurement process in order to facilitate a fair and honest competition for government contracts. Secrecy at this stage is clearly essential to the process itself, and is in the public interest. However, the public interest in maintaining this wall of secrecy diminishes rapidly once a decision on the merits has been reached.

The court ultimately required the government to disclose the bidding documents while ordering the redaction of some of the more sensitive data contained within them. As this case illustrates, like other jurisdictions across Canada, Nunavut's common law and statutory obligations require it to balance the confidentiality obligations owed to suppliers against its public transparency obligations. Determining the dividing line between information that can be disclosed and information that must be protected will continue to be a delicate balancing act for all public bodies in the years to come.

Building a Bid Dispute Protocol: Complaint Procedures Under Trade Treaties
By Marilyn Brown

Most public sector entities are aware of their basic obligations under applicable trade treaties – the common principles of non-discrimination, transparency and fairness are generally understood and respected. However, in some cases, details of specific requirements under applicable trade treaties can be overlooked. For example, many Provincial and MASH sector (municipal, academic, school board and health sector) entities covered by the procurement provisions under the *Agreement on Internal Trade* ("AIT") have not yet fulfilled the requirement to have documented complaint resolution procedures in place and available to suppliers.

What's Required?

The complaint procedures regarding procurement by Provinces are set out in Article 513 of Chapter 5 of the AIT. The first requires entities covered by Chapter 5 of the AIT (such as Provincial agencies, boards and commissions) to have in place a process for receiving complaints in writing, acknowledging the complaint in writing within five (5) working days and providing a response to the complaint within twenty (20) working days. The "5 and 20 rule" is considered a good standard for any public sector entity, whether or not it is governed by these provisions of the AIT, to adopt in its procedures for dealing with procurement complaints.

MASH sector entities covered by the procurement provisions in Annex 502.4 of the AIT are required under Section "M" (Dispute Resolution) to "document their non-judicial complaint process and provide this information to suppliers or Provinces upon request." Apart from a requirement under this Section that the opportunity to challenge contract award decisions must be equally available to suppliers from all Provinces, the Annex does not dictate the specific content that must be included in complaint resolution procedures.

What's In?

Complaint procedures may vary in their details, but there are some basic elements that ought to be addressed. The procedures should:

- not be limited to bidders in a competitive process, but be available to any supplier raising concerns with respect to the institution's procurement, whether a competitive process or a direct award (i.e. a sole-source or single-source contract);

- provide direction to suppliers on how to initiate the complaint resolution process – typically by writing to a designated contact within the institution, identifying the procurement in issue and explaining the nature and details of the complaint;

- include timelines for responding to complaints – the "5 and 20 rule" is recommended;

- identify the individual that will manage the complaint procedures – responsibilities may include receiving the complaint letter, sending an acknowledgement of receipt, preparing materials setting out the background of the procurement in issue, and co-ordinating the review of the supplier's correspondence and pertinent materials; and

- establish the review committee – typically consisting of the head of the purchasing department, legal counsel and a third senior employee or official of the institution – to conduct a review, consider the merits of the complaint and determine the appropriate response.

What's Out?

The procedures should provide for the establishment of a committee to consider the complaint and provide a response to the supplier – it seems straightforward enough, but this is where the process can become tricky. If the complaint is without merit, the response is relatively easy to prepare. But what happens if a supplier's complaint raises a legitimate concern with respect to the procurement? What are the options for attempting to resolve the complaint? What is the appropriate response to the supplier? These are difficult issues that, unfortunately, do not lend themselves to "one size fits all" solutions. The response will depend on the specific facts of the procurement and the complaint in issue. Responses to complaints therefore need to be carefully considered by the institution on a case-by-case basis.

What's Accomplished?

Unfortunately, not all supplier complaints will be resolved by an institution's complaint resolution process. All the institution can guarantee is that complaints will receive careful consideration and a timely response. At the end of the day, if a supplier is not satisfied with the institution's response, there are options for escalating the complaint, including proceeding with a challenge under applicable trade treaties or before the courts. While institutions need to allow themselves the flexibility to respond to complaints in the manner determined to be appropriate under the circumstances, any complaint found to have merit should be carefully examined by the institution and lead to the internal review and improvement of policies or practices that have failed to meet legal standards or best practices in public procurement.

Federal Crackdown Targets Bid Rigging and Conspiracy Scams

While many procurement professionals would assume that bid-rigging and price-fixing conspiracies are rare events that occur in exotic offshore locales or in Hollywood movies, the reality is that these scams are closer than you think. In fact, your institution may be a victim without even knowing it. The following discussion highlights the federal crackdown against these commercial crimes and provides an overview of some of the warning signs that can assist you in detecting and reporting the anti-competitive practices that cost us millions of dollars a year.

Bid Rigging: A Federal Offence

The federal *Competition Act* establishes a number of "Offences in Relation to Competition" including "bid-rigging" and "conspiracy." As the federal Competition Bureau states:

> Bid-rigging is a serious crime that undermines competitive markets and has serious negative economic consequences for businesses and for the public, which cost tax payers millions of dollars annually. It is a form of conspiracy that occurs when bidders secretly agree not to compete or to submit bids that have been pre-arranged among themselves. Firms and individuals convicted of bid-rigging face fines at the discretion of the court and imprisonment for up to five years.

As detailed on its website (see www.competitionbureau.gc.ca), the Competition Bureau has successfully conducted many prosecutions that have led to multi-million dollar fines and even jail sentences. Prior conspiracies have impacted many significant construction projects, including Pearson International Airport, the Toronto Skydome Hotel and BCE Place, along with a broad range of industries and goods and services including re-enforcement cable, flour milling, electrical contractors, timber, paper, compressed gas, concrete, fax paper, ambulance operators, pharmacies, waste disposal, snow removal, bulk vitamins and notary services.

Types of Bid Rigging

In April 2008, the Competition Bureau launched a free online *Bid-Rigging Prevention Tool* that identifies a number of common forms of bid-rigging including:

- *cover bidding*, where the same or related companies submit fake bids to create the appearance of competition to disguise the fact that a fix is in place;

- *bid suppression,* where competitors agree to withhold their bids to allow a pre-selected competitor to win uncontested;

- *bid rotation,* where competitors agree to take turns submitting the best bid; and

- *market division,* where competitors agree to divide up the market to avoid competing head-to-head.

Risk Factors and Telltale Signs

The following list, which was derived from the federal government's *Supply Manual* and from the Competition Bureau's *Bid-Rigging Prevention Tool*, summarizes the top five telltale indicators of potential bid-rigging and price-fixing conspiracies:

1. *Standard Buys From Limited Supplier Pools:* industries with standard goods or services that remain relatively unchanged over time and are supplied by a limited supplier pool with few new entrants are particularly susceptible to bid-rigging and price-fixing conspiracies.

2. *Active Associations Promoting Fixed Pricing*: the presence of an active trade association, coupled with supplier references to "standard industry pricing," can be a telltale sign that the fix is in on pricing.

3. *Evidence of Common Authorship*: the use of identical wording to describe non-standard items, the presence of identical irregularities or idiosyncrasies in bid documents or the indication that suppliers are aware of competitor pricing can all be a warning sign of an unnaturally cozy relationship between supposed competitors.

4. *Suspicious Bidding Behaviour*: multiple bids submitted in the same package or at the same time, instances where regular bidders fail to participate for no apparent reason, situations where a typically unsuccessful bidder repeatedly wins a particular category of contract, situations where the same winning bidder repeatedly awards subcontracts to its competitors, award patterns that suggests a pre-determined rotation of successful bids or other indicators that reflect a pre-determined market division amongst a group of suppliers are all signs of possible bid-rigging.

5. *Suspicious Pricing Patterns*: pricing that is consistently higher than prevailing industry rates, unexplained sudden price escalations, pronounced gaps between winning bids and other bids, identical bids from losing bidders and identical transportation costs from local and remote suppliers are all examples of suspicious pricing patterns that could suggest the presence of a price-fixing conspiracy aimed at stifling competition and inflating costs.

Buyers Beware

As the Competition Bureau notes, "buyers can play a major role in combating bid rigging." If you suspect the presence of bid rigging or price fixing, the Bureau advises against confronting the suspected participants directly. Instead, purchasing institutions should make a thorough written record of all relevant details, contact their legal advisors and contact the Competition Bureau. Proper training and increased buyer vigilance can help assist in federal law enforcement efforts and significantly reduce the anti-competitive practices that undermine open competition and unnecessarily cost institutions, consumers and taxpayers millions of dollars a year.

Competition Act Amendments Spotlight Bid Rigging Risks

Amendments to the federal *Competition Act* in March 2009 put the spotlight back on the area of bid rigging, highlighting the risks faced by unsuspecting purchasing institutions in falling prey to unscrupulous suppliers. This section provides some recent examples of bid rigging drawn from a high-profile lawsuit involving a government institution that successfully recouped damages against a party who illegally used insider advantage to win phantom contracts and purchase government land at a bargain basement price.

The federal government recently enacted a number of amendments to the *Competition Act* that target anti-competitive practices in the marketplace. While most of the amendments deal with supplier conduct outside of the bidding process, the bid rigging amendments are squarely directed at creating a greater deterrent against illegally manipulating the competitive bidding process. In fact, the new amendments significantly increase the penalties relating to bid rigging, upping the maximum term of imprisonment from five years to fourteen years. This amendment should provide the Competition Bureau with additional leverage when negotiating plea bargains with unscrupulous suppliers caught red handed in tainted tendering procedures.

In addition to criminal prosecution, parties that engage in bid rigging can also face civil action. The 2009 Ontario Superior Court of Justice decision in *Ontario Realty Corp. v. P. Gabriele & Sons Ltd.* offers a high profile case study. In this case, the defendants were found to have engaged in bid rigging in connection with a contract with an Ontario Realty Corporation ("ORC") soil remediation contract. The ORC was awarded $350,050 after the court found unlawful conspiracy in relation to that contract. The ORC was also awarded additional damages for unjust enrichment in relation to a second contract for the sale of land. Both of these tainted tenders are described below.

In the first claim, the court found that the ORC made payments but received no work after the defendant supplier was awarded a contract based on "a phony tender process". The court drew "the inescapable inference that there was collusion" between the supplier and an employee of ORC which included the employee preparing false competing bids to paper the file prior to awarding the untendered contract to the supplier. The court also found "overwhelming evidence" that no work was actually done on that contract and that "ORC received nothing in return for the payments made." It found the supplier liable for fraud in the amount of $350,050 in connection with the false invoices.

In the same lawsuit, the court also found that ORC was entitled to damages for unjust enrichment in connection with a bid rigging swindle involving the sale of government land. While there are numerous reported cases dealing with the improper use of post bid "clarifications" that enable bid repair and result in the improper award of a contract, this particular case took post-bid clarification abuses to new depths. The court found that an ORC employee served as an inside accomplice and allowed the defendant supplier to improve its bid after close to beat out a superior competing offer. To make matters worse, the price was then readjusted downwards after the award of the contract to make it less attractive than the original competing offer. As the court found, the defendant supplier made out with a bargain, purchasing the land for $1,922,000 before flipping it less than eight months later for $4,390,000. The court concluded that "the bidding process was manipulated to harm ORC" and recognized ORC's claim against the supplier for unjust enrichment, thereby entitling ORC to the return of the profits obtained from the tainted tender.

As these bid tampering swindles illustrate, tendering abuses can cause significant harm to an institution. While such conduct is subject to serious criminal and civil sanction, these deterrents can only be effective if potential perpetrators feel that there is a real likelihood of detection. To reduce the risk of falling victim to the next tainted tender, institutions should implement the following due diligence measures:

- obtain the necessary internal training to assist in detecting bid rigging;

- implement proper reporting procedures to alert the authorities; and

- notify suppliers that bid tampering barriers have been put in place.

While no institution is immune from bid rigging and other tendering conspiracies, proper due diligence can go a long way to reducing the risk of falling victim to the next swindle. As is often the case, there is no substitute for being prepared. The following section contains the relevant bid rigging provisions from the federal *Competition Act*.

Canada

Competition Act
Bid Rigging Provisions

47. (1) In this section, "bid-rigging" means

(*a*) an agreement or arrangement between or among two or more persons whereby one or more of those persons agrees or undertakes not to submit a bid or tender in response to a call or request for bids or tenders, or agrees or undertakes to withdraw a bid or tender submitted in response to such a call or request, or

(*b*) the submission, in response to a call or request for bids or tenders, of bids or tenders that are arrived at by agreement or arrangement between or among two or more bidders or tenderers,

where the agreement or arrangement is not made known to the person calling for or requesting the bids or tenders at or before the time when any bid or tender is submitted or withdrawn, as the case may be, by any person who is a party to the agreement or arrangement.

Bid-rigging

(2) Every person who is a party to bid-rigging is guilty of an indictable offence and liable on conviction to a fine in the discretion of the court or to imprisonment for a term not exceeding 14 years, or to both.

Exception

(3) This section does not apply in respect of an agreement or arrangement that is entered into or a submission that is arrived at only by companies each of which is, in respect of every one of the others, an affiliate.

(24) Effective Use of Technology

Is your organization keeping up with industry practices and leveraging technological innovations to enhance and accelerate its tendering cycle?

There is little doubt that technology is taking us into a new era in automated procurement. To avoid being left behind in a tendering time warp, purchasing institutions need to be ready to quickly adapt to this new reality. The following section highlights some of the legal and industry developments that are accelerating the evolution towards paperless procurement.

Paperless Procurement: Clearing the Path to Paperless Bidding

The paper-based bidding process hasn't changed much with the times. In fact, bid submission practices remain trapped in a tendering time warp, frozen throwbacks to the pre-internet era. That's about to change. This article explains how inherent systemic inefficiencies, accelerating timeframes, trade treaty developments and technological innovations are all converging to convert our out-dated bidding systems into a paperless procurement process.

Systemic Inefficiency and Waste

It's a tale of two technological eras trapped within a single tendering cycle. While electronic *posting* may have become a mainstream standard for many public institutions, this technological advancement has only served to obscure the technological atrophy that continues to plague the bidding stage of the tendering process. While tender calls can be downloaded electronically at any time of day and night, public institutions continue to manage manual bid receipt processes, where bids are only accepted in paper form during business hours, at prescribed locations, within strictly enforced timeframes. In addition to being slow and inefficient, this paper-based bidding process creates a colossal carbon footprint. Add up the thousands of bidding processes run by public institutions across Canada every day, multiply those competitions by the number of suppliers who respond to each tender call, and then multiply that number by the multiple copies of each bid that has to be shipped to the purchasing institutions only to be shredded after the evaluation of tenders and what you get is a T-Rex sized mountain of waste. Time is running out on these soon-to-be-extinct paper-bound tendering practices.

Increasing Time Pressures

With ever-accelerating time-pressures, institutions need to increase tendering cycle efficiencies somehow. The planning and drafting stages of the procurement process are already squeezed to the breaking point, as are the post-bidding evaluation and contract finalization stages. This puts purchasing institutions under greater pressure to shorten the period between tender call posting and bid submission. However, in a system where the bidding window can determine whether a supplier responds to a tender call, and in an environment where lawsuits are fought over bids that are submitted even seconds after a bid deadline, timing is everything. Shortening the posting period threatens to undermine the open competition value-for-money objectives that lie at the heart of the public procurement process. Purchasing institutions need to buy some time somewhere without compromising open competition. Electronic bidding offers a clear solution for accelerating the bidding process while preserving an adequate window for bid submission.

Trade Treaty Developments

These timing pressures are compounded by the ever-expanding network of open procurement treaties. Within Canada, the *Agreement on Internal Trade* ("AIT") requires reciprocal non-discrimination for all Canadian suppliers, which means that suppliers from coast-to-coast are entitled to an equal opportunity to compete for public sector work. Under the AIT, institutions must keep their bid opportunities open for a "reasonable time." Those institutions that set their bid submission deadlines to the minimum amount of time required by local suppliers may actually be setting themselves up for a bid protest by engaging in a form of prohibited local preference. Enabling electronic bidding will help institutions address this risk by giving all eligible suppliers, regardless of location within Canada, an equal opportunity to submit their bids.

If the domestic trade treaty obligations under the AIT aren't enough to tip the tide towards electronic tendering, then international treaty developments soon will be. The 2010 *Canada-U.S. Procurement Agreement* (which applies to sub-federal public bodies) and the treaty negotiations between Canada and the European Union (which are intended to also expand open competition to sub-federal institutions across Canada) will open the floodgates to an expanding pool of international bidders and create an irresistible pressure to adopt electronic bidding procedures.

Legal and Technological Enablers

Fortunately for procurement professionals, technology is catching up to the tendering cycle to provide the three missing links required to complete the transition to paperless bidding. Firstly, encryption technologies are helping to preserve the reliability and confidentiality of electronic bids, which is essential to preserving the integrity of the paperless bidding process. Secondly, key public infrastructure protocols are enabling the electronic signatures required to provide legal certainty and enforceability to paperless bids. Finally, industry groups are quickly working out the technical and contractual intricacies for converting paper-based bid bonds to digital bid bonds that can be attached to electronic bids. These legal and technological enablers will soon serve as the final catalysts for launching us into a new era of paperless bidding.

UN Model Law Launches a New ERA of Online Bidding

The new UN Model Procurement law defines an "electronic reverse auction" ("ERA") as "an online real-time purchasing technique utilized by the procuring entity to select the successful submission, which involves the presentation by suppliers or contractors of successively lowered bids during a scheduled period of time and the automatic evaluation of bids." As the new UN protocols recognize, public institutions should be leveraging the use of technology and enhancing price competition by utilizing ERAs to seek multiple real-time bids from competing suppliers. The UN Model Procurement Law recognizes both Stand-Alone ERAs, which utilize electronic bidding for new publicly posted opportunities, as well as Second Stage ERAs, which use similar electronic bidding protocols but invite a pool of prequalified suppliers to bid under existing framework agreements. The UN Model Procurement Law provides detailed protocols for administering both types of ERAs. Those protocols are reproduced below.

United Nations

UN Model Procurement Law

Article 31
Conditions for use of an electronic reverse auction

1.   A procuring entity may engage in procurement by means of an electronic reverse auction in accordance with the provisions of chapter VI of this Law, under the following conditions:

   (a)   It is feasible for the procuring entity to formulate a detailed description of the subject matter of the procurement;

   (b)   There is a competitive market of suppliers or contractors anticipated to be qualified to participate in the electronic reverse auction, such that effective competition is ensured; and

   (c)   The criteria to be used by the procuring entity in determining the successful submission are quantifiable and can be expressed in monetary terms.

---

2.   A procuring entity may use an electronic reverse auction as a phase preceding the award of the procurement contract in a procurement method, as appropriate under the provisions of this Law. It may also use an electronic reverse auction for award of a procurement contract in a framework agreement procedure with second-stage competition in accordance with the provisions of this Law. An electronic reverse auction under this paragraph may be used only where the conditions of paragraph 1 (c) of this article are satisfied.

Chapter VI. Electronic reverse auctions

Article 53
Electronic reverse auction as a stand-alone method of procurement

1.   The procuring entity shall solicit bids by causing an invitation to the electronic reverse auction to be published in accordance with article 33 of this Law. The invitation shall include:

(a)   The name and address of the procuring entity;

(b)   A detailed description of the subject matter of the procurement, in conformity with article 10 of this Law, and the desired or required time and location for the provision of such subject matter;

(c)   The terms and conditions of the procurement contract, to the extent they are already known to the procuring entity, and the form of the contract, if any, to be signed by the parties;

(d)   A declaration pursuant to article 8 of this Law;

(e)   The criteria and procedures to be used for ascertaining the qualifications of suppliers or contractors and any documentary evidence or other information that must be presented by suppliers or contractors to demonstrate their qualifications in conformity with article 9 of this Law;

(f)   The criteria and procedure for examining bids against the description of the subject matter of the procurement;

(g)   The criteria and procedure for evaluating bids in accordance with article 11 of this Law, including any mathematical formula that will be used in the evaluation procedure during the auction;

(h)   The manner in which the bid price is to be formulated and expressed, including a statement as to whether the price is to cover elements other than the cost of the subject matter of the procurement itself, such as any applicable transportation and insurance charges, customs duties and taxes;

(i)   The currency or currencies in which the bid price is to be formulated and expressed;

(j)   The minimum number of suppliers or contractors required to register for the auction in order for the auction to be held, which shall be sufficient to ensure effective competition;

[(k) If any limit on the number of suppliers or contractors that can be registered for the auction is imposed in accordance with paragraph 2 of this article, the relevant maximum number and the criteria and procedure, in conformity with paragraph 2 of this article, that will be followed in selecting it;]

(l)   How the auction can be accessed, including appropriate information regarding connection to the auction;

(m) The deadline by which suppliers or contractors must register for the auction and the requirements for registration;

(n)   The date and time of the opening of the auction and the requirements for identification of bidders at the opening of the auction;

(o)   The criteria governing the closing of the auction;

(p)   Other rules for the conduct of the auction, including the information that will be made available to the bidders in the course of the auction, the language in which it will be made available and the conditions under which the bidders will be able to bid;

(q)   References to this Law, the procurement regulations and other laws and regulations directly pertinent to the procurement proceedings, including those applicable to procurement involving classified information, and the place where those laws and regulations may be found;

(r)   The means by which suppliers or contractors may seek clarification of information relating to the procurement proceedings;

(s)   The name, functional title and address of one or more officers or employees of the procuring entity who are authorized to communicate directly with and to receive communications directly from suppliers or contractors in connection with the procurement proceedings before and after the auction without the intervention of an intermediary;

(t)   Notice of the right provided under article 64 of this Law to challenge or appeal decisions or actions taken by the procuring entity that are allegedly not in compliance with the provisions of this Law, together with information about the duration of the applicable standstill period and, if none will apply, a statement to that effect and the reasons therefor;

(u)   Any formalities that will be required after the auction for a procurement contract to enter into force, including, where applicable, ascertainment of qualifications or responsiveness in accordance with article 57 of this Law and the execution of a written procurement contract pursuant to article 22 of this Law;

(v)   Any other requirements established by the procuring entity in conformity with this Law and the procurement regulations relating to the procurement proceedings.

[2.   The procuring entity may impose a maximum limit on the number of suppliers or contractors that can be registered for the electronic reverse auction only to the extent that capacity constraints in its communications system so require, and shall select the suppliers or contractors to be so registered in a non-discriminatory manner. The procuring entity shall include a statement of the reasons and circumstances upon which it relied to justify the imposition of such a maximum limit in the record required under article 25 of this Law.]

3.   The procuring entity may decide, in the light of the circumstances of the given procurement, that the electronic reverse auction shall be preceded by an examination or evaluation of initial bids. In such case, the invitation to the auction shall, in addition to information listed in paragraph 1 of this article, include:

(a)   An invitation to present initial bids, together with instructions for preparing initial bids;

(b)   The manner, place and deadline for presenting initial bids.

4.   Where the electronic reverse auction has been preceded by an examination or evaluation of initial bids, the procuring entity shall promptly after the completion of the examination or evaluation of initial bids:

(a)   Dispatch the notice of rejection and reasons for rejection to each supplier or contractor whose initial bid was rejected;

(b)   Issue an invitation to the auction to each qualified supplier or contractor whose initial bid is responsive, providing all information required to participate in the auction;

(c) Where an evaluation of initial bids has taken place, each invitation to the auction shall also be accompanied by the outcome of the evaluation, as relevant to the supplier or contractor to which the invitation is addressed.

Article 54
Electronic reverse auction as a phase preceding the award of the procurement contract

1. Where an electronic reverse auction is to be used as a phase preceding the award of the procurement contract in a procurement method, as appropriate, or in a framework agreement procedure with second-stage competition, the procuring entity shall notify suppliers or contractors when first soliciting their participation in the procurement proceedings that an auction will be held, and shall provide, in addition to other information required to be included under provisions of this Law, the following information about the auction:

   (a) The mathematical formula that will be used in the evaluation procedure during the auction;

   (b) How the auction can be accessed, including appropriate information regarding connection to the auction.

2. Before the electronic reverse auction is held, the procuring entity shall issue an invitation to the auction to all suppliers or contractors remaining in the proceedings, specifying:

   (a) The deadline by which the suppliers or contractors must register for the auction and requirements for registration;

   (b) The date and time of the opening of the auction and requirements for the identification of bidders at the opening of the auction;

   (c) Criteria governing the closing of the auction;

   (d) Other rules for the conduct of the auction, including the information that will be made available to the bidders during the auction and the conditions under which the bidders will be able to bid.

3. Where an evaluation of initial bids has taken place, each invitation to the auction shall also be accompanied by the outcome of the evaluation as relevant to the supplier or contractor to which the invitation is addressed.

Article 55
Registration for the electronic reverse auction and the timing of the holding of the auction

1. Confirmation of registration for the electronic reverse auction shall be communicated promptly to each registered supplier or contractor.

2. If the number of suppliers or contractors registered for the electronic reverse auction is insufficient to ensure effective competition, the procuring entity may cancel the auction. The cancellation of the auction shall be communicated promptly to each registered supplier or contractor.

3. The period of time between the issuance of the invitation to the electronic reverse auction and the auction shall be sufficiently long to allow suppliers or contractors to prepare for the auction, taking into account the reasonable needs of the procuring entity.

Article 56
Requirements during the electronic reverse auction

1. The electronic reverse auction shall be based on:

   (a) Price, where the procurement contract is to be awarded to the lowest-priced bid; or

   (b) Price and other criteria specified to suppliers or contractors under articles 53 and 54 of this Law, as applicable, where the procurement contract is to be awarded to the most advantageous bid.

2. During the auction:

   (a) All bidders shall have an equal and continuous opportunity to present their bids;

   (b) There shall be automatic evaluation of all bids in accordance with the criteria, procedure and formula provided to suppliers or contractors under articles 53 and 54 of this Law, as applicable;

   (c) Each bidder must receive, instantaneously and on a continuous basis during the auction, sufficient information allowing it to determine the standing of its bid vis-à-vis other bids;

   (d) There shall be no communication between the procuring entity and the bidders or among the bidders, other than as provided for in subparagraphs (a) and (c) of this paragraph.

3. The procuring entity shall not disclose the identity of any bidder during the auction.

4. The auction shall be closed in accordance with the criteria specified to suppliers or contractors under articles 53 and 54 of this Law, as applicable.

5. The procuring entity shall suspend or terminate the auction in the case of failures in its communication system that put at risk the proper conduct of the auction or for other reasons stipulated in the rules for the conduct of the auction. The procuring entity shall not disclose the identity of any bidder in the case of suspension or termination of the auction.

Article 57
Requirements after the electronic reverse auction

1. The bid that at the closure of the electronic reverse auction is the lowest-priced bid or the most advantageous bid, as applicable, shall be the successful bid.

2. In procurement by means of an auction that was not preceded by examination or evaluation of initial bids, the procuring entity shall ascertain after the auction the responsiveness of the successful bid and the qualifications of the supplier or contractor submitting it. The procuring entity shall reject that bid if it is found to be unresponsive or if the supplier or contractor submitting it is found unqualified. Without prejudice to the right of the procuring entity to cancel the procurement in accordance with paragraph 1 of article 19 of this Law, the procuring entity shall select the bid that was the next lowest-priced or next most advantageous bid at the closure of the auction, provided that that bid is ascertained to be responsive and the supplier or contractor submitting it is ascertained to be qualified.

3. Where the successful bid at the closure of the auction appears to the procuring entity to be abnormally low and gives rise to concerns on the part of the procuring entity as to the ability of the bidder that presented it to perform the procurement contract, the procuring entity may follow the procedures described in article 20 of this Law. If the procuring entity rejects the bid as abnormally low under article 20, it shall select the bid that at the closure of the auction was the next lowest-priced or next most advantageous bid. This provision is without prejudice to the right of the procuring entity to cancel the procurement in accordance with paragraph 1 of article 19 of this Law.

CONCLUSION:
BUILDING A RAPID ACTION PLAN

Ultimately, the solutions to achieving due diligence in the tendering process must be found from within the institution, by taking local conditions into account, if the objectives of self-governance and self-sufficiency are to be achieved. Purchasing institutions need clear rules that support the organizational objectives and meet their due diligence duties, but they don't need to be unnecessarily entangled in red tape. Accountability must be balanced with efficiency if the public interest is to be served. To accelerate their tendering processes and meet their due diligence duties, public institutions need a rapid action plan that is tempered with an understanding of the organization's existing conditions and unique challenges.

As discussed in the Introduction, the first step in a three-stage strategy is to take a clear snapshot of existing conditions. The case studies in the last eight chapters surveyed the eight critical target areas and twenty four due diligence indicators that help inform how an institution measures up to its due diligence duties. By gaining a clearer picture of how your organization measures up, you can build an internal governance framework based on a process roadmap and deployment strategy that:

- aligns your budget approval process with the procurement cycle to create an effective early warning system for proper procurement planning;

- establishes clear and accessible procurement policies that address ethical considerations while identifying roles, responsibilities and accountabilities within the institution for the project planning, document drafting, tender posting, bid receipt, bid evaluation, contract award and contract management phases of the procurement process;

- develops a broad range of procurement templates and related procurement protocols to help establish consistent standards within the procurement cycle; and

- implements a practical training program that increases institutional awareness of proper procurement procedures across the entire organization.

Internal Governance Roadmap

To be effective, an institution's internal governance roadmap must be clear and accessible to all users of the procurement system. To accelerate the tendering cycle, we need systems built for speed with policies built with precision. We need to clearly map out a step-by-step process that identifies who does what and embeds due diligence into the procurement process. The clear alignment of roles and responsibilities in an internal governance roadmap helps ensure an efficient tendering cycle and an effective accountability framework. To operationalize that framework, organizations also need to update their procurement playbooks.

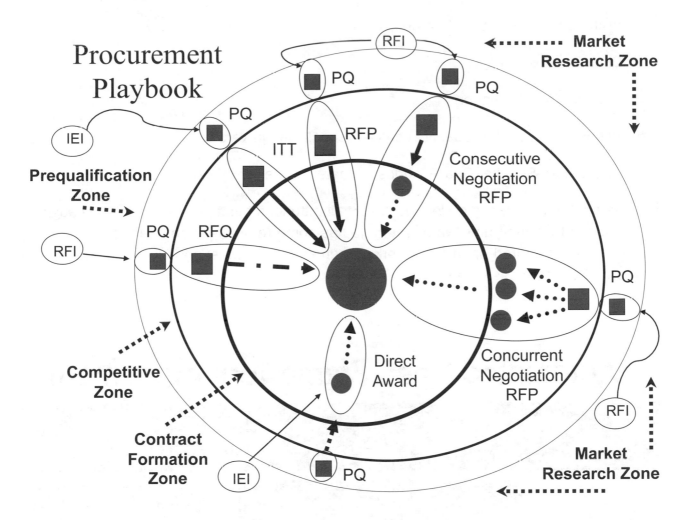

Purchasing institutions should overhaul their procurement playbooks with a professionally designed set of tendering templates that meet the broad challenges of an increasingly complex, diverse and dynamic marketplace. In this regard, no two institutions are the same. There is no substitute for a direct knowledge of an organization's inner workings and an understanding of market conditions. While tendering templates should be tuned up to prevailing due diligence standards, they should also be tailored to meet the organization's unique operational requirements. They need to be calibrated to address the challenges that are distinct to the particular industries that the purchasing institution is buying into. Those formats should be properly adapted for use within the Canadian legal context and should be drawn from the following menu of options:

- Invitation to Tender

- No-Negotiation RFP

- Consecutive Negotiation/Rank-and-Run RFP

- Concurrent Negotiation/BAFO RFP

- Invitational Request for Quotation

- Open Request for Quotation

- Request for Information

- Request for Supplier Qualifications – Prequalification Version

- Request for Supplier Qualifications – Master Framework Version

To accelerate their tendering cycles, purchasing institutions must also avoid getting caught in a paper-bound tendering time warp. The time has come to finally adopt electronic tendering and establish automated open framework agreements with transparent protocols governing the award of discrete assignments.

Automated Open Framework Agreement

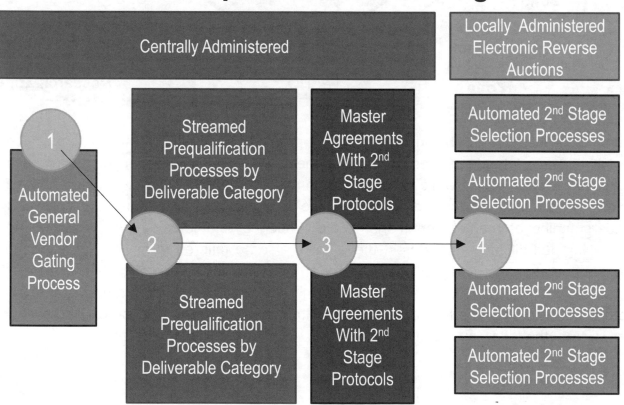

Open frameworks allow vendors to quickly prequalify and be streamed through an online evaluation process into category-specific standardized master agreements. These framework agreements can facilitate accelerated second-stage competitions. Where appropriate, these second-stage processes can utilize electronic reverse auctions to enhance competition for the award of discrete assignments. Automated open framework agreements can help take considerable pressure off the procurement system by standardizing and de-centralizing repeat purchasing across the organization. This way, core procurement resources can be deployed more strategically to focus on more complex, high-risk procurement projects.

A public institution's procurement governance framework should also include clear protocols governing bidder debriefings and bid disputes. To bring the procurement process full circle, the governance framework should also integrate effective contract management mechanisms for monitoring vendor performance under both discrete contracts and automated framework agreements.

Once the internal governance framework is built and the second stage of the rapid action plan is completed, the internal governance roadmap, supporting tendering templates and related policies and protocols should be operationalized through the deployment of a clear training program. The deployment stage should be aimed at promoting a broader organizational awareness of the "who-does-what" of the internal governance roadmap. The deployment stage should start by bolstering the training of core procurement staff so they can serve as the due diligence hub of the procurement cycle, delivering transaction-specific procurement services and training to the broader organization. In this manner, the procurement operation can gain better traction in the use of an updated suite of templates and in the implementation of accelerated document-drafting protocols.

While at first glance this may appear to be setting a high bar for what can be accomplished within the procurement cycle, the fact of the matter is that many organizations are already implementing these strategies and realizing significant downstream benefits from doing so. It is now incumbent upon all public institutions to meet the due diligence challenge. In the coming years, those institutions that proactively implement systemic enhancements and put a premium on accelerating their tendering cycle will be the ones that set the standard in serving the public interest.

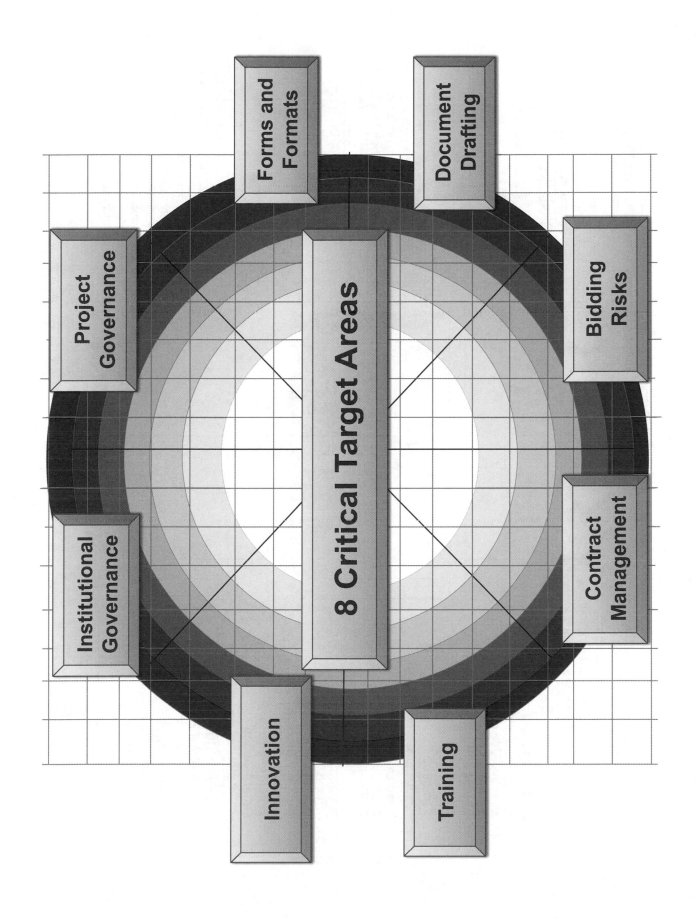

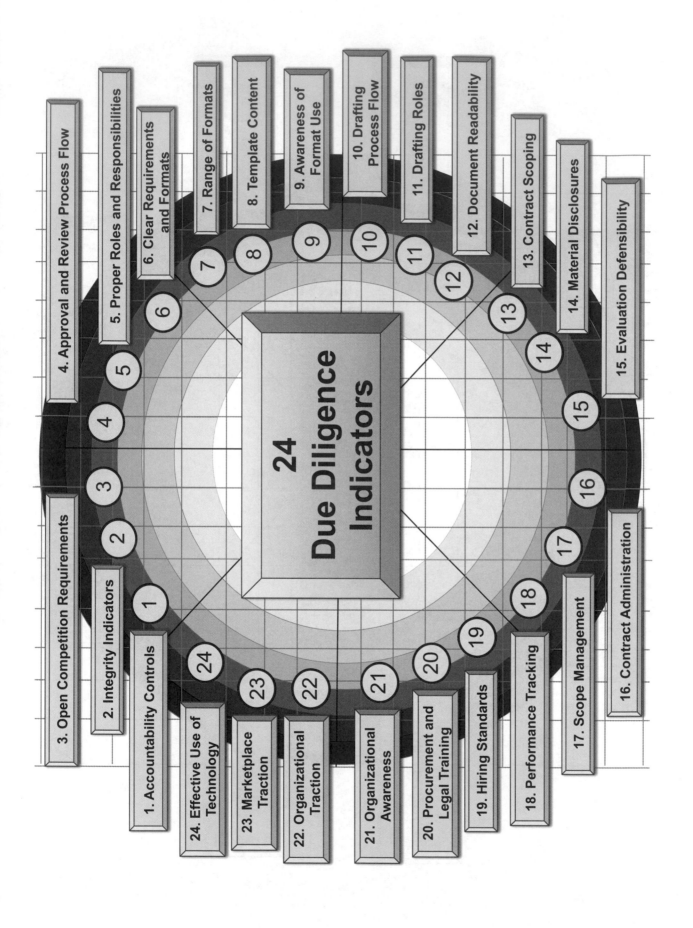

24
Due Diligence
Indicators

1. Accountability Controls
2. Integrity Indicators
3. Open Competition Requirements
4. Approval and Review Process Flow
5. Proper Roles and Responsibilities
6. Clear Requirements and Formats
7. Range of Formats
8. Template Content
9. Awareness of Format Use
10. Drafting Process Flow
11. Drafting Roles
12. Document Readability
13. Contract Scoping
14. Material Disclosures
15. Evaluation Defensibility
16. Contract Administration
17. Scope Management
18. Performance Tracking
19. Hiring Standards
20. Procurement and Legal Training
21. Organizational Awareness
22. Organizational Traction
23. Marketplace Traction
24. Effective Use of Technology

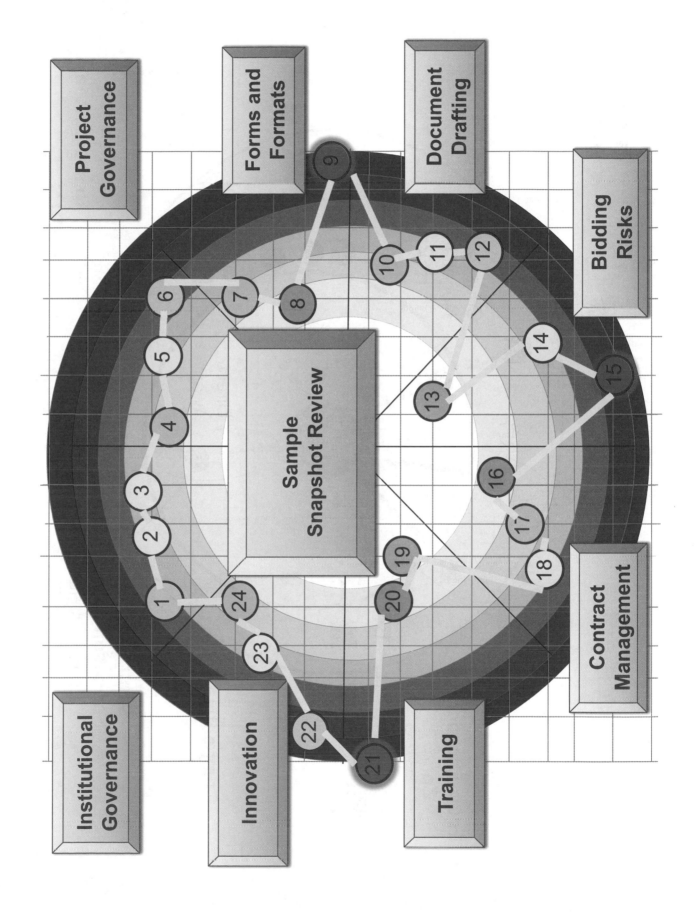

Project Governance

Forms and Formats

Document Drafting

Bidding Risks

Sample
Snapshot Review

Institutional Governance

Innovation

Training

Contract Management

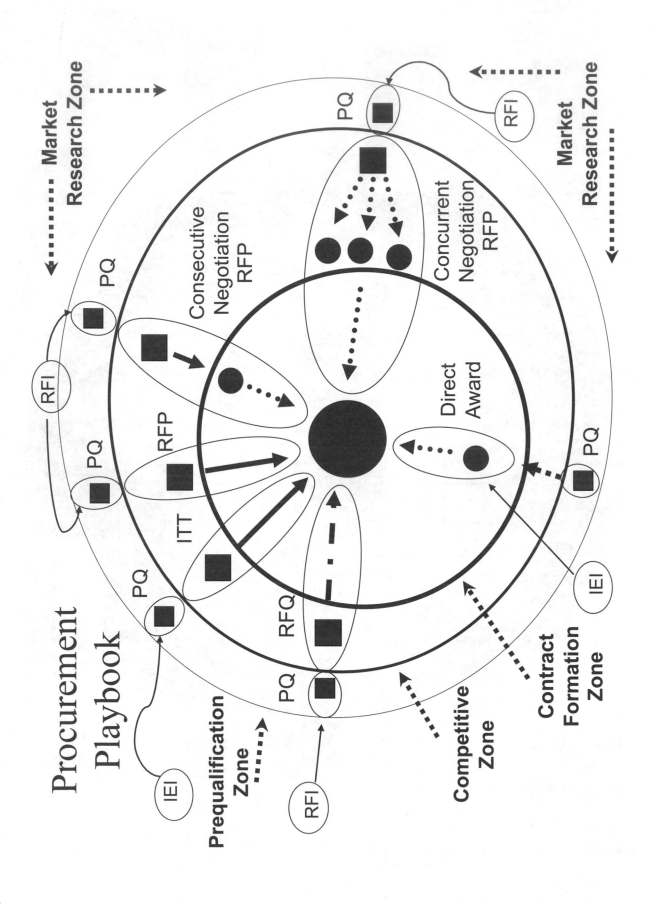